A LIFETIME
IN A RACE

MATTHEW
PINSENT

A LIFETIME IN A RACE

EBURY
PRESS

First published in Great Britain in 2004

10 9 8 7 6 5

First published by
Ebury Press
Random House, 20 Vauxhall Bridge Road, London SW1V 2SA

Random House Australia (Pty) Limited
20 Alfred Street, Milsons Point, Sydney, New South Wales 2061, Australia

Random House New Zealand Limited
18 Poland Road, Glenfield, Auckland 10, New Zealand

Random House South Africa (Pty) Limited
Endulini, 5A Jubilee Road, Parktown 2193, South Africa

The Random House Group Limited Reg. No. 954009

www.randomhouse.co.uk

A CIP catalogue record for this book is available from the British Library.

Cover design by Two Associates
Text design and typesetting by seagulls and Textype

ISBN 0091901499

Printed and bound in Great Britain by Clays of St Ives PLC

Papers used by Ebury Press are natural, recyclable products
made from wood grown in sustainable forests.

contents

Acknowledgements

I want primarily to thank Ebury and Hannah MacDonald for agreeing to take this on, I'm sure I didn't make it easy. Matt Parker for his patience and diligence in his editing, hopefully he doesn't hate rowing now. For Neil, Diana and Dee with their gentle critique, and for pointing out the howlers before they made it into print.

I want to thank my parents for so much, not least the money to start senior international rowing and the support to continue it. Maybe one of these days I will actually be able to spend time with them.

To my wife and family

*To my rowing partners with whom I have
shared my Olympic dreams: Steve, James,
Tim, Stevie, Ed and of course Alex*

To all those who know a double from a pair

competitive
record

OLYMPIC GAMES

2004	**Gold**	Athens	Coxless four with James Cracknell, Steve Williams and Ed Coode
2000	**Gold**	Sydney	Coxless four with James Cracknell, Tim Foster and Steve Redgrave
1996	**Gold**	Atlanta	Coxless pair with Steve Redgrave
1992	**Gold**	Barcelona	Coxless pair with Steve Redgrave

WORLD CHAMPIONSHIPS

2003	**4th**	Milan	Coxless pair with James Cracknell
2002	**Gold**	Seville	Coxless pair with James Cracknell
2001	**Gold**	Lucerne	Coxless pair with James Cracknell
	Gold		Coxed pair with James Cracknell and Neil Chugani

1999	**Gold**	St Catherine's, Canada	Coxless four with James Cracknell, Ed Coode and Steve Redgrave
1998	**Gold**	Cologne	Coxless four with James Cracknell, Tim Foster and Steve Redgrave
1997	**Gold**	Lac d'Aiguebelette, France	Coxless four with James Cracknell, Tim Foster and Steve Redgrave
1995	**Gold**	Tampere, Finland	Coxless pair with Steve Redgrave
1994	**Gold**	Indianapolis	Coxless pair with Steve Redgrave
1993	**Gold**	Roudnice, Czech Rep.	Coxless pair with Steve Redgrave
1991	**Gold**	Vienna	Coxless pair with Steve Redgrave
1990	**Bronze**	Tasmania	Coxless pair with Steve Redgrave
1989	**Bronze**	Bled, Slovenia	Coxed four with Terry Dillon, Steve Turner, Gavin Stewart and Vaughn Thomas

WORLD JUNIOR ROWING CHAMPIONSHIPS

| 1988 | **Gold** | Milan | Junior coxless pair with Tim Foster |
| 1987 | **4th** | Cologne | Junior eight |

introduction

4.30 a.m., 21 August. Attica Beach Hotel, Athens
Four hours to the Olympic Final

You are awake instantly. The butterflies that have accompanied you for the last week are there straight away as well. For once, there is no stiffness in your limbs. You lie there in the semi-darkness listening to the regular breathing of your roommate. Periodically, he drinks from his bottle on the bedside cabinet. It is not the only sign that he is awake. There has been none of the usual snoring or muttering, and the room doesn't have the usual accoutrements of careless sleep. Bedclothes are not scattered, there are no books left face down on the floor and yesterday's clothes are tucked away rather than left where they fell.

The alarm has no purpose today. There was no chance of oversleeping, but who would risk it? Even at this hour it barely begins to squawk before one of you silences it. You sit up and swing your legs onto the floor. The packing and setting out was all done last night. Neatly folded on the floor is your warm-up kit: a Lycra rowing suit, a T-shirt, a long-sleeved top and then a waterproof suit. Even here in Athens you will need them until about eight in the morning. Shoes are flip-flops. Cheap and untidy-looking, they are the uniform of swimmers poolside and of rowers at anything but a black-tie function. You don't need to pack the fancy trainers – your race shoes are

I

attached in the boat 20 miles away. The rest of the race kit is in the backpack. In addition there is the water bottle, accreditation and sunglasses – these have been with you every waking moment since your arrival ten days ago.

Dressed, you pull back the curtain to the balcony that you share with Ed's room. They are already up and out; the light is left on but the room is empty. Four years ago, you could look out across a wide-open area and see the fence of the Olympic Village, and beyond that Stadium Australia. Here the view is of a car park, a dusty road and the back of a nightclub.

For the umpteenth time you ask yourself what is going to happen today. For the umpteenth time you cannot come up with an answer. Thousands of hours in the boat, millions of strokes throughout your career and only one thing is for certain. This is the most important day of your life.

Today is the Olympic final.

I

steve

If anyone else were writing this story, they would make more of the first time I set eyes on Steve Redgrave on the television. Here was this guy, a legend already, on the screen, and the school rowing coach was desperately trying to interest us in the sport and the race. It was 1984, and after signing up for a second term of rowing, there were about thirty of us in the classroom in front of the television. It was the Olympic final of the coxed fours, and Great Britain was charging through the mist against the Americans to win the first Gold medal in rowing since 1948. The commentary would have helped but the coach had it turned down so that he could explain what was going on. The four were a study in contrasts. The bowman, Martin Cross, looked small on the screen, dwarfed by the oarsmen giants around him. But you could see the intensity of his efforts, his body lurching and straining with every stroke. Richard Budgett was bigger, certainly, and you could see that it was much less effort for him. His rowing seemed more natural and carefree. But the real focus of attention was in the stern, the combination of Holmes and Redgrave. Sandwiched between two giants, Andy Holmes looked smaller and less powerful, but the intensity of his rowing sprang off the screen. He would look at the opposition, then turn back to his oar and spend a few strokes driving hard. With Redgrave in the stroke seat, he had good rhythm to follow, but you could see how much Holmes brought to the crew. That is, if you were at all interested.

It should have been a 'Road-to-Damascus' moment in my life. Here was the very sport and the very person who would dominate my life for nearly twenty years. All the meaningful events of my late teens and beyond would be set against a backdrop of day-to-day rowing and its effects. And yet there was no blinding flash of light, no voice from above, no sudden realisation that this sport and these people would soon be role models for me. All I was interested in was how soon the video was going to end. There was a rumour going around that this was the day the coach was going to announce the line-ups for the eights. Last year there had been three crews, so even with my maths, I could figure out that this was the end of the line for six of us. But I also knew enough to assume it was unlikely to be me. There were plenty of guys who were bigger than me, and plenty more who rowed better, too. But even so, I reckoned I had a good chance of the second boat. This was good news. Even in the second boat you got to go and race at events outside the school. One guy had even heard that after you raced they let you drink beer from the tankards you won. And everyone knew the school eights missed lessons on Saturdays. I didn't love rowing but I certainly hated Latin, and that was one of the lessons that could kiss my arse when we packed up for Burway Schools Head of the River.

It had all started a few months before in my first summer term at Eton. In winter you played football for a term, then in the New Year a mysterious concoction called the Field Game, of which only a select few seemed to know the rules. It didn't stop it being compulsory, and the non-football-skilled in the team were forced to run around the centre of the field chasing the ball, while those who could kick played a kind of long-range tennis over our heads. Someone had cunningly combined all the most pointless elements of both football and rugby into one game and it was torture. In the summer term the choice was between cricket and rowing. I'd embarrassed myself aged 12 being captain of a team that was all out for fourteen, so to choose rowing was a straightforward decision.

Nobody in my family, myself included, had ever rowed, but the Pinsent household was no different from any other, religiously tuning in to the Boat Race on one of the spring weekends to cheer on Cambridge, normally in those days in vain. Why? Because my dad's nanny had once lived near the city and had handed down the association to the Pinsents like one of our odd Christmas traditions. No Pinsent had ever been to either Oxford or Cambridge yet there was a genuine feeling of disappointment when the Dark Blues, coached by Dan Topolski, used to win year after year.

Once signed up for rowing, all the novices were taken down to Rafts, the big boat house in the shadow of Windsor Castle, and shown the rudiments of getting a single-seater scull onto the water and moving it around. The first few weeks were going to be based exclusively on single sculls and that meant trouble for me. I developed a hate-hate relationship with sculling, and single sculling in particular, which I've never got over. The first time I tried it, I fell in within swimming distance of the dock and in the end spent longer in the water than out of it. I got better but it never got easy.

The older oarsmen, boys of 17 or 18, set up a points system to make sure you did enough rowing each week. You got one point for reaching the road bridge, two for the corner by the racecourse and four for getting to the lock. You had to get 15 points in a week to keep up, and after a fortnight we found we could do it easily. By then we could go out in other boats, too. The favourite in our group was the coxed pair. It was a huge behemoth of a craft. Its wooden-plank construction made it unwieldy but stable and we could easily swap seats in the middle of the river. It became a happy way to fritter away a sunny June afternoon with a couple of mates, rowing out your time in the working seats before taking control of the rudder strings and having a break. We would chat on about schoolwork, our least favourite teachers or how many points we were going to give ourselves.

The only target was getting to the island that the college owned near Maidenhead. It was called Queen's Eyot and was an idyllic combination of pavilion and lawn. On a summer afternoon you could spend two hours getting up there in steady fashion (with at least three turns in the cox's seat), spend two hours toying with a chocolate bar and a drink on the lawn and then come gently back.

Racing wasn't really a priority to begin with. For sure, there were inter-house trophies that were up for grabs but no one from my house was going to win the sculling cup, and our junior four, with me rowing in the middle, was stuck in the slow lane of the river while the good ones swept past taking the piss.

But one thing was beginning to annoy me. I didn't like losing.

It frustrated me that I had no chance of winning the sculling trophy. It got to me when our four failed to qualify from the preliminary rounds of the competition. It would be a very long time before I could say that I was a winner.

In the first year, losing races was just part of the appeal. There were going to be more in a week or so, so why get stressed about it? The winners only got tinny little medals on string that only they were impressed with, so it didn't matter, right? Within minutes of losing I could laugh it off, or blame something or somebody for our misfortune. 'If only our three man hadn't caught a crab, we would have won,' or 'You should have seen me. I was so bad I nearly fell in!'

But within a couple of years there were events that I wanted to win, regattas on the Thames that other schools and crews would go to. We were training more seriously by this time, spending afternoons rowing in eights trying to get everyone to do the same thing at the same time. The rowing was fun but losing hurt. I couldn't pretend it didn't matter. I could no longer look crewmates in the eye and laugh about it.

The first time I ever went to the National Schools Regatta it was the premier event of the year for us. I was in an eight where all of us were under 15 years old. We were the 'B' crew, an assortment of athletes either too small or too mal-coordinated to be considered for the 'A' line-up. I had a great summer never quite winning but always aware that the Nationals were the focus.

The blessing was that at the Nationals we had an event designed for Under-15 'B' crews. I was getting annoyed and frustrated being put out as cannon fodder for the 'A' crew in training, and then having to race them or some school's 'A' crew at regattas. This time the event was restricted. We had a secret plan for the middle of the race that was going to be a 'burn' – a massive effort and energy expenditure that we were sure would give us the lead with 400 metres of the race left.

We didn't take a lead in the opening 500 and were rowing in a pack of eights when our coxswain announced the burn. 'Okay, guys, here it is. Legs 20 in three ... two ... one ... now!'

We sprang at the water, throwing caution to the wind with our pacing, but it was worth it. With a frantic burst of speed, we captured the lead from the opposition and the adrenalin was flowing. We were all thinking the same thing. We can win this thing. But then the guy behind me had a disaster. Rowing too enthusiastically, he lifted his body off the seat for a moment and came crashing down on the runners. With him off his seat, this left him and the rest of the crew in trouble. He couldn't move up and down the boat in the same rhythm as everyone else. He couldn't use his legs at all and tried for a stroke or two to keep in time with just his arms. But when it became evident that it was no use, he reached down to try to sort out the problem. But by now the seat was damaged and he couldn't get it back on the runners. We all tried to make up the deficit in power and timing but there was too much lake left. The lead, which we had been so excited to capture, was gone within a hundred metres. For a time, there was still hope for a second place but soon that, too, was gone. There was no hiding the disappointment, no joking, just tears and recriminations. What did he do wrong? Why didn't he get it sorted? If it had been me, I would have done something different.

In retrospect you might think that it should pale into insignificance. But I would still have a lively conversation with an opponent from that race today if they remembered it. I'd still try to claim that we could and should have won. From that moment losing never sat comfortably.

By the time I wanted to know more about Steve I certainly did love rowing. The patchy and unimpressive Under-15 'B' eight had engendered an enthusiasm for the sport that pretty soon became obsessional. Every event entered – and usually lost – was now followed by a frantic scrabbling in the pages of the library's copy of *Rowing* magazine. There was never a mention of us or even, come to think of it, of the competitions we had entered. The pages were given over to the big events of the month. Headlines ran 'Interview with Head Coach' or 'Results from Trials' and there was always coverage of Redgrave. Within a year he had gone into a pair with Andy Holmes, one of the other guys from the 1984 Olympic four, and their boat manufacturer ran a big ad on the back cover of *Rowing* each month. It was a photograph taken from behind the crew so that they faced the camera, Steve at stroke, Andy at bow. Redgrave, with shoulders like a Spanish fighting bull tilting gracefully towards his rigger, his mouth set in a tight line with his bottom lip over his top teeth. Holmes is tilted out further, almost as if he is trying to get into the picture. He is small in comparison but his expression dominates the photograph. Despite all the things that could take his attention – the oars, the boat or his strokeman – he is staring almost manically back into the camera. When I at long last plucked up courage to steal a back cover from the library and post the photo in my room, Holmes's eyes would catch my glance several times a day.

It was only towards the end of my school career that I really started getting good for my age. The Under-15 'B' crew had been followed by a year in the 'A' crew at under-

16 level. In that season I won my first tankard at Bedford Star Regatta. They were (and still are) sinfully ugly things: squat blue china with a rim lined in gold. Going home we must have looked like a bunch of Knightsbridge dowagers cradling their pug dogs in the park, no one plucking up the courage to tell us that our pride and joy was in fact frighteningly hideous.

By the time I got into the first school eight in 1987, selection for Britain was at least a possibility. That year saw my international debut in the eights in Cologne at the Junior World Championships. Like all such international events, it was a race over 2000 metres. We nearly won a medal, but finished in the worst possible position, fourth. By the time I was leaving school the following year after 'A' levels, I was rowing in a pair with Tim Foster. My school coach, Paul Wright, had put us together. By the summer of 1988 we had done enough to convince the selectors that we were the best hope for a Gold at the Junior World Championships. Paul coached us on the river at Windsor in the few weeks that we had at home before leaving for the competition. One afternoon we had just finished our row when he called us into the boat house for a talk.

'Good. Well done, it's coming along nicely. I think we need to take the riggers off and put the boat on the trailer.' Tim and I look confused. The boat wasn't going anywhere for a few days at least and we had all planned the outings that we had left. We turn to Paul with quizzical expressions.

'We are going to Molesey tomorrow,' he said. No help for us. We knew roughly where it was but no more. 'I was on the phone to Mike Spracklen and we have been invited down there to train with Steve and Andy.' Slack-jawed, we nodded our heads and walked out to the boat to begin loading it. Then it hit us properly and the dam was broken.

'This is so cool.'

'What if we beat them?' Laughter all round. Then a silence as it sank in some more. 'We are really going to go up against these guys?'

We arrived at the club around 11 in the morning in time to join in with their second session of the day. The national coach Mike Spracklen, who looked to me alarmingly like Yoda from *Star Wars*, was standing on the side of the river on the concrete apron in front of the clubhouse. 'Okay guys, we are going to do quite a simple training session this morning. Do you know the river?' He looked at us both with questioning eyebrows.

'No, we've never rowed here before.'

'Okay, that's fine. I'll steer both pairs from the launch, so if you hear me shouting at you, you know what that means. We will warm up to the top of the river in that direction.' He pointed off to the right upstream. 'On the way back we will do a piece of harder rowing. There will be five minutes at 22 strokes a minute, then three at 24. We will finish with a minute at 28. Okay?'

Then, before we could ask any questions, he turned to face the boat house. 'Oh, here they are now.'

With trepidation we turn round to find them stalking towards us. Steve, massive as I expected him to be, especially in his shoulders, and Andy, smaller but intense, impressively so. We all shake hands and quickly run over what is going to happen. Us on one side of the river, them sticking to the other bank. Then it's a mad dash for us to get going. They seem to have everything sorted and ready in an instant, clothing arranged, oars down by the water and coaching launch pulled alongside the jetty. We are flustering back and forth, forgetting things in our haste and excitement.

We row like dogs on the way up to the top of the river. Although neither of us can say it out loud, we are both thinking – WE ARE TRAINING WITH HOLMES AND REGRAVE. WE ARE TRAINING WITH HOLMES AND REDGRAVE. Their rhythm seems to dominate us. It is like being in a disco and trying to dance the samba. By the time we get to the end of the warm-up, our rowing has been to hell and back and we have just about got the boat running the way we knew it could. Both pairs pause to spin round at the top and Steve peels off his tracksuit bottoms. 'Oh God, look at the size of his legs,' I think. Our school coach Paul is giving us the look a dad might give his scrawny kid about to join in a game of British bulldog in the street.

The boats paddle downstream and Mike gives us a countdown to the start. A good second before he says 'Go!', we tear off at a much higher rate than anyone had planned, especially us, and probably row 30 strokes in the first minute. We also take the lead (WE ARE BEATING HOLMES AND REDGRAVE, WE ARE BEATING HOLMES AND REDGRAVE). After two minutes of rowing they are beginning to catch up. Like a cartoon giant chasing a mouse, their huge strides are more effective than our scamper. We quickly run out of energy. The bubble of confidence and bravado that had carried us through the first part of the piece bursts in sudden style. The pair come up level with us and, without pausing or looking at us, sweeps past. There is little we or the coaches can do about it; our limbs are heavy with dejection. In a final insult, we make a mistake with the steering and find ourselves on the wrong part of the river, heading down a different channel on the wrong side of the island. By the time the frantic waving and gesticulating from the launch has been translated between us, it's all over. We paddle back up again and round the right side of the island and into the dock. The Olympic pair is even more efficient in clearing up than in setting out, boat and oars packed away into the boat house within seconds, then one trip back to sort out the launch. While we fuss over getting the boat up and out near the trailer, Steve wanders over.

'Did you enjoy that?' He is nearly deadpan but his mouth has a smile struggling up from one corner. We can't raise a smile in response. 'Yes, thanks. Shame about our steering.' He seems to keep himself in check, unwilling to rub salt in our wounds but not hiding our defeat away, either.

'Listen, good luck at the championships.' That makes me perk up. 'Yeah, you too. Have a good Olympics.'

I can't quite shake the impact as he walks away to his car and, best of all, gives us a thumbs up as he leaves.

We were ecstatic, bugging Paul endlessly about how good we must have looked for that brief spell when we were looking down on the World Champions. A few weeks later, having won Gold in our own junior event, we both stayed up late in the night to watch them attempt an unprecedented double: two Gold medals in two rowing events at the same Games. They won the first in fine style, their giant strokes outclassing the Romanian pair. But the Italian Abbagnale brothers were too quick in the start of the Sunday final in the coxed pairs, and the Brits never looked like winning. We shouted and cheered at the telly anyway, and for the first time the relevance of the Olympics hit home. Here was the sport I now loved, and a pair I had at least raced, winning the ultimate event. We took great pride in the fact that our winning time at the Junior Championships over 1500 metres would have had us leading the Olympic final in Seoul with only 500 metres left. Different weather and water made no difference to us, we argued, and the fact that Tim had been nearly unconscious at the end of our shorter final did not dent our joke that we were in fact the quickest pair in the world.

2

cyprus diary

Saturday, 18 October 2003
On the way home from Cyprus
308 days till the Olympic Final

Knackered again. This camp has really been tough. It was the first foreign training camp of the Olympic run-up, a chance for the group to come together to blow away the cobwebs that three weeks of holiday had gathered. The training was based in the gym on rowing machines and on cycles criss-crossing the hills north of Paphos. The gym was a great place to look out of and we got amazing sunsets through the windows, but if you were in the first group, you got absolutely baked. I reckon I was losing up to 5 kilograms a session in sweat.

We had a discussion last night about the training today. We didn't leave till noon, so we had plenty of time to train and then catch the bus, and in addition we get tomorrow off. Brilliant! Dee will be happy. Our wedding anniversary as well.

Haven't told her yet. Managed to get her a really nice watch. Had to make a special trip to get it but I know she will like it. I knew what I was looking for and it only took an hour. Apart from the cycling and going to watch England play rugby, it was the only time I left the hotel .

Anyway, last night Dunny started discussing the training and suggested we do another cycle instead of a last rowing machine session. It was 16 kilometres on the programme. I was not that bothered as long as we stayed on the flat and did those 6-kilometre loops that we started out on, but Jürgen, our coach, insisted on the hill route. For the third time! I was dead set against it, along with the larger portion of the group, but Dunny persisted until it was decided.

Early start for the cycling group (seven thirty). Breakfast arrives and there's Dunny bold as brass saying he can't come – he has a sore back and good luck, etc. etc. Bastard. We tell him that the hills will echo with his name.

We get into three seeded groups this time (slowest to head out first) and my group is second to go. We are already past the first group by the lowest village on the first climb and I'm leading out of it when I begin to get the same rhythm as I had on the first time up there. For a minute or two I'm leading on the road, then Tom James comes past like his bike's on fire. Up to the top by the town I get a bottle fill from Gunny and say, 'Tom's going really well'.

'Robin is out on his own,' he replies. The last group went another way up the first hill and we never saw them!

Furious now. Ride along for the next hour cursing Robin, Hodgy, Gunny, Jürgen and especially Dunny. But the descent is good. Get to the trucks at the halfway stop to find none of the bloody cheats (that's what they are by now) have waited to allow the group to reassemble. Find the last 10-kilometre climb a hell-hole. But get to the top with the fantastic views over Paphos knowing that we are done for this camp.

Get back and half-heartedly get a 'you lot are cheats' campaign going while we pack up the bikes. Ed starts chipping that missing bits of kit must have been stolen by them. Bus journey takes forever across to airport. Can't sleep, so send flirty texts to Dee.

touching distance

Rowing after I left school was a much more individual effort than it had been from the comfort of the school boat club. Gone was the camaraderie of the guys I had learnt to row and race with and gone, too, was the daily guiding influence of my coach Paul Wright. In September 1988 I joined Leander, the premier rowing club in the country and home to most of the men's Olympic team. They had a cadet rowing scheme to take aspiring youngsters and try to turn them into senior athletes. The routine was pretty simple: everybody got together on a Saturday morning to row twice on the river at Henley and then again on Sunday for two more stints. Monday to Friday was left up to you. Some of the guys were at college or university, some had jobs, and I fell into the second category. I had started work in a cake factory near my parents' house in Hampshire to get some money together, with the plan of travelling the world. While I waited for the post office account to fill up to a necessary minimum, I could feed my rowing habit at the weekends.

The cadet group was imposing. No one seemed to know or give a damn that I had won a Gold medal at the Junior Championships, and I certainly didn't want to come across as some public school twit. I resolved fairly early on to keep my head down and enjoy the company of the newer, younger guys. The older, more experienced rowers dominated the humour of the group but it was an atmosphere I felt I could laugh in as much as anybody else. Advice or help didn't come from within the group, and bad results or rowing were cauterised by the liberal treatment of group piss-take therapy. The whole set-up was different from anything I had experienced before. Everyone was serious about getting high up on the rowing ladder; they talked in terms of winning at Henley Regatta, or even making the team for the World Championships.

During the second month the guys who had actually competed at the Olympics returned from holiday. They added a top layer to the club, which made weekends in the changing room a mixed bag. The Olympic group were quieter than the younger guys; some of them were nursing the results from Seoul (when all the men's boats bar Steve's finished fourth – the worst possible result) but they had an assurance about them that was compelling. They had their own group briefing with Mike Spracklen and seemed to do their own thing.

Steve was in the group, too, but you had to recognise him to find him. He was quieter and more assured than any of the others. By this stage, he and Andy had split up. Andy had unofficially retired, and rumours flourished about how the partnership had come to an end. We all knew that even though they won two Gold medals together, they weren't even on speaking terms any more. Don't allow anyone to tell you precisely what went on between those two. I'm not sure even they know. So Steve was now trying new partners, and the current favourite was Simon Berrisford, one of the Olympic coxless four. The cadet group was snide and impressed in equal measure when it came to Steve. It was almost as if they couldn't bring themselves to love or hate him publicly. Steve's aloofness only stirred the mix. I had been there a few weekends and had had no sign from him that he remembered or cared to remember that we had met on a training outing. I didn't broach the subject, preferring to watch from afar. He didn't mingle with the cadet group, and even got dressed in a quiet corner of the changing room.

On one weekend just before Christmas the coach of the cadet group was waiting for me when I arrived at eight on Saturday morning. He took me to a secluded corner of the changing room before saying that I wasn't going to be part of the group any more. I was stunned and furious milliseconds apart. How could this be right? I was young, sure, but I was more than punching my weight in the cadet group. I was set to have an angry outburst over him and his coaching when his face softened a little. 'You are not going to row in this group any more because Mike Spracklen wants you in the Olympic group.' This time I was stunned and terrified moments apart. But with what I hoped was a confident stride I walked past the other cadets and out onto the concrete apron between the club and the river. There stood a group of the men I had watched compete on the television only months before: Berrisford, Mulkerrins, Stewart, Burfitt, Dillon, Turner and, of course, Redgrave. These were all people who had years of international experience behind them.

'Morning, Matthew,' said Spracklen. 'I want you to row with Steve Peel.' Peel was a Cambridge Blue and Olympic oarsman who had been in the coxless four at Seoul. He was tall but not thickset, and as soon as we went out I knew I could learn a lot from him. It wasn't as if he was talking all the time during the training (believe me, you don't want one of those), but in the pair I had to match his technique and strength.

In a coxless pair half the power is your responsibility, and half the rhythm, too. The balance can be dominated by one person, but it's hard work if you do it that way. In a good pair the rowing is seamless between the two partners. To begin with, I really struggled. My hands were moving the oar too slowly after the blade left the water, I was rowing a lot shorter than Steve Peel and he was out powering me quite considerably.

It can't have been easy for him to be given the task of pairing with some unknown junior guy. He didn't grumble, at least not to me, and I began to think I could recover after a bad start when he abruptly retired. There was no meeting, no announcement made, I certainly wasn't in the loop. I just turned up to find he was no longer around. I don't think even now that I had much impact on the decision; at least I hope I didn't. I just reckon the time running up to an Olympics is the longest and hardest to deal with in the winter after the previous Games. The memory of the flame is going cold, and all you are faced with is four winters of hard slog.

A few weeks later I got home late on a Friday night to find a message from my mum on the kitchen table. Andy Holmes had called. This wasn't just unexpected, this seemed as likely as the Queen calling to invite me for tea. As far as I knew, Andy wasn't in any group or club at that stage, and him calling me could mean only one thing: he wanted to row in a pair with me. It was after ten o'clock, so I decided that I would give it a night to think over what I would do. By the time I had driven up to Leander on the Saturday morning the decision had been made for me. There was already a rumour going around that the stroke of the Olympic eight, Nick Burfitt, had left the Henley group to try a pair with Andy. There was no antipathy towards Nick. Anyone given the chance to pair with a guy like Andy should go, but the plot line was obvious: it was a clear challenge to Redgrave and Berrisford in the pair, and, if one were needed, a final nail in the coffin of any future rowing partnership that Steve might have had with Andy.

I often wonder what would have happened had I got back

home in time to talk to Andy. Would he have invited me to row with him and, if so, how would it have turned out? One thing is certain: challenging Steve so openly and early might have jeopardised any partnership with him later on.

In the end, Andy and Nick didn't get beyond a few weeks together, and despite a spring season back rowing in the squad, Andy retired in the middle of the summer. I only remember him as a quiet guy who got on with the job; we never spoke about the message, and before long he had removed himself so far from the rowing world that no one knew what he was doing. He was quoted in a newspaper article before the 1992 Olympics saying some really complimentary things about me, and I never had anything but respect for him. Eventually Andy would become one of the very few things Steve and I didn't talk about. In future years I always held the position that it is inexcusable to fall out with someone with whom you have won an Olympic Gold medal. You don't have to like them, you can disagree with them on lots of things. But the bond that is created in competition at that level is like a family one – whatever happens you are part of a team. But Steve obviously felt differently and I didn't see it as part of my job to educate him on this.

But a proper relationship with Steve was still some way off. The summer of 1989 was a big time for me. Little did I know it, but I was fast becoming a senior athlete. The gangly, mal-coordinated teenager, who had so struggled with a boat early on, was getting to grips with it. That's not to say I was a polished rower. I never shook off the issue of my slow hands at the finish of the stroke – a habit I fight to this day. Mike Spracklen was so exasperated with my efforts in the Great Britain coxed four of that year that he took a length of rope and attached it to the outside ends of the oars. My job was to ensure the rope stayed taut and never dragged on the water. If it did, he would shout, 'No! ... No! ... No!' every stroke. It was a fairly degrading experience but richly deserved, and the four went on to win a Bronze at my first World Championship in Yugoslavia.

Relations with Steve had at least moved up a notch. An appearance in the team of 1989 would mean I could justifiably expect to get recognised by him. However, Steve treated every member of the squad with caution. He knew only too well that the majority wanted him and Simon Berrisford to fail. For some it was jealousy plain and simple; for others the failure of the top boat with Steve in it meant the pecking order of the squad would be adjusted in their own favour. Any chance that Steve would be incorporated into a bigger boat meant more seats in the boat alongside him. It all added up to a lot of pressure for Simon and Steve.

Simon was a talented individual but he was nothing like Steve. Outgunned in the boat and quietly ridiculed by the younger members of the squad in the changing room, he felt the pressure worse than most. It's not as if the pair were terrible either. They performed well in the season of 89, winning a series of races, including Henley. But they were well beaten by an East German pair at the World Championships, and it became clear that only a radical rethink would improve them to Gold medal class.

In the winter of 89/90 Simon hit another boat while out training in his single scull. Though it did not cause a career-ending injury, it hurt his back and was something he struggled with that season and beyond. The rest of the squad smelt blood in the water. Surely there was never a better chance to beat Redgrave on home water? I was rowing in a pair with Pete Mulkerrins, who had, like Peel, been in the Olympic coxless four. He was taller than almost everyone in the Team, and rowed well because of it. His stroke was languid and rhythmical, which was a revelation to me. With Pete at stroke, we could get a lot of boat speed if I simply followed. At Spring Trials we ran Steve and Simon close but couldn't beat them. The cracks in their crew were beginning to show, however. Steve was obviously trying to coach Simon in the boat. This is a delicate balance: you want your partner to encourage, cajole and criticise, but coaching was a no-no. Coaching somehow indicated a lack of respect, a situation where one guy felt he was better than the other, and it was music to our ears. There was one point where they were sitting out in the middle of the lake at Nottingham with Simon screaming and ranting in frustration, whether at himself or at Steve we didn't know, but it was all good.

Being in the ranks of the Team was increasing my confidence and skills rapidly. I was no longer the learner in the group, the one being singled out in the crew for individual treatment from the coach. I was far from being the best, but it all made me louder in a group situation than I had been before.

Pete and I hatched a plan to compete with Steve and Simon as much as we could. At this time we were also in a coxless four with Tim Foster and Martin Cross. They were as keen as us to upset the apple-cart, and though we rowed in the four successfully through the early summer, the pairs competition at Henley in 1990 was seen as a big opportunity. Henley was perfect for us, a home crowd and therefore lots of pressure for the favourites, but, more importantly, one-on-one racing where only the winner progressed. The draw came out with Martin and Tim seeded to meet Steve and Simon in the semis if all went according to plan. As Pete and I saw it, we had to deal with the Austrian pair on semi-final day and we would race a tired Redgrave and Berrisford in the final. So much for the plan. Steve and Simon made it through the first two rounds without incident and then withdrew. Simon's back had become so painful that he was unable to row – early estimates were talking weeks out of the boat. The whole balance of the event shifted. Tim and Martin now had a row over the course at their leisure on Saturday, and we knew they would be fresh as daisies for the winner of the semi between us and the Austrians.

As it turned out, the Austrians were a hard nut to crack. Locked together side by side for three-quarters of the race, we put in an effort with 600 metres to go that we had always imagined would be the beating of Steve and Simon. It was a high-risk strategy designed to buy a lead but the cost in energy was immense. With 300 metres to go, we were a length up but hanging on for dear life. For a moment I thought we had them, but the bowman, Karl Sinzinger, turned and must have sized up the situation pretty well. From then on, it was one-way traffic: they kept on attacking and despite the roars of a few thousand well-wishers in the grandstand, they took the lead with three strokes remaining. We folded completely and could only summon the energy to look each other in the eye 40 minutes later.

Tim and Martin had to deal with the same finishing sprint from the Austrians on the Sunday. I found myself in a not unusual quandary for the rowing team. Did I want our crewmates to win and publicly prove they were better than us? Or did I want the Austrians to charge through to show that at least we had lost to the eventual winners? In the end, I opted for the former, but the fact that I had to think about it shows something of the mindset of the rowing team then.

Despite my support, Tim and Martin went down fighting to the Austrians and we all consoled ourselves in our win in the fours later in the afternoon. Despite our best scheming, we had not brought about the demise of the pair, but the result was in some ways even better. Redgrave was footloose and fancy-free.

· · ·

As a squad of 15 athletes, we had been invited to be part of the Goodwill Games in Seattle in the summer of 1990. The selectors, as we had expected, had persuaded Steve to be part of the team if only as an interim move while he waited to see how Simon progressed. For the first time in anyone's experience, Steve was part of the group rather than someone to race against. To begin with, few knew how to deal with him. His seeming arrogance and aloofness that we had all experienced in different ways was actually shyness to a great degree. That, combined with the very real (and justified) feeling on his part that we were all out to get him, made life a little tense at first. But a few training sessions did wonders, and I in particular wasn't going to let a few group loyalties get in the way of spending time with my schoolboy hero.

That summer broke down the myths that surrounded Steve. Yes, he felt pain when he rowed (there was an oft-quoted theory that so gargantuan was his oxygen uptake that it defused any pain during a race). Yes, he was massively and quietly proud of what he had achieved, and he pretty much didn't give a stuff what anyone in British rowing thought of him. Over the years he had put the back up of almost everyone around with varying degrees of justification. Administrators, coaches and other athletes were just bit players in his plan to win Gold medals. Given the fact that even at this stage of his career he was the single most successful rower Britain had produced, he had both the power and the experience to plot his own path. The rest of us were channelling much of our energy into fighting the system and each other, yet his focus on everything outside the narrow confines of British rowing was a revelation. He had a quiet confidence about him in a sporting situation and in the boat, but it seldom appeared in the setting of the club or the group.

As we were travelling home, the news came that Simon's back was worse than anyone had expected. He would be out for the rest of the season and there would be the trials in a few weeks to decide on the crews for the forthcoming World Championships. Pete saw it way before I did. He commented to me that the next available oarsman to pair with Steve would be me. I outwardly dismissed him but found myself brimming with excitement.

The head coaches announced a small rowing trial at Henley to test two options for Steve's new combinations. The new unit would then go to Nottingham to be trialled against the other British pairs and might, in fact, be rolled into a four or even an eight. Both Pete Mulkerrins and I were invited to Henley to pair with Steve. At this stage Steve had the ability to row on stroke side, as he had with Holmes at the Olympics, or on bow side, as he had with Berrisford.

Steve always said that the morning in question was a nightmare for him. Pete phoned through the night before to say he wasn't coming. I think he felt that there was going to be an outright winner in the race-off and it wasn't going to be him. As 8 a.m. came and went, Steve became sure that I was not interested either. But a quick call to my house in Oxford confirmed that I had been seen a few minutes before running out of the house shouting 'shit' over and over again.

The first outing was surreal. Steve was bending over backwards not to be imposing and I was hanging on for dear life. His power and attack in the boat were unbelievable. His stroke wasn't as long as Pete's, but it was more dynamic, and the precision with which he repeated every one was impressive. I soon realised that if he or the situation fazed me, as they had in the pair with Steve Peel, then this was going to be a very short collaboration. I began to enjoy it. Within certain technical parameters, there were moments of the stroke when I could pull as hard as I liked and have it matched by the guy sitting ahead of me. Steve was doing all the hard stuff – he was stroking and setting up the rhythm and also doing the steering. This meant he had to look round to judge the river and the traffic and use the rudder to manoeuvre the pair accordingly. I just had to row.

By the end of the session I was getting cocky. 'Let's row ten strokes and see who pulls the other one round,' I suggested. Steve agreed, and I got a box seat for the biggest shoulders in the business doing their stuff. After about three strokes it was clear I was not going to win this one. The boat was carving round to me, and no matter what I did I couldn't stop it. Stunned and disappointed, I called a halt and it was only when he turned round that I realised he was using all his strength and the rudder to move the boat in a tight semicircle. From then on the tone was set between us. We competed against one another in everything. Only when we raced did we join forces against the rest.

Two weeks later after the promised trials in Nottingham the selectors decided that double Olympic and World Champion Steve Redgrave would be joined by Matthew Pinsent for the upcoming World Championships in Tasmania.

I was 19 years old.

training

Training is the most dependable and consistent part of life in our sport. Through thick and thin, home and abroad, good weather and bad, training is a constant. If you rowed under our training scheme for four years, you would travel about 35,000 kilometres on water and rowing machine. If you add in the time spent doing weights and running, stretching, cycling, swimming or cross-country skiing, it means that for every stroke in an Olympic final you have trained for 15 hours. Rowing is one of the sports where training is not the remit of the champions alone. I'm pretty certain that all the people who rowed in all the finals I have contested have done as much.

The central demand of rowing is all-round fitness. Anyone who has sat on a rowing machine for even a few minutes gets a clue about that. The rowing stroke needs first a dynamic push with the legs from a bent position to straight. This is then combined with a pull by the arms and, in addition, an extension of the back. Add in the use of the shoulders and you have the complete body work-out in one package, as they are keen on saying on the Shopping Channel.

Unfortunately, this is only part of the story. This fitness has to be combined with good technique. Technique is a bitch to nail down. At times it feels like juggling five or six balls. No sooner do you have the entry of the oar sorted than the finish goes to pot. Some parts of the technique seem impossible to combine – a relaxed float as the blades are out of the water combined with a powerful drive with them in. After a while rowing can become an almost existential search for the perfect technique.

We were always expected to be at the club at eight in the morning. The common misconception is that rowers start at five in the morning, but as the cars queue to get over the bridge and go to work, so do we. The day starts in the changing room with sleepy 'Good mornings' exchanged, and perhaps a quick conversation about yesterday's football. Steve Redgrave follows Chelsea, Tim Foster is a Tottenham fan and James Cracknell is Wimbledon. I haven't really been to enough games to call myself a proper supporter of any one team, so I remain an impartial bystander, able to hand out criticism to all the guys but share in none of the glory.

The arrival of our coach, Jürgen Grobler, hurries the onset of the training. The first session of the day is always on the water. We row between 16 and 20 kilometres, which takes between 70 and 90 minutes in a pair. This is not 'train till you drop'; you are not pushing yourself to the limits. Your body will only take so much of that. The idea is to build endurance. Every session has an intensity band stipulated by the coach's programme, and this is usually expressed by heart rate. The higher your heart beats, the harder you are working. We try to hold it in a zone where the body is forced to adapt the lungs, the blood and the vascular system to cope. For me, this means anywhere between 130 and 165 beats per minute. Once out on the river, we spend a few minutes getting warmed-up then break into a steady row. The heart rate rises slowly onto a plateau, and at 18 or 19 strokes a minute we have to work to keep it there. The body quickly starts sweating, and even in cold winter weather the first stop after twenty minutes is a chance to peel off the top layer of clothing. The breathing is steady rather than rushed and after a while the boat can take on a relaxed loping rhythm. For us in the boat, at first the mind is concentrating on the here and now. Am I in time? Am I changing this or that nasty habit? But after a while a significant part of the concentration need not be on the rowing. For me training is a means to an end, racing, so I project the boat into the future and a big competition environment. I picture the World Championships or the Olympics, and in my mind's eye there will be the opposition, the course and a race. There then follows the best attempt I can muster on the Thames in January. If you get really good at this kind of rehearsal, you can spend minutes at a time away in your imagination and the rowing doesn't suffer. On the other hand, if you start thinking about the football game last night or tonight's date, then the rowing disappears down the plughole.

By the time we reach the end of the session the legs are drained and the mind is certainly ready for a break. We row the boat back up past the picturesque boat houses on the town side of the river and back into Leander. The oars stay on the pontoon ready for the next session and the coach, who has been cycling the whole session, on the towpath, chairs a quick debrief. It is usually quick. Jürgen is not keen on long speeches; but a quick assessment of what he thought opens up a discussion between the crew members. Sometimes people are itching to say what was on their minds, to bring out a trend or a pattern that they were happy with. Steve and, to a less extent, James are on the glass-half-empty side of the fence. For them, every stroke needs to be the very best, and anything less than a perfect outing is to be criticised. Tim and I are much more optimistic about our assessments. We are happier to concentrate on the good patches of a bad outing, urging the crew towards the positive patterns rather than the negative. The contrast is useful, and whether in the pair or later in the four, I've always needed to have a strong critical eye to get the best from me. Some people call it laziness but I hope that from a different angle I give as much to the boat as the 'let's go quicker brigade'.

The post-outing talks can escalate into a clash quite quickly, however. Everyone has the right to criticise someone else for the way they are rowing, or behaving, or training. It becomes a necessary medium for the angst and aggression that top-level sport produces. You want the other guys to be as committed and passionate about things as you, and nothing hurts more than the feeling it is not going right. A good crew will argue, compromise and discuss its own destiny to death. The idea is that it all happens right there, in the boat house while the sweat is still in your clothes. It has an urgency then, and can defuse issues that might otherwise fester into massive arguments. I have never hit anyone in a rowing boat, or been hit, but I have seen crews dissolve into nothing in their frustration with each other. I have even known crew members to give up in the middle of the river mid-training and mid-stream and slip into the water and swim away. Drastic and, in team terms, terminal.

Jürgen might chip in with the times that he has taken from the bank. These are never precise, not because he is inaccurate, but because we train on a river and the water is always moving. But after a few months you get used to the variables and can assess them fairly well. All our speeds can be compared to a gold standard. We know even at 18 strokes a minute and at heart rate 145 we should be producing 75 per cent of world-record speed. A quick glance at the chart and Jürgen's times and we can sign off the session as a success or otherwise. It is a tribute to Jürgen that the system is so simple to use and yet hard to set up in the first place. We had used a gold standard before to train to, but the idea that every session, irrespective of the intensity, could have a benchmark was new. Jürgen had the whole spectrum laid out for all the differing boat classes, single scull through to eight. This then also allows us to race each other when we are not side by side. In a pair we might do seven minutes for a piece of rowing over 2 kilometres that the eight then does in six. By reading across the percentage chart, we can see that we have achieved 78 per cent of Gold-medal speed and they have done 77. Therefore we 'win' the piece. Even though they went a minute quicker, we get the bragging rights.

After the debrief, we wander in to change kit and have something to eat. Leander has a fully staffed kitchen and club facilities upstairs to cater for the 3000 members who might care to avail themselves of the cooking. When I first joined, rowers were catered for on sufferance, but Jürgen changed that pretty quickly. With the support of the committee, he set up a crew room that was our space with no dress code, organised the chef to provide food at breakfast and lunch times and at subsidised prices, and in a single stroke changed the relationship between the club and its athletes. We now get the service and support of a club determined to help us compete at the highest level. I get to bore the younger crew with stories of how it used to be and how lucky they are. Breakfast can be toast, cereal or porridge, and we can order anything cooked from the chef. We have a dietary target of 6000 calories a day, and though it sounds as though you can eat anything you like, you must try to get 70 per cent of that total in carbohydrate. If you can't cheat by piling on the sugar, then it is a massive challenge to eat enough. Breakfast is all washed down with plenty of fluids. Even at home in the mild British weather we are losing 2–3 kilograms of fluid every session.

After breakfast we get some downtime. The TV will usually be on, and those with a penchant for *This Morning* can get their fill. Some guys sleep off the night before. Some read the paper. If we have a media interview to fulfil, now is a good time to spend half an hour doing so. Mail sent to the club can be read and replied to. The majority are autograph or interview requests; the hard ones are the charity letters.

Eleven o'clock heralds the start of the second session. Three times a week, except in the racing season, we do weights. We have a gym, which is part of the ground floor of the club, and we go there to do either circuits or heavy weights. Circuits came as a bombshell when Jürgen first got Steve and me to do them, and they remain that way now. We take 15 exercises – sit-ups, press-ups, squat jumps and bench presses – arranged in a rough circle. Each exercise has a certain number to be completed before you can move on. We do 1200 or 1500 lifts or repetitions in total, and we get competitive, too. One guy leads off and then everybody follows at minute intervals. All the way round the four or five circuits you are assessing the lead he had and trying to see if you are catching up. Within a crew there is no bragging or gloating if you win, but everybody knows the score. It's one of the few times that we brazenly compete with each other. Encouragement between you is scarce and you haven't got the breath anyway. After 45 minutes or so it's over and you can rest.

Heavy weights are more sedate and less competitive. There are only about half a dozen different exercises. We usually lift pretty much the maximum weight, and this is repeated some 40 times for each exercise. This power training drains the energy steadily. There's less sweat than doing circuits, but it's tiring all the same.

If we have done a weights session second then, sure as eggs are eggs, we have a third session to do. By the time weights are over it's lunchtime, so there is a chance to get in more food and drink. The last session, especially in the winter months, is on the rowing machine.

The 'ergos', as the rowing machine sessions are known, are the least favourite test of the athletes because there is nothing to beat but the machine, and it always wins. They are loved by coaches because they provide a rare opportunity to rank the athletes on a test where there can be no argument over the result. There is no weather that can interrupt it, no blaming a dodgy partner or boat. Just you versus the machine. The display shows not only how many strokes a minute you are rowing (the rating), but also how hard you pull every stroke, and expresses it all as a time per 500 metres.

We use the same machine as everybody else – the black Concept II one. It is hard by this stage in the day to keep the energy going, but the instant feedback on the screen lets you know exactly what you are pulling each stroke. For a third session, the distance is unlikely to be less than 12 kilometres. It is usually 16.

This goes on for seven days a week. Jürgen Grobler's approach was that if you were keen on winning, then mileage made champions. The old system was to do nothing all week, then train so hard at the weekends that you needed a chair to sit on in the shower. A full-time programme from Monday to Friday, with light sessions at the weekends, was a sea-change from what anyone, with the exception of Steve, had been doing up to that point. But the pay-off was immense.

We get a day off every three weeks. And it goes fast. By the time you have had a nice lie-in and spent a few hours reading the Sunday papers, the impending start on a Monday seems just a few minutes away. Monday comes and the body creaks back into action. The harsh bit is that after a while your body becomes more used to the training than life without it. A day off is an interruption in the addictive hormones that your body produces, and the irony is that after a hard week, your body actually prefers a lighter day of training to a day of complete rest. The mind, on the other hand, cries out for a change.

I've lost count over the years of the weddings I've missed, evenings I've cut short and promises I've broken. The grind of training is the thing that Steve always said he would miss least when he retired. The offers we get to do cool stuff are incredible – golf days, trips abroad, test drives and so on. But

99 per cent of the time we turn them down. We used to have a saying in the University Boat Club at Oxford: 'The rowing gods are hungry'. The amount of time we sacrifice on their altar, we should be high priests by now.

Bad days can be just awful. The alarm seems to break into a sleep that should have been left to carry on for hours more. The rain is pouring down, and even though I am about to spend three hours in it, I run from the car into the club. Every last excuse has to be employed to delay the start of training in case the weather breaks, but in the end we just have to get on with it. My backside gets wet first sitting down on the seat that already has beads of water on it. Within a minute or two the water is beginning to trickle down my neck so that I have to squirm to get my shirt to absorb it. After 15 minutes all my kit is drenched, and though I don't get cold, the fabrics cling to my arms, back and legs. The boat is going badly too, and it becomes impossible to get any rhythm going. The water seems to drag the boat back and make the effort almost futile. The trees and bushes crawl past. And through it all comes the thought that I have to do this all today and tomorrow and the next.

When training goes well it gives you huge confidence in your fitness and your ability to win. We know going to the line that no one is going to be fitter or stronger than us. That you can't buy. You also get a kind of grim satisfaction from training. Each session is a tiny little step along the road – one that, on balance, I want to be on. Rowing at top level is binary: it's either a one or a zero. Either you are in and in to win and it takes first priority, or you're not and you can have off all the days you like.

I only have to step back to realise the position I am in, and when training gets me down I go through a reasoned argument in my head. It goes like this.

On balance I don't know anyone who loves their job every day. Sure, there are bad days where it seems like a meaningless treadmill, but the good days outweigh the bad. Best of all, every four years I get to go to the Olympics with Great Britain on my back, and, what's more, if I do it right, I win. No matter how bad the weather or how hard the training, you can't put a price on that. Competing for your country is an honour and a responsibility; if I can't do it justice, then I should just pull the duvet over my head and go back to sleep. At that point I usually get out of bed and go training.

5

jürgen

We were all sitting in the cafeteria when he first came over. It was 1990 at the Goodwill Games in Seattle and we were all enjoying the village format, the secure accommodation, the entertainment areas and, of course, the food. The cafeteria served food twenty-four hours a day, and, despite the linoleum floors, plastic chairs and even more plastic food, we gorged ourselves for three meals a day. The conversation lulled as he approached; everyone knew who he was and that most of us would be coached by him within a few months.

'Hello, Steve I just wanted to shake your hand and wish you good luck for this week,' he said in his thick German accent. He was smaller than one might imagine, but stocky. He had never been a great rower but his magic was in his eyes. You were first attracted by his smile, quick and dynamic, augmented by a gold-capped tooth. But his eyes were the real ice-breaker. He had a comedian's twinkle, an ability to confer any amount of issues and quips with a look one way or other. His English was stilted but passable; most important of all, he spoke rowing.

Steve got up out of his chair to shake his hand and they talked for a few minutes in front of the whole group about the Goodwill Games and the boats we planned for the summer ahead. Then he waved to us all, quiet and respectful, and took his leave.

When the Berlin Wall had come down in 1989 I had been a student at Oxford, happily throwing myself into studies and the Boat Race. Well, let's be honest ... just the Boat Race. A bright spark at Leander realised that if the whole East German system was merging with the West, then there was some fairly serious coaching talent up for grabs. The club had survived on the expertise of volunteers and part-timers, but with the increasing numbers and expectations from the squad, it was decided that the coaching should be consolidated into one first-rate, full-time individual. It represented a cultural shift within the famous club. Determined not to become a dusty shrine to past rowing glories, Leander was determined to be at the cutting edge of modern rowing.

The club quietly organised for a prospective coach to come over at Henley Regatta time to see the club and the river in full swing. He was met at the airport by a driver and a Jaguar and driven through the leafy 'A' roads to Henley. The contrast with Berlin must have been immense. He did all the right things. He sat patiently as the old duffers took him through their vision of what the club needed, he shook hands with the sponsors and met all the athletes. He had all the rowing credentials you could want – his crews had won Gold medals for two decades, he had even been chief coach of the all-powerful women's team in East Germany from 1980 to 1990. His wife spoke very good English and they seemed to enjoy the atmosphere of Henley. To put it in perspective, it was like taking a football manager to the Cup Final and saying, 'This is your job: do you want it?' They must have known that it was not going to be blazers and Pimms every day, but on the Sunday night of the regatta, Jürgen Grobler signed a contract that would guarantee him a salary and accommodation in Henley for him and his family. It would start at the beginning of the calendar year 1991. Up to that point the East German oarswomen would continue to compete for the GDR, and, as their chief coach, he should be at the helm.

He was there in Tasmania to see Steve and me win a rather unremarkable Bronze medal in the 1990 World Championships. We struggled all week to get a grip with the same East German pair of Jung and Kellner who had beaten Steve and Simon in 1989. With me in the bow seat of the pair, it was my job to do the calls; in other words, do the job of the cox in a coxed boat. It demanded encouragement, tactical awareness and a bit of grit to deal with the physical demands of the race and not turn the calls into a breathy, panicky warble. Needless to say, I was not up to the job. The race was delayed for rough water and when the final did get under way it was still choppy down at the start. The more polished East

Germans leapt out to a lead that they never relinquished. I managed to get some of the race plan out in the middle part and we seemed at least to hold the Germans at some points, but they were in the driving seat. I had sized up the finish area and picked a red advertising hoarding as a mark to begin the finishing sprint. But the hoarding in question had been blown flat in the wind, and we floundered in the last 300 metres. The Soviet pair of the Pimenov brothers swept past us in the final few strokes and we crossed the line in third.

It was the first time in twenty races with Steve that the Pimenovs had beaten him. It seemed a disaster at the time. We consoled ourselves that we could and would do better, and essentially committed to each other for the next season. Looking back, it seems hard to justify how we would ever have won. We were up against a pair that had won the World Championships the year before and, what's more, rowed really well to do it. They rowed with the confidence of champions – long, relaxed and powerful. To make it worse, they had beaten us in their spare boat. Their race boat had been damaged on the trip to Tasmania, so they had rigged up their spare and just got on with it. There were many, many lessons we could learn from them, and Jürgen's arrival soon afterwards meant we got the blueprints to a big part of their performance – the training programme.

I returned to the UK and went back into the Boat Race training with Oxford. It was great to spend the winter with a completely separate group, but the distance between the pair of us was unusual. Steve had taken a short holiday in Australia, where he started his family, and returned to the beginning of the Jürgen Grobler era. To start with it was hard to get information about what was going on at Henley. There was only a small group there and Steve was reticent on the telephone. I got edited highlights of the training – lots more distance work, a lot less intensity and the possibility of weights in the programme. Then Steve came to see me in London when I was training in January, and for the first time I was able to hear what was going on. Yes, it was true there were much longer outings in the sculling boat for Steve, as much as 24 kilometres at a time. Worse than that, there were sessions on the rowing machine that blew your mind: 100 minutes at a time. Given that a long session on the Ergo up to that point was considered to be an hour, this was depressing. But Steve was far from depressed. He liked the attitude of the new guy, his English was improving and he expected his athletes to train in a professional way. Jürgen treated Steve with respect – a first in Steve's dealings with coaches. Most were either too scared to coach him at all or scored cheap points (not usually within his earshot) about what he was doing wrong. The list of coaches in the world acceptable to Steve was very short. His mentor for the first decade of his career, Mike Spracklen, was in Canada, and training with him would have meant us going to him. Steve proposed a simple plan – we would follow the German for a year with US marine-like stupidity, never question anything. We would take for granted that he knew what we needed and should do everything he asked. This licence would last a year; if we were unhappy in 1992 with eight months left to the Olympics, we could rescue something.

But Steve saved the biggest bombshell till last. He and Jürgen had had a discussion over the seating in the pair and Jürgen had essentially announced his intention to move the seats over so that I was in the stroke seat.

Stroking a pair is in almost all regards the same job as in the bow seat. The timing and coordination between the two rowers is up to both people. It is hard to argue in a pair that one person is late or early. In a bigger boat rhythm becomes a matter of numbers, the majority ruling the errant minority. In a pair both people govern the rhythm equally. The job of a stroke-man in a pair is to shoulder the workload. The mechanics of a small boat mean that the leverage the bowman has is much better and easier. If the bowman wants, he can dominate the strokeman with quick movements, and this means the stroke-man has to be determined to continue no matter what the pain or the pressure. For the strokeman the limits are physical; for the bowman they are technical. A good bowman will extract the absolute maximum from his strokeman while doing as much of the work as his seat will allow. The strokeman has to trust that the bowman is going to back him all the way and not abuse his position. If a pair gets it wrong, the strokeman can end up in all sorts of trouble in the later stages of the race.

For me to be in the stroke seat went against many of the

rules. I was clearly behind Steve in almost every physical respect. He was stronger by a long way, he had an edge in endurance and technically he was in a different league. The only thing you might think was that removing me from the bow seat at least took me away from the position of calling the shots in a race. This was something I couldn't help but smile at. Steve was not unhappy, at least to my face; he felt it fell fairly under the 'we do what he says' policy. It meant I spent the night nervous and excitable, knowing that the new coach had some level of confidence in my ability.

When we got together in late March after the Boat Race many of my worst fears were confirmed. I had to work at what felt like 115 per cent to offset the power being shovelled down from the seat behind me. I had to attack the water at the beginning of the stroke, otherwise we would jink off to my side by about 10 degrees. And I had to put up with Steve's advice and attitude from the bow seat. On the face of it, he was supportive, but he didn't suffer any drop in power at any stage, and after a short while he left me in no doubt that he wasn't keen on the bow seat. It didn't bother me one bit. I knew the best way for me to improve was to get stuck in, and if we argued or I caved in, it would hurt us both in the long run. I could understand his position, but I had already learnt that the best way to deal with stubbornness was just quiet confidence.

My only supporter was Jürgen. He was everything we wanted in a coach. Self-assured and confident in what he was doing, yet willing to listen to our comments and complaints. There was only one problem: his English. He was learning quickly, but stops on the water for technical tuning was peppered with lots of 'How do you say...' and accompanying (polite) hand gestures. We laughed at times when his coaching tips across the river were unintelligible: we would just be trying to work out what he had asked us to do when he would announce, 'Yah! Better so!'

There was one pivotal session where Jürgen stopped the pair and instead of concentrating on some technical angle or other he simply stated, 'You will beat Jung and Kellner'. It was a ringing endorsement, given that we had not even raced in the new set-up, and it was a huge boost for me. I had always relied on a coach to give me a jolt of confidence, and Jürgen was quick to pick up on this. Even years later, nothing seems to quiet a troubled racing mind like his take on things. He backs it up with a good technical eye for a boat so that he can see what you feel in the water without any conversation. Bad coaches are forever asking how the boat feels and if the crew agree with what they are saying. Jürgen did so little of this it was scary. He would bring the boat in towards the towpath and give you a few pointers, nothing outlandish but definitely taxing. Most often he wouldn't open any negotiation with the crew at all; it was a swift monologue and then off you would go again. It didn't take very long doing this to find out if the guy was a faker or the real thing.

He drove us through more training than either of us had

attempted before. Technique was always a part of the training, so you were expected to work your body and mind at the
same time. In, too, came circuit training for endurance and
heavy weights for power. Steve hadn't done weights in almost
ten years and had always loudly professed the maxim that if
he wanted to be a weight-lifter, then he would do weights:
until then he could be found out on the river. But under
Jürgen's programme his prodigious power increased
markedly, as did his fitness.

When we did go to race abroad, Jürgen was amazingly
simple and straightforward in his tactical approach. A
normal race plan, as described by any other coach that we
had had, would be detailed to the point of prescribing a
target for this ten strokes and that marker. You could often
go into a race juggling a dozen themes and targets for a race.
Jürgen sent us out with, 'I want you to lead the race by one
length at halfway and then open up the lead. You are the best
in the race – no one can beat you.' And they didn't. We went
to the old East Germany specifically to find Jung and Kellner
and although they were a shadow of their former selves, we
beat them handily. We won races in Cologne, Duisburg, at
Henley and in the big European race in Lucerne. When we
turned up for our second World Championship final in 1991
in Vienna we were a different unit from that which had
competed in Tasmania. We were fitter and we had a much
larger cache of experiences together, both racing and training, which allowed us to deal with almost any eventuality.

The final didn't exactly go according to plan, however. In a stiff tailwind, the Slovenian pair took a lead, which was different from any race we had had with them in the season. We loitered in the pack during the middle of the race, and we found ourselves in fifth place with 500 metres to go. The only good news was that we were just half a length from the lead. I got and deserved a bollocking from Steve, with an unusually gruff, 'C'mon Matt. Last 500. Let's go!' and we hit the gas with everything we had. It wasn't pretty, it wasn't efficient, but we surged to the front of the race. With ten strokes to go, Steve screamed, 'You are a World Champion!' And I was, too. We crossed the line in 6 minutes and 21 seconds, a new world record. My face is a classic on the TV coverage, an overjoyed kid who didn't know what had hit him. Steve is in a more slumped position. He knew we didn't row to the plan, and even though he hadn't won a World Championship since 1987, it took the shine off it.

But I was on cloud nine and wouldn't come off. We all went out for a beer that night, and when Jürgen made a trip to the toilet, I took a cigarette from the team doctor and, to wind him up, was smoking it when Jürgen returned. Despite the alcohol and the hour, he didn't see the funny side. He snatched it from my mouth and pressed his face close to mine.

'Massew, we go now and try to win zee Olympics. It will be bloody hard, I tell you, but we do it, I'm sure. So enough of zis,' he indicated the cigarette, 'bullshit.'

It's safe to say his English had improved.

henley diary

Friday, 19 December 2003
Henley-on-Thames
246 days till the Final

Last day of organised training today but what a finish. Two-kilometre ergo race on the rowing machines, the last ritual of the calendar year before the Christmas break. Did a programme on Radio 5 last night. I thought I was going to be incredibly serious and get an early night for once. But they offered wine in the studio and that pretty much sealed that one. Decided to stick to the tried and tested 'relax and it will happen routine'.

Show was really fun – Coe, Jackson and eventually Steph Cooke, but she's a doctor and had a few lives to save in Bath first! Good chat with Saggers, the presenter, for 90 minutes on all things Olympic. Garry Herbert and Martin Cross have a great little job of reporting on Olympic sports.

Beer and, after call to Dee, curry in Shepherd's Bush. Nothing off limits: had fantastic gossip about Rio Ferdinand, with all chipping in with their two pennyworth. Got back around one.

Had a lie-in and then the drive to the gallows at Leander. True to tradition, Jürgen has four rowing machines on the platform. A few non-showers: Kieran, Dunn, Lawson, Partridge – but at least 20 to get through. Did 30 minutes with no bursts at all. Then drank water and lay in crew room. Felt fine for hydration but didn't fancy toast or cereal, and had a power bar instead. Mistake.

Had the last heat with Josh West, James Cracknell and Rick Edge. Didn't feel nervous but had my usual negative thoughts about the gallery of people that show up on ergo day just to see the show. Athletes competing is fine, coaches, of course, but we had way more than that. There was a film crew too, BBC regional, I think. They behaved, though. Picked a newer ergo between James and Rick, but was adamant I didn't want to row their rhythm, unlike in Birmingham. Was hoping for under that score (5.47 for the 2 kilometres), and Jürgen was pushing for 5.45. If I want to go sub 5.42 in April, then I know he's right.

Start was really strong and low – no higher than 42 strokes a minute. James was way over but scores similar. Did 500 metres in 1 minute, 25.1 seconds. Then had always planned to eat up the middle 1000 metres at 1.27 per 500 metres pace. Held that well, but rating 31 strokes a minute.

Had an average at 1500 of 1.26.6 or so and knew it was on. Cranked it in and actually enjoyed the sprint for the first time in ages – good sign. 5.44.3 for the whole 2000 metres. Excellent. Jimmy was second with 5.47 and seemed happy. Threw up the power bar afterwards into the bin. Jürgen looked concerned as it was the first time he had ever seen me do that.

Had a last chat to Jürgen at lunch before he goes to Germany tomorrow. He was very happy with the winter session, despite the slight illness that I had in December. A good 5-kilometre ergo in Jan, and 9-kilometres in 30 minutes at altitude would be a really great start to 2004.

Disappointed to be missing another row in that four with Steve Williams and Toby Garbett. Both did well today. Can't help but wonder about what would happen if it is a four. Would we win with those guys?

the 1992 season

The World Championship win in 1991 gave us a huge jolt of confidence. Our relationship with Jürgen was now unquestioned. He was our coach and his licence had been extended indefinitely. I got a year away from Oxford, which cleared the decks for both Steve and me to be in full-time training. We sat down with Jürgen and planned our year. He was keen on a trip to South Africa in the winter months, which traded three weeks of winter misery on the Thames for three weeks of southern hemisphere sun. For many of us it was the first time we had been on a winter training camp, and Jürgen mixed the water sessions in with plenty of time for excursions and beers. We had a trip down a gold mine, where the guides had been specifically told to work us hard. We walked for miles and miles along dark, hot tunnels to experience the working environment that so many South Africans queued to be part of. We spent a few days on a game reserve, where we had special permission to run in the evenings for training. Only when they told us that they would be providing armed guards against the possibility of lion attack did we prefer to have a couple of quiet days with no training at all.

One of the group was a young guy called Cracknell. He was fresh from school and sporting the most ridiculous haircut any of us had seen. It was a grade one cut all over, apart from a horseshoe of hair that ran around the front of his head. He was confident enough to take the flak from the guys, and good enough to quieten it, but his potential was only partially fulfilled for another few years. At one point in South Africa he fell foul of Steve in the pool playing water polo. He tried to hold the big guy under to win the ball and found that 16 stone of angry Redgrave was a handful. Steve reared up, grabbed James around the waist and dunked him to the left and then to the right, lifting him bodily in the air with each twist. It was like a scene from a nature programme, with a killer whale toying with an unfortunate seal pup in the surf. The only difference was that on *Wildlife on One* the pup isn't saying 'Sorry, sorry, sorry, sorry' every time it's out of the water.

In the second year of training under Jürgen I was coming on dramatically, the scrawny teenager being replaced by a much more mature athlete. My powering of the boat, although still nothing like Steve's, was improving rapidly. In endurance terms I was his equal, able to get through a 20-kilometre row and feel as tired as he looked. Even on the rowing machine on a good day I could give him a race. The physical gap between us narrowed so that I now felt I deserved to be his strokeman. Steve, too, had given up the attitude with the seating arrangement. He handed out criticism and encouragement without reference to it, and genuinely felt the pair was set up in the quickest way. It gave me the confidence to joke that with me at stroke, the pair had broken the world record and he was only now, thanks to me, finding his true potential. We were becoming a close team through friendship and a healthy dose of competition. It didn't matter what the event was – it could be cards – we were each only interested in finishing ahead of the other. But once in the pair it was different. We harnessed the competitive spirit to go toe-to-toe with the rest of the world together.

The winter had gone well and we arrived at the Spring Trials in fine form. The trials are an event designed for all the British oarsmen to have a race-off in pairs. The pair that wins can effectively call the shots about what they want to do. For us the equation was simple: win and we would be given the slot to race at the Olympics in the pair. Easy.

We hadn't counted on a London-based pair of brothers called Searle. Well, in fact we had known about them. We just underestimated them. The elder brother was Jonny, a successful Boat Race Blue for Oxford. We had rowed together in 1990. His younger sibling was a star throughout his career, had a fistful of junior medals and was the only oarsman to be selected for the senior team when he was still only 18. He was a giant of Redgrave-like physical proportions, and totally outsized his brother who sat at bow. We thought it looked like one of those Victorian street scenes with a dog riding a bear. They were based at Molesey Club, bitter rivals of Leander, and though I had every reason to like them, I didn't, plain and simple. They were the enemy, the shit stirrers who were happier battling against us than anything else. In retrospect they were only doing exactly what Pete Mulkerrins and I had done in 1990, challenging the status quo. On the receiving end of the challenge, I was just as uncomfortable as Steve and Simon Beresford had been.

When we got to the final race of the trials we started the race well, taking a small lead. But as we tried to hit our rhythm, it was like in *Star Wars*, when the *Millennium Falcon* won't go into hyperspace. As hard as we pulled, the speed would not come. The Searles passed us quickly, and within a few hundred metres had got a lead that we could never overtake. Confused and tired, we crossed the line as the Searles howled their victory to us across the water.

But Jürgen was amazing. I was sure we would get a dressing-down for making mistakes, either technical or tactical, but he was very calm and assured. It was the first time I was ever exposed to one of Jürgen's best attributes – his ability not to panic, even when things seem to be heading for disaster.

The selectors were not keen to take the pairs slot away from the World Champions on the basis of one race, and sent both pairs to the Cologne regatta a month later. It remained uncontested there, however, when the Searles fluffed the start and were left on the starting line as the field disappeared over the horizon. The showdown was now set for the Essen regatta a few weeks later. But this time the Searles did not qualify for the final. We were left on our own to race off against the field, but despite our ten weeks of hard training and 'putting things right', the exact same situation occurred against the Slovenians, who had won the Silver behind us in 1991. They were good, the second quickest pair ever, but until now we had never lost to them. On a good row we could open up a 5-second margin on them, but here they passed us as if we were standing still.

When we had the chance to talk after the race, we both pretty much blamed each other, which in itself was unusual. I thought there was no power coming from the bow seat and Steve felt there was no drive and rhythm coming back the other way. Yet despite our misery, the selectors felt we had done enough to prove we deserved the slot, and on the Sunday night in Germany we were told we were going to the Olympics. But there was no feeling of celebration or success – we had issues to sort out. We didn't want to go to Barcelona to lose to the Slovenians.

Steve had been feeling generally below par for a while, which can just be the training load or fighting a cold, but something about his body worried him after the Essen weekend. Soon after, he went to the doctor, and over a period of a few days was passed along a chain of specialists. Eventually he found himself in hospital being told he had colitis. It must have been misery for him. He took a fierce pride in being strong and healthy and now, at the very least, he was going to have to take medicine for the rest of his life. The Olympics were a secondary issue to begin with. It was a hammer blow for me, too. I literally wept out of concern for Steve and the mess our dreams were in. To see Steve in hospital on a drip with his wife Ann, normally the least panicky person, fussing over him was a sight that I never want to experience again.

The concern over our rowing seemed immediately selfish and childish given the fact that Steve was so obviously and seriously ill. Jürgen set me a vicious programme on the rowing machine and told me to throw myself into that. He added that if Steve wasn't ready to train within a month, he would arrange for me to go to the Olympics in one of the fours. This was scant consolation to me. The fours were good medal chances but little more. There was precious little chance of winning an Olympic Gold now. It was then, and remains now, the low point of my career.

But within a week the news was better. Steve had been referred to a colitis specialist, who reckoned he could get him on a fast track of medication in order for him to compete. He would delay long-term analysis and treatment to get him back in the boat. From the very first few strokes back on the water I knew there was a different athlete behind me. There was oodles of power again and a fresh, relaxed and excitable voice making the calls. It was game on.

the barcelona olympics

From the moment you step off the plane, an Olympic city feels different from anywhere else. We had all been to Barcelona before, even to the site of the rowing, but never in that atmosphere. Everyone passing through the airport was interested in what we looked like, which country we were from and which sport we were there to compete in. The rowing team was large: 40 or so athletes and about half that number again of coaches, medics and administration staff. We moved with the habits of a tour group – frequent stops, frequent counts. Dressed to the nines in Olympic kit, we felt and looked the part.

We were all herded into the accreditation area to be issued with our Olympic passes. I produced my passport and my name was checked off on the list, then it was on to stage two. I had my photo taken by a digital camera (which seemed revolutionary at the time) and was issued with the essential item for anybody who is anybody at the Games. The pass was about 5 x 7 inches and a photo, barcode, sport name and level of entitlement jostled for position on the front. I got a chain to thread through the top and hang round my neck. Except to wash and sleep, I wouldn't take it off for nearly three weeks.

We all got loaded onto buses and left the airport. As we pulled onto the motorway, a police escort took up position and prevented traffic from getting in the way or in between the buses. After a while, we bored of watching them and dozed in the sunshine. We were not going to the Olympic Village in Barcelona – rowing had a distant venue in Banyoles and we had been allocated a separate mini-village there. Despite the fatigue of the journey, I felt invigorated by the prospect of the Olympics. Steve was quiet as ever, but both he and Jürgen seemed happy with our times in training. The illness that had so blighted our racing season now seemed from a different time zone. Nevertheless, we both felt the pressure. Steve was putting together a run of Olympic Golds that no Briton had achieved since the Second World War, and yet his hopes were inextricably bound up with a cocky youngster who knew it all. I'm sure that he had doubts both about himself and our combination, but he was very careful to keep them quiet.

The heat was immense, not humid, but strong enough to make you squint and sweat. The bags got taken to some other entrance and we passed through the pedestrian gate of the mini-village. It was the usual security routine: bag on the belt, metal in the tray and walk through the hoop. A police guy checked the accreditation around my neck and we were in. Inside, it looked like a film set. Apartment blocks rose four storeys either side of a street empty of cars. Shop fronts lined the pavement, but only a few were occupied: a bank, a hairdresser's and a launderette. Steve and I were in an apartment with the coxed four – three twin rooms, a kitchen and two bathrooms. There was a living room with picnic furniture and a TV, and a balcony overlooking the street.

We dropped what bags we had and found the others being delivered to the street entrance. Time to change and go for a row. The joy of a separate village was obvious straightaway – it was a two-minute walk from apartment to the boat yard. Not for us an Olympics on the buses or sitting in traffic. Jürgen helped us rig up the boat that had travelled by road from our final tune-up camp in Italy, and then we were off. The water was perfect: flat, warm and clear. The boat sang with the energy of two psyched-up oarsmen just itching to get going. But we would have to wait another few days to race, so we contented ourselves with a loose paddle over the track. The finish area was impressive. Large grandstands over on the left side dominated the last 200 metres, and Steve told me quietly what to expect in the final: crowds so large you won't be able to hear, and enough atmosphere to last four years of Jürgen's training.

After the row we found the food tent, a communal mess offering all sorts of grub. Everything was free, of course, so the big temptation was to fill up and overeat, but we tried our best to restrain ourselves. We found the ice-cream freezers quickly and began an experiment with the varieties on offer that would last a few days. Someone told me years later that the rowing village averaged five ice creams per person per day.

I felt good about the way the boat was going, Steve seemed relaxed and I took my cues from him. We spent a few hours inspecting the village and its pools, games and computer rooms, then sleep beckoned.

Within twenty-four hours we had a nice routine going. Early row as the sun rose, breakfast and then a long period of relaxation before an evening paddle. The pool and other outdoor pursuits were banned. No one wants sunburn. The TV could provide only Spanish soap operas and even I got bored of those. I got a haircut that was way too short and then had to wear a cap all the time. On about the Wednesday afternoon we were sloping in from our evening paddle when a cup of water slanted across our backs and the road from our block above. We stared up and caught the Searles, wind-up merchants as ever, grinning over their balcony at us. They were in the coxed pair with Garry Herbert after our trials against one another and had a good chance of winning. They were bored, too, apparently.

We got up onto our balcony and one cup became two as

some of the guys from the eight started coming back. Within minutes every returning Brit coming around the corner was heralded with a riotous cascade into the street. This was interrupted only by a revenge attack from the men's eights balcony immediately above ours. It got me square on the head, so I retreated inside to find a suitable response.

A few minutes later and I was climbing the back stairs with a bin full of water and making my way up onto the roof. As I emerged above the eight's flat, I realised that all the French were out on their balconies watching the commotion opposite. They quickly spotted me and I began to play to the audience. Using the reflections from their block, I positioned myself above the eight and in one deft move got the bin swinging in a high arc up and over the guardrail. With me bent double at the waist, arms straight out ahead and the still-full bin upside down, the scene went into a kind of slow motion. I realised two things: one, I was going to get the eight, in fact all of them, and most of their flat as well; and two, no one else was throwing water because the police and our team manager were now in the street below. The water crashed down on the intended victims and most of the others on the balconies below them and I swung back up out of sight of the street. The French block broke out into applause and with a quick bow I left the scene for (what could be more innocent I ask you?) a shower. Revenge was, however, in the remit of the Spanish police, as halfway through the shower the water to the whole block was switched off and I had to rinse soap off me with bottled water from the fridge. The water wasn't returned for a few hours but it all calmed down without my being found out.

The next morning Steve was offered the job of carrying the flag for the team at the Opening Ceremony. Barcelona was a good two hours away and the ceremony finished at midnight. Anyone who went would interrupt his or her routine just 48 hours before the first race. We talked about it between the three of us. Steve was flattered that he had been asked, but was unsure about the late night. Jürgen was adamant that he should go, and then he turned to me. His expression was different and straight away I realised that he didn't want me to attend. He persuaded me that it was better for the boat if I stayed behind. Steve was carrying the flag and I would just have been marching in the team behind him; there will be other ceremonies, he said. I reassured him that it was fine, but felt a little disappointed all the same.

In the team, some boats went en masse, some stayed. Those who remained watched on TV, and when Steve appeared, a cheer went up in the room. Only when it died down did I realise that the French block opposite cheered, too. A few hours before he went, Jürgen had told Steve about the German discus thrower who carried the flag one-handed and straight-armed all the way round the track. Sure enough, there he was. Everyone else was using the white holster over their shoulder but not our Redders.

● ● ●

The day before the heat, as usual, everyone starts getting nervous. You can't escape the fact that four years of training are about to be tested on the biggest stage of them all. For me the appetite drops considerably. It becomes hard to concentrate on anything that isn't the race. We have drawn the Slovenians, the very crew that beat us in the last race we did, so our mission is clear – 'Prove to the world and ourselves that we can win this whole effing thing.'

And that's exactly what we do. At last, given the chance to race with full tanks of energy and clear heads, we lunge away from them early and carry on moving through the middle of the race. It is only when Steve calls a cruise in the last few hundred metres that they begin, for the first time, to move back at us. But there is nothing to rescue from the ashes. The adrenalin rush of crossing the line is almost bigger than before the start because we both know the significance of what we have done. We have silenced the doubters and moved into a position of red-hot favourites for the Gold medal. For a half hour after the race one of the Slovenians sat under a tree near the dock with his head in his hands. We wandered back and forth, extra nonchalantly going about the post-race routine. Steve told me straight away that the challenge from them at least was gone.

The feeling of euphoria lasted a few short hours. But the nerves return on the Tuesday morning in the long lead up to the semi on Thursday. By a quirk of the draw we get the Slovenians again and, despite the nerves, we can't summon quite the same intensity for the race. We know and they know what is going to happen. The others in the race are bit part players, as we do the same demolition job again. This time crossing the line there is no adrenalin, just a sense of anticipation for the final in 48 hours' time.

We do a pittance of training the day before and, apart from 12 kilometres on the lake, we have to sit out the day in the flat yet again. I'm fast learning that one of the attributes demanded of an Olympic athlete is the ability to waste time without wasting energy. We have a detailed talk with Jürgen the evening before the race about what might happen. As the Slovenians were handsomely beaten in the heat and the semi, they can't come out and expect to beat us with the same plan. They could try a high-risk sprint early on. It's the tactic of the desperate, but what would you do? Settle for Silver and race everyone else in the field, or try something new to rattle our cage and see if our race plan is brittle? The Germans have had a good regatta and may challenge too, but we had them in the semi and they didn't show either. Jürgen is adamant that we row our own plan and that if we do, we will win. His grit and confidence is ringing in our ears as we head back to bed. I can't help noticing the starlit sky, and the thought occurs to me that by the time the next night falls, all this will be over. I will either be a Gold medal winner or I won't. It's a realisation that won't leave and I start applying it to a shortening list of daily events. We go through the routine of going to bed in methodical fashion. There is no noise in the flat or, in fact, the whole village; everyone, it seems, is held in suspension over the racing tomorrow.

It's a ten o'clock start to avoid the heat, so the day begins with our usual dawn paddle. But this time there's no point going to the food tent. I just have to watch Steve wordlessly munch his way though his cereal. I am so nervous that even the thought of food makes my stomach churn. A couple of hours in the flat are torture. I can't sit still and don't want to waste energy moving around. All the time I have these two voices in my head, one telling me that we are going to crush them, the other telling me that it is all going to go wrong. The success of the heat and the semi seem in a different world. The labels of 'World Champion', 'World record holder' and 'favourite' are liable to sink you in the lake. It also strikes me that this is the Olympics, the pinnacle of mine and many other sports, and, as far as I can tell, this is far from fun. This is purgatory.

At last it is time to go to the boat, and there is Jürgen, having checked over everything a dozen times. Equipment failure is rare but usually terminal. An hour before the race he gives us our talk. It's not fire and brimstone but it's intense and just gets me feeling worse. My job is simple, Jürgen says. Don't start the race crazy, but take control after a minute of rowing. That's where the fitness and the strength we have will be effective. I suddenly realise Steve is pacing and jigging about almost endlessly. I have never seen him this bad and I can't look at him any more, never mind speak to him.

Nine fifteen and we are moving towards the lake. Jürgen pushes us away from the raft with a final and not very helpful 'Have a good row'. He can't help us now. He has to watch on TV with the rest of the world. The warm-up is pretty rubbish, all in all. Steve has to keep telling me to relax. The practice bursts we do are way over the rate he specifies. What was supposed to be 28 strokes a minute comes barrelling out at 36. It's not a good sign; we want to race at around 37. If I start bashing away at 40, then we won't make it past 1000 metres in first place. By the time we get on the start pontoon, I'm struggling to keep it all together. I keep telling myself that I'll do this race and then get out of the sport for good. This can't be healthy. I join together a few simple checks in the boat, then the starter calls us to order. I realise with a jolt that this is it.

We put in a fantastic start and within a minute of fast rowing we are in the lead – just. With Jürgen's instructions ringing in my head, I focus on the call I know is coming from Steve after a minute, and start driving my legs with all the pent-up energy the last week can supply. We start moving away from the field, and in an amazing moment of clarity I realise it's going to take an earthquake to stop us winning this race. We are moving so powerfully, and what's more, the others haven't changed their plans at all. They are all racing for the Silver.

It is a career-defining moment. All my dreams of an Olympic Gold medal are coming true as I race along, ahead of the world, knowing, just knowing we are going to win. My legs seem rejuvenated and it feels as if I could row like this forever. Steve is roaring the commands that we practised, but we never had anything like this. Steve has said throughout his career that he had only one perfect race, and this was it.

We cross the line 4.99 seconds ahead of the German pair, who pip the Slovenians for the Silver. We are arms aloft by the time they get there. I turn to Steve and we both say 'Yes!' We agree the race felt amazing. We are both buzzing. Within a few seconds, though, the physical toll hits and we have to spend a few seconds breathing deep and trying to get our legs feeling like they will bend again. Both the German and Slovenian pairs wave their congratulations and we turn and paddle slowly past the grandstand.

It is then that a complex mixture of emotions begins rattling round my system. I am, of course, physically tired from the exertion of the six-and-a-half minute race. Also, I am relieved. We had been the favourites and everybody expected us to win, but we did not crumble under the pressure. Then it hits me that after this race I would be everything I had wanted – a winner, a Gold medallist, an Olympic Champion and, beyond all question, the best in the world at what I do. All of this hits me as we sit out in the lake, awaiting our medal ceremony, and I have to double over to cry quietly in the boat. Steve is quiet and I half believe he was crying too.

Things then begin to move quickly. The next race passes us on the way to the finish and it is our cue to move to the medal pontoon. We go separate ways to congratulate the other medallists in person. To a man, they are sincere in their handshakes and seem happy with their races. We group in the middle of the pontoon and, in a flash it seems, the ceremony begins. We get our medals from an Australian dignitary and then the anthem starts. We turn to face the flagpole and stand stony-faced as the flag rises up to the top.

Then the cries of the photographers begin and we have to coordinate where we look to try and give everyone the shot they want. Steve's wife comes down to the pontoon and embraces us both. The photographers go crazy all over again for a shot of the two of them and I step away to try and spot my own parents and family in the stand. Faced with even a few thousand, it becomes impossible. I have to satisfy myself that waving enthusiastically at every Union Jack will have to suffice for the moment. We are shooed off the stage by an official keen to get the next ceremony under way and we paddle slowly back to the boat yard. Jürgen is waiting and we take turns to exchange hugs. I cannot summon the right words to explain to him what I'm feeling and he stumbles over his own congratulations, but we all know what we mean.

Some of the boatmen appear to take away our boat for us and the press reporters then descend en masse. They are all polite and excited and want some sort of sense from us about what we did and how it feels. For the first time they want to talk to me as much as they want to talk to Steve. They have been organised into two distinct groups so that the Sunday papers with their tighter deadlines go first. For us it means that 20 minutes after it began we have to tell our stories and say our quotes all over again for the weekday papers. Steve starts talking earnestly about carrying on together in the pair until the Olympics in Atlanta. It is not something we ever planned but it seems totally naturally to say it. We love competing in this boat. After today it has the labels of World and Olympic Champion and we want it to stay that way.

Steve is taken away to have a drugs test and I am left to find my parents at the entrance to the rowing village. They look drained but happy and I spend an hour or so talking to friends and family who have come out to show support. My girlfriend, Ash, was persuaded by a fellow doctor to get on a plane at the last moment and managed to get tickets to watch. It transpires that Jürgen knew she was coming and ordered everyone not to tell me; he knew more than anyone that I didn't need anything else to think about. It is great to see her. All my family are staying with Steve's in a farmhouse about 5 miles away, so we agree to meet there later for a meal. I suddenly realise that for the first time I have no plans, no schedule, my time is my own. Just two hours ago every minute was mapped out and now I have no idea what I'm going to do in the following weeks.

I went into the village and suddenly felt self-conscious walking around with the medal on. I knew what I would have felt like if someone had done that on the day before our race, and with half the rowing world preparing to race on the Sunday it didn't feel right. I tucked the medal away beneath my shirt and went to take a shower in the flat. Immediately afterwards I found myself on the end of the bed dripping water onto the floor and holding the medal in my hands. All the work over four years and this was the result. It seemed anticlimactic in lots of ways. Later, I was to find out that the medal ceremony, the national anthem and even the medal itself are only a very small part of the experience of winning. Everybody wants to know about those parts, of course, but the biggest joy of winning at the Olympics is one that lasts the rest of your life. You know that you came through all the training and the pressure and succeeded. That satisfaction, sense of accomplishment and all the confidence that goes with them never leave you.

But I was far from realising all of this as I sat on the end of that bed in the village. All the adrenalin and the excitement had died down and I was about to experience the first surreal moment of winning. Stuck for anyone to share the moment with, I walked quietly down the stairs to the village laun- derette, and while the machines hummed and hissed their way through my dirty kit, I sat out in the sun and wrote post- cards. One of the first was to my school rowing coach, Paul Wright: 'I became Olympic Champion three hours ago,' I wrote. 'I wanted you to know how much you had to do with that. Thank you.' Just as with Jürgen, it was really hard to tell Paul exactly what impact he had had, but at least he would know I was thinking of him at the time.

st moritz diary ⁹

Thursday, 15 January 2004
Hotel Sonne, St Moritz
219 days till the Final

Haven't been this tired for a long time. Started day with circuit weights (all 24 of us in the gym at the same time) 24 stations and a minute on each on. Most were fine but there were some new exercises that the coaches popped in to make life interesting. We had to do three circuits, though, which was a bit rich for a supposed warm-up session. Most of the guys were dodging it as much as possible. I caught Matt Langridge doing the most ridiculous impression of a press up but we just smiled because I was trying not to do straight arm dead lift at the time. Gunny was fine today and seems to bear no grudge at me for shouting at him yesterday.

Came back for second breakfast and lay on my bed feeling more nervous than I had for a training piece than ever before. Next was the hardest part of the camp, the 30-minute test at a fixed 20 strokes a minute. At sea level a few of the squad, including me, can break the 9000-metre barrier in the time, but at this altitude of 2000 metres above sea level, no one has got close. There is 7 per cent less oxygen, and oxygen is the only fuel available for your aching muscles. I had attempted to do it a year ago but folded with 15 minutes to go. This time I was determined it was going to be different, but now rued the fact that I had told Jürgen all those months ago that I wanted to do 9000. Got down to the ergo room about twenty minutes before to find everybody there and warming up. Did a half-hearted minute or two but what are you going to learn? You only really find out after ten minutes. Started first out of the group and pulled 1.38 for a minute or so, then down onto 1.40. First ten minutes were okay and then I had to fight really hard for the middle ten. Bad gut ache but it never spread to my legs. Had James behind me for the last ten, which was good timing, as I had a deficit of 10 or so metres with eight minutes to go. Even Jürgen starts giving me a shout. Had to pull 1.38 again for the last two minutes to get over nine and did 9007. Felt rotten for a long time. It was worth a handshake from Jürgen, though. Praise indeed.

James did 8952, which looked painful, but we were both happy to finish first and second. After getting beaten by all sorts of people at the beginning of the camp I was very happy to finish first. It just showed how bad the Christmas and New Year illness was. Two weeks out and it took all of this camp to get it back.

There was supposed to be two and a half hours of cross-country skiing this afternoon but it was cut to two because of late lunch. Most of the top group went out to Pontresina and up the valley to Roseg. Pace much slower than on previous days, which no one was complaining at. Was getting massive grip on uphills and no glide speed on descents, which was okay, and preferable to sliding around like on Tuesday. Found out that Biff had exacted his revenge for Norway by waxing both my skis from tip to tail. Said he was pissed off when I came past him in first five minutes.

Everybody shattered by five. Really happy with it, though. Reckon there can't be many people in the world who can do what I did today. Shame the Olympics aren't a half hour ergo at altitude.

Had a meeting in the evening with Jürgen who said he was more than happy with the progress of both of us. We plan to row the pair, with James stroking for a while.

coming home

Life was different after the Barcelona Games. The jumble of emotions I'd experienced in the village soon settled into a much more manageable and enjoyable post-Olympics glow. It was unlike any other race I had won. The World Championships in 1991 had provided a peak of enjoyment and satisfaction that was at least on the same scale as the Olympics, but we couldn't revel in it. Then, by necessity, the concentration had shifted to the Games in Barcelona. After 1992 the rules were changed. For once, Jürgen, now the national coach, didn't seem worried about our training regime in the short term. He was keen for us to attend as many of the celebrations as we could, and there were plenty. Marlow rolled out the red carpet for their favourite son and an open-topped bus was laid on for Steve to be applauded by the town. I was invited along with Jürgen, and we all spent a hugely enjoyable day waving back at those who knew what was going on and waving medals at the 80 per cent of people who didn't. All the town's dignitaries were out in force to garland both of us with certificates and mementoes, including an honorary pass to all of Wycombe District Council's sports facilities. Trouble was, neither of us felt like doing any training for a long time.

The demands on our time were increased by television. We were both asked to go on *Question of Sport* in the winter season following the Games. Steve had been on before a couple of times but it was a huge deal for me. As a competitor from a small sport, I had always marked *Q of S* (as I liked to call it within about ten seconds of finding out I was going on) as a threshold of some kind of recognition. At that time it was still the era of Botham and Beaumont, and I acquitted myself reasonably well. They never ask you hard questions on your own sport because it would quickly become boring for the average punter, and it would also make the guests look stupid, and sportspeople hate that.

The Sports Personality of the Year was another threshold that I had reached the previous winter after the win at the World Championships. Despite Steve's scepticism, I genuinely believed that we stood a chance of the 'Team of the Year' in 1991, but in the end the seating plan should have told me the truth. They seldom seat the winners in row Q. For the programme in 1992, the two rowing pairs of us and the Searles, who had won Gold in Barcelona in the coxed pairs, were set to have a race-off on rowing machines in the studio. We hadn't raced each other since the early part of the year and it was an attempt to settle the 'Who's the best pair?' argument that was, in theory at least, raging in pubs and bars. The problem was that rowing machines are pretty much all about power, and of the four of us Jonny Searle was by far the worst on it. He was only keen to do it if he didn't trail in last by a long way. So Greg Searle broke the ice between us and phoned Steve to offer a deal. They would happily take the challenge on live TV if we fixed the outcome. Steve was to win, Greg was to come second, me third and Jonny last, but not by much. We instantly agreed and on the night we refined the race fix to provide a bit more drama. The trouble with a 500-metre ergo race was that it lasted only 1 minute and 20 seconds; there wouldn't be much time for any tactical battles, so we invented some. We agreed that Jonny should lead at the start by hammering off in the first 30 seconds, then I would overtake and be leading up to a minute. Then Greg and Steve would charge past me in the last 20 seconds and Steve would just pip Greg to win. We could do this because all the machines were linked up to a screen and each person was represented by a little boat on a racecourse.

It was all going so well. Jonny led away and the three others bided their time to allow him to do it, then at 30 seconds I pulled the machine as hard as I could and leapt out to a lead. But at the minute mark I was suddenly so far ahead I had to fake a fade of near-death proportions to allow the other two through. As we collapsed over the line, in my case in an Oscar-winning display of exhaustion, Steve whispered,

'I thought you had won it there!' But as it turned out, the BBC loved it and everybody commiserated with me afterwards about how close I'd come and how bloody marvellous Steve was and so on. I just had to bite my tongue.

The fixing format was a method that Steve and I developed, though. Real competition between us was something that we couldn't necessarily be bothered with all the time, especially for a TV programme that might say, 'That was great, can we just do it one more time?' So whenever we were asked to race off, we alternated who got to win and always made it close. If we did it well, it added to the drama and it devalued the competition in our eyes to the point that you didn't mind losing if it were your turn. The challenge between the pairs, however, was never really settled. The Searles continued in the coxed pair in the 1993 season but we beat them at trials in the spring of that year. Though we raced against one another several more times, we never lost to them again. At one point, there was a plan to have a big challenge pot to race for in a TV special, but in some ways I'm glad it didn't happen. The time spent together at dinners and events as equal Olympic Champions was healing the rift between us and it felt better because of it. By now the squad was developing a more harmonious way of operating together, and although there were flashpoints and competition between crews and different people, the early '90s were a low point that we have not sunk to since.

There were other benefits of having won. Eton asked me

back to the school to speak at assembly. In my honour the Headmaster gave the school a day off and called it the Pinsent holiday. The only commitment I had that day was to speak at the assembly and then they could go. Teenagers are a tough audience at the best of times, but these assemblies, as I could well remember, had a kind of 'Okay, impress me then' quality that we, as pupils, hoped would intimidate the speaker. I gave a 15-minute presentation about how I had had no idea I could be a champion in my sport, and went on to say that I reckoned there had to be one guy in the room who could be on the plane to the Sydney Olympics in 2000. I was wrong. There were two. Ed Coode and Andrew Lindsay were in the hall that day and they were both in the rowing team that competed in Sydney. I would love to take some credit for what they did but I can't – they got there through their own hard work. I can't really claim even a small role, as they were already keen rowers by that stage. But it became a theme for any school talk that I did going forward from there. My dream is that someone will come up to me and say, 'You came to my school and inspired me to get to the Olympics.' Still waiting for that.

My own education had been put on hold for the Olympics. Way back in 1991 I had realised that the chances of being successful at both the Olympics and my finals in the summer of 1992 were slim, so as I was pretty sure the International Olympic Committee were not going to move the Olympics, I asked Oxford if I could delay my finals. I was impressed that both my tutor and the Master of St Catherine's College were totally behind me, but really disappointed that there were others who were not. When I left after the academic year in 1991 I was given the same letter as someone who had been thrown out on a disciplinary matter. All the rules of what I could and couldn't do were there, and it was signed without anything like a 'Good Luck'. When I returned after the Olympics St Catz had a celebratory dinner in my honour. The academic tutor who signed the letter sat directly opposite. It's safe to say we didn't talk much.

But in October of 1992 I was back on the academic lists, and in work terms it meant I had eight months to go before my geography finals. In rowing terms it meant I had six months before the Boat Race.

the boat race

The Boat Race is a 4¼ mile test of sporting courage and pain that can be compared to nothing else in rowing. Sure, the rowing is not of Olympic standard. The race carries the baggage of a Victorian gentleman's challenge, but you should never underestimate the dedication it takes to take part. The Boat Race demands a level of training and time that would be a solid winter for any aspiring international, and yet the rewards, even for winning, seem small. The reward for losing, as I was to find out in the 1993 race, is a bitter pill indeed.

The Oxford Boat Club runs on a rather bizarre basis, whereby the student president, who is elected each year, essentially runs a professional sports outfit. Coaches are hired and athletes selected ostensibly on his authority. He can delegate as much as he likes, to the point of not racing in the crew himself if he sees fit, but one thing remains sure – he's in charge and the buck stops with him. When I arrived in 1989 it was actually a system of the 'buck stops with her' as Oxford had elected its first-ever woman president. This would have made happier news had she not fallen foul of the examiners once too often and been asked to leave. Soon after, Jonny Searle, the wiry-haired dynamo who was yet to make waves with his brother, was elected in a hastily convened vote and took up the reins of the presidency.

The routine was fairly simple because we were still students, and though studies could be crammed into brief sections of the day, there was no way we could train full time, not during term at any rate. Fitting in training meant an early start at around six in the morning. You don't need to see too many early British winter mornings for them to lose their charm. We always started in the gym, as this was based in Oxford at the Iffley Road sports centre. Early in the academic year there might be 40 guys who turn up to see if they can make the grade. But within a week or two the president posts a list of the top 24 so that the group can become more manageable.

After the morning session finished it would probably be about 8.30 or so. We'd have time for a quick shower, a breakfast on the run, and could just about make a nine o'clock lecture. Once the morning lectures were over it was another quick meal and then to the meeting point in town. There were two minibuses ready to take us on the 15-mile journey to Wallingford, where the river is longer and less crowded than the Isis in town. The daily afternoon row lasted from two till about four and then it was back in the buses for the trip back to town.

The evenings were the first time we could slow down and choose our activity, whether it was the bar with friends, a meal or some work. It was obvious that those involved with the Boat Club were willing to sacrifice a lot to be part of the race; there simply was not time to fit much in around the sporting and academic mayhem. It was also a prerequisite that you had to have the ability to focus on the job in hand. Your degree was going to collapse quite quickly if you spent all the time thinking about rowing, and you sure as hell were never going to win a Blue if you spent time on the river trying to finish an essay in your head. Contrary to the reputation of university sportsmen, the majority of the guys I rowed with were incredibly bright, and most have gone on to be doctors, lawyers and one even a rocket scientist.

Within the university the rowers were admired and derided in equal measure. Some people thought we were big, stupid oafs who got drunk all the time, while some were in awe of the reputation of the biggest university sporting event in the country. It was hard to know what reaction to expect when you told your tutors you rowed. In my first year some knew from the start that I was not going to be able to make afternoon tutorials while other (thanks to creative time management on my part) never knew until I popped up on the TV in March rowing for the university.

In my first year the Boat Club consisted of a fairly broad-ranging group of international talent, good schoolboy rowers and guys who had come up through the ranks during their time at Oxford. It is another facet of the race that each boat that represents its university has a wider range of talent than any other crew. Olympians rub shoulders with near novices and have to make the best of it. I certainly wasn't going to start throwing my weight around with any of the guys, especially given the success of my 'keep your head down' principle during my early months at Leander. There were plenty of people who were not so happy to work to the same principle.

Oxford were in the middle of a winning streak that had seen them win every race but one since the 1970s, and everyone was confident about what they were doing. It was infectious. It became easy to talk about winning and training as if they were part of a recipe. Put in the right ingredients and the result was a given.

We had certainly cornered the market in talent. All our team for the 1990 race were either recent internationals at junior or senior level, or had already raced and won the Boat Race itself. Jonny had the job of corralling all the egos into a cohesive unit and making it race well. In the end, there simply weren't enough seats to go round. Several guys who had pinned their hopes on a Blue retired on being told they were not going to win one. Cambridge, by all accounts, were much less experienced but were not going to be overawed by us. They had six months to get used to the idea that we were going to look impressive on paper, and they formed a race plan based around asking us to prove our form on the day.

We did, but we only did enough to win. We had been raced against a really quick eight full of Steve and the national team a few weeks before the Boat Race and got thumped. It proved to us that no matter what the talent in the line-up, we couldn't take things for granted. Nevertheless, Cambridge were lighter, younger and less experienced and it was a one-sided battle. No matter what they threw at us early in the race, we could respond and we ran out winners. It was altogether a fairly flat experience, as Jonny Searle put it within days of the race: 'A huge amount of training to prove we are better than Cambridge.' By now both of us were hungry for international racing.

By the time I returned to college in late summer 1990, I knew that I was going to go to the World Championships with Steve in the pair. They were the very last championships of the year – in November. This pretty much tore apart my Michaelmas term but I wasn't going to let a few environmental and social geography lectures get in the way of rowing with the most famous oarsman in the world. Tasmania didn't go according to plan, of course, when we finished third, and in the event the Boat Race provided a refuge from the self-doubt and worries of defeat. The Boat Club was a younger group in 1991 and I felt at home straight away. Given my international and Boat Race experience, I was always going to be part of the final crew, so I was free to be a quiet member of the squad for a while. There were a few Americans we would gang up on mercilessly over guns, drugs and intelligence, and they would fight back with plumbing, the Royal Family and the Second World War. It made the daily bus trips fly by. The crew that was chosen was feisty but a lot smaller than the 1990 boat.

We were given a good hiding by a University of London crew in the last run-up to the race, and many of the press reports were very doubtful of our abilities. Relations with Cambridge were also at an all-time low. There is such little contact between the two camps that rumour and gossip spread quickly. In our camp we had Richard Young, who was about to become the second man to row for both universities in consecutive years. He was able to give us an inside line on what Cambridge were doing and thinking. What little contact we did have with the opposition was clouded by stares, bad jokes and outright hostility. It was all rapidly getting out of hand. Both camps felt that they were: a) the underdogs; b) the good guys; and c) going to win. In our boat every quote made by a Cambridge man was dissected and analysed for any wind-up potential, and as we approached the race there was a genuine 'let's do them over' feeling in the camp.

Race day for the Boat Race is surreal. After months of training, it seems half the country has shown up to watch. The pressure for the mainly young and inexperienced rowers can be immense, and the fact that nothing but a win is worth anything makes it worse.

The day begins with a short paddle on the first part of the racecourse by Putney. Then it's back to the house that Oxford uses in Barnes. It is a huge, five-floor town house let out to the crew for the final fortnight by its owner, Heather. She and her family give up their rooms and their privacy for the comfort of the nine guys, who are getting more nervous by the day. She has to cook three square meals a day for the eight huge crew, and even goes to the point of cooking different low-fat food for the little coxswain. The dog and cat and, to a certain extent, the children all became mascots for the crew, which lent an atmosphere to the place that a hotel could never match. Heather was there to listen to our love-life problems, our rowing worries and then to celebrate or commiserate when it was all over. On the stairs she keeps the race photos of all the crews she has hosted, and these were a reminder every time we went to bed that there really was a point to all the work we were putting in.

Race day is, of course, a different atmosphere throughout. The children were all packed off to stop them losing limbs to some tense bowman, and everyone settles in around the house to wait out the remaining hours.

When the departure time comes we get into the bus and are driven with a police escort through the race traffic down to Putney embankment. The university teams base themselves with different Putney clubs: Cambridge at London Rowing Club and Oxford in the Nat West Bank Club. On race day our host club is filled to the rafters. The bar is doing a roaring trade and the towpath pundits are arguing about who is going to win and why. The crew appear at the door, then thread their way through the Mêlée and shut themselves into the changing room at the back. The guys get changed slowly and carefully. It is not particularly difficult but it feels better to be doing something than sitting quietly and stewing. The older, more experienced rowers might have a few words with the first-timers, not in a condescending way, but just reminding them of a really simple idea to focus on. Meanwhile, the president goes out onto the embankment in front of the early crowd and the BBC cameras for the coin toss. The crew will have a plan for both the Middlesex and the Surrey stations. They are not much different: the race is seldom won because of the side of the river that you have, but being on the outside of any of the bends makes you concentrate, that's for sure. The longest on the course is the Surrey bend from just east of Hammersmith all the way round to within sight of the railway bridge at Barnes. The Surrey station gives you the inside of that one, which is great, but it's a one-hit deal. You have to wait out the first bend at Fulham football ground within two minutes of the start, and then seize your advantage when you reach the Surrey bend. By now you have been rowing for the best part of six minutes, so you never tend to feel fresh as a daisy, but you have to dig deep and finish the race. If, on the other hand, you get Middlesex, you have two choices. Either you decide to go hell for leather in the first part of the race and use the first bend in your favour, or you take the ballsy route and determine to wait it out. That means staying alongside the opposition for 12 minutes with five of those on the outside of the Surrey monster, and then taking your advantage of the last bend. It really is a choice between the devil and the deep blue sea on Middlesex, and most presidents who win the toss go for Surrey.

The Boat Race essentially boils down to one critical moment. It is not like an international race where the first across the line gets the Gold, second Silver and even the last-placed can persuade themselves that they did well to get to the final. The Boat Race is winner most certainly takes all. The winner is the crew that can get its boat in front of the opposition's at almost any point on the course. As soon as that happens, the crew ahead can see the opposition and, more importantly, disturb the water of the other crew. Rowing behind another eight is like trying to walk a tightrope in a crosswind. As soon as the wash hits you, the balance of the boat suffers. It begins to roll from side to side and it becomes impossible to match the other guys in the boat. This imbalances makes the boat feel heavy and your effort inefficient. It is the beginning of the end. A crew in the trailing boat knows the statistics: only one crew in a hundred comes from behind to win the Boat Race.

This fact alone puts huge pressure on the race tactics. In a usual rowing race you can devise a plan to get from the start to the finish line as quickly as you can and hope the other guys don't do the whole race even faster. In the Boat Race you are trying to get a length up without ever giving the others the chance to get a length up on you. All this means the crews are throwing out any sensible race plan. If you asked a Boat Race crew to row flat out for two minutes, it wouldn't go much quicker than it does in the first two minutes of its race. If you then tack on a six-minute row as quick as you can go, that gets you to Hammersmith. The good news is that you have only another two minutes till you get halfway. The bad news is, of course, that if you have used more energy than the opposition, you are on a quick route to a Boat Race Silver medal.

When our president, Rupert Obholzer, came back to the changing room in 1991 he was grinning from ear to ear, which meant only one thing. We had won the toss and had chosen the inside lane on the Surrey station. We had a simple task: win the race when the corner favoured us. It would take five minutes of rowing to get to it but then we had to seize it and make it count.

Cambridge started faster and had a lead of about half a length after three minutes. They also had the advantage of the first bend, and we rowed well to stay with them and start coming back at the Mile Post. At the beginning of the bend in our favour at the Harrods Furniture Depository the advantage swung in our favour. One of the Americans rowing behind me shouted, 'Bye-bye, Cambridge! See you at the finish!' It was the first and only time I have ever been in a boat that actually called out to the opposition during the race. It hardly set new standards of sportsmanship but we loved it. We never lost the lead and it was the fifth consecutive victory for Oxford.

In the run-up to the Olympics in 1992 I went to the meeting of all the Boat Race oarsmen and announced my intention of running for president the following year. It was something I had gone for and lost to Rupert Obholzer the previous year, but I knew beyond all question that I was qualified for the job. Once elected, I began by trying to continue the summer rowing programme for the more junior guys in the club throughout the summer months. However, with my absence in Barcelona and a dearth of real upcoming talent, it was hardly successful. But when I returned to the university in the winter of 1992, the Boat Club formed up with more promise than it had had since 1990. In addition to myself, we had a graduate Canadian, Bruce Robertson, who had won an Olympic Gold medal in Barcelona in the men's eight. We had a South African international who had also been to the Olympics, and the spare man from the British squad for Barcelona. We had four returning Blues from the 1992 race, and the possibility of a fifth who was studying languages abroad. Even early in the winter people were whispering about the best Boat Race crew ever.

I elected to stay with the same coaching staff who had been so successful in previous years. Pat Sweeney had been an international cox and in fact had steered Steve and Andy in the 1988 Games in their unsuccessful bid to win two Gold medals in one Olympics. He was not a natural coach but had a simple and effective way of dealing with the athletes. He was brutally honest and treated everyone the same. I, as president, was just as likely to be called a wanker as the most junior person in the squad. I certainly liked his approach, but his lack of technical coaching was a concern to some. I had to listen to complaints from some of the guys over why they weren't improving or why the squad didn't do this, that or the other. I was beginning to find out why the president very seldom rows his best during his year in office.

The worst job of president was the selection time. The days on which the cuts were made were well known throughout the group. First, in November, the group would be trimmed to around 24 so that there could be three eights training each day. I stayed behind to have a meeting with Pat rather than travel back to Oxford in the van, and we discussed the relative merits of the oarsmen ranked 20 through to 30. For most, this was their first year in the system. They would have another chance next year. Having established exactly who was going to be cut and why, I travelled back to Oxford and began the job of tracking them down. I didn't want to post a notice with the three remaining eights until I had told the unsuccessful guys, so I spent a couple of hours going round colleges and houses to see them face to face. They all knew exactly what was going to happen: there could be no other reason for me to show up than the end of their Boat Race dreams for 1993. One guy wasn't at home but his flatmate told me where to find him. I had to walk into one of the libraries and have a hushed conversation over why this guy couldn't come to training the next day.

As Christmas came and went, the group was performing okay. Okay but nothing more. The results from the rowing machine were impressive, but on the water the combinations were not flowing the way everyone wanted them to. There was a wide variety of styles to accommodate and I, for one, was not brutal enough with the more experienced people in getting them to change. Worst of all, I wasn't leading by example. My rowing had slipped back to a bad impression of myself when I first started rowing with Steve. Poor timing and coordination of the different elements of the stroke are bad news for any boat, but for a big guy like me it was a death sentence. The trouble is that inefficient rowing spreads like a plague. As soon as you are not pulling your weight, you are asking some-one else in the boat to do it for you. They then find that the boat feels heavier and heavier and are then, in turn, likely to start missing the stroke. Within a few hours on the river the whole boat starts to row short and the rhythm suffers.

As president, the position was confusing for me. I knew in my heart that the first attempt at a Boat Race line-up was not feeling right, but the crew were excited about the prospect of training and preparing together and it seemed a really bad time to alter the line-up. Pat seemed calm about the situation and pressed me to leave it for a while. But after a week or two we decided to have a change. The first one was small: up in

the bow seat we decided to take out one of the least experienced guys, Ed Haddon, and replace him with a small but
effective Blue from '92, who was in the reserves. The trouble
was, they were two of my best friends. I steeled myself for the
chat with Ed and invited myself to his room, before interrupt-
ing tea with a massive change in topic onto selection. Ed knew
at that moment what was happening. He was devastated. He
had been through the exact same thing the year before, missing out on a seat by the narrowest of margins. As much as I
persuaded him that it could only be temporary, we both knew
the score. If you are changed out, it is highly unlikely that you
will get another look in. It was a measure of Ed that he
commented before I walked out that he didn't want it to affect
our friendship. Happily, it didn't, either in the short or the
long term, and I still count him as one of my closest friends.
But changing Ed out didn't seem to solve the problems. The
crew still felt sluggish and the timing bordered on the novice
level at times. But the more I tried to fix it, the less settled the
crew felt and became. The surplus of talent was throwing up
more options than we had the time to try, and the quicker we
changed, the quicker the problems returned.

Everybody seemed to have an answer and an opinion,
and I eventually had to call a halt to the experimentation in
the last month running up to the race. In the end the line-up
was strong and included four of the successful 1992 Blues,
including the strokeman Ian Gardener and two Olympic
Champions – Bruce Robertson and myself. Left out were Ed

Haddon and a South African international, Andrew Gordon Brown. With the line-up confirmed, we went to the Challenge – when the two varsity presidents formally agree to race each other. In 1993 this was held at the House of Commons, and the usual array of television and newspaper journalists turned up. One of them had the most unusual question I have ever been asked.

I can't remember his name or even his face but he approached me to ask if I would spend few minutes with him one on one. I agreed and we walked apart from the group to a small staircase where he asked me, 'How much of this is to do with your brother?'

My brother, Thomas, four years older than me, had been a huge influence as I grew up. He was a twin to my middle sister, Emma, and they had both gone to join my elder sister, Kathy, at Durham University in 1982. He had even joined the boat club there and done some rowing. He suffered from leukaemia and in 1984 he died in Newcastle General Hospital. It was a huge blow to our family and we still miss him, but it simply was not something that I spoke of easily to friends or rowing crewmates. I don't know how this reporter found out about it, and I was so shocked that I could only blurt out something about how my brother had little to do with my rowing career and pretty much left it at that. But in the van home I was seething with anger. How dare he ask me that? Not only did he presume to ask about my brother, but what's more, he hoped to make some sports story angle from it.

It has happened only once since then and that was later the same year when a reporter from the *Daily Telegraph* asked me again about Thomas. This time I was prepared and told her that if we were to continue the interview, it would be without reference to him. She persisted that it shouldn't be taboo and that it was only part of my background and motivation. In the end, after a bit of toing and froing we continued the interview and she telephoned later to confirm that no mention of Thomas would be made in the piece. I was relieved. It's not that I am set against discussion about my brother. What infuriated me was the inference that somehow his death was a motivation for me. I didn't want to see some sick-making piece about how I was winning Gold medals for my older brother. Nevertheless, I have always expected such a newspaper piece to appear one day, and have gone to the extent of talking to my family about that possibility.

The 1993 crew continued its rather rocky preparation with a race practice against Leander a fortnight before the Boat Race. We lost the fixture, and though a boat with Steve Redgrave on board is never going to be a pushover, we should have at least got closer to winning. The boat continued to row in a short and lethargic way, which is a double blow to speed, rather akin to shooting and hanging yourself at the same time.

The final change of crew happened in the last fortnight, while we were in residence at Heather's in Barnes. The coxswain, Gordon, had made a bit of a meal of the Leander race, and Steve had even had cause to shout over, 'You had better not steer like that on race day, Oxford!' The coxing is a massive part of a boat race. Coxes have to implement a race plan that takes 17 minutes. They have to cajole and encourage a crew that, by necessity, puts itself on the brink of exhaustion, and they have to be the tactical brain amongst them. In addition they have to position the eight accurately on a piece of water that is more than 100 metres wide. The stream is at best 10 metres wide and both crews want the fastest water. Therein lies the source of all the clashing and controversy that the Boat Race throws up. The cox treads the fine line between the fastest water and a disqualification for fouling the other crew. Gordon was not so much treading the line as watching it in his rearview mirror and the boatman who was teaching both coxes the river in the last few days took me aside to talk about his reservations. Bert Green had been the Oxford boatman for nearly 40 years. He had seen all the crews both good and bad, and he told me that Sam Benham, the reserve cox, was learning a lot quicker than Gordon. He also said that he had never had cause to do it before, but he recommended changing coxes. I was stunned. Could I really snatch a Blue away from someone who was within grabbing distance of it? Could I really do it so publicly? I thanked Bert and told him that I would think about it. In the end the decision made itself. The very next training session Gordon knocked the boat's fin out when he brought the craft in to land at Putney. This is pretty much akin to knocking the front bumper off a Formula One car, and it was all the reason I needed. I sat Gordon down in the house that night and told him to pack his bags. He simply moved over to the reserves and Sam came to steer us. She was a better coxswain but in retrospect by this stage I was rearranging the deckchairs on the *Titanic*.

We were nervous for the race, with good reason. We had a long Oxford run of victories to continue and a Cambridge crew who were sniffing the scent of an upset. In the event, it wasn't close. We rowed so badly that it shames me even now. It wasn't as if we suddenly rowed badly, either. We just continued what we had been doing all along. Cambridge took an early lead and we never fought them for it. As they established control, we gave up the struggle. It was the most disappointing Oxford row for a decade, if not longer, and we spent the last 12 minutes of the race facing that fact.

When at last we crossed the line we found that we had been beaten by five lengths. It was the crowning and most public moment of my failed presidency.

windsor diary

Saturday 31 January 2004
Dorney Lake, Windsor
203 days till the Final

It's not often I have an argument with Jürgen, but I did today. James Cracknell and I are in a pair preparing for a winter trial on Valentine's Day. The whole men's group is out in pairs aware that every session is being watched by the man who decides who goes to the Olympics, in what boat class, and who stays behind.

Winter rowing is miserable for many reasons. The rain can lash down on us for hours each day, the sleet can chill our fingers and toes within minutes of starting a session, and sweat can often freeze in our hair. But nothing will drive us off the water except high wind. Wind, and the waves that accompany it, makes a rowing boat unsteady and it becomes impossible to tell what movements are the elements and what are ours.

As soon as I got up today I knew the lake was going to be terrible. The wind was blowing 20 miles an hour, gusting double that, and by the time we got down to the lake it was just getting light enough to see that the waves weren't bad but the wind was blowing right across the lanes.

We get out there as usual for the three intensity pieces: first 2 kilometres at 26 strokes a minute, second at 28 and then 1000 at 30. It's raining hard and by the time we get down to the start it's hard to look upwind, never mind row there. We can hardly keep the boat in lane as we do a couple of bursts, but a couple of the others seem keen to get going and start off down lane two. They are getting blown all over the place, with blades washing here, there and everywhere. We give it a go but get caught in a gust, and I can hardly keep my blade off the water on the way forward. We give it 200 metres and then stop and paddle. We try again around the 1500-metre mark but same deal. Jürgen is waiting at 500 with a full argument face on. He opens with, 'Where are you going?'

'In,' I reply. 'Where do you think? This is shit.'

'What's the point? Why are we coming here at all?' Jürgen responds.

'Good question when it's as bad as this.' He doesn't like that.

'All the others have come past, doing the pieces.'

'Even Kieran's pair?' I know they have paddled in in despair. Crafty.

'What, is Kieran your hero now?' Gauntlet down good and

proper. James is already paddling the boat round to point back up to the start.

'What about Tom and Robin?' Weaker argument now. I'm just hoping they went in after nearly capsizing off the start of the first one.

'No. They've gone back up. Go on in if you want to. Go home.'

The lowest blow of all – calling you soft for even thinking about cutting the session. We row back to the start, me calling him all sorts of un-PC names.

We win the first piece by almost 4 per cent, but mainly because we avoided most of the gusts. Beat some of the other pairs by 20 seconds. After it was all over the timesheet was a mess. Pairs were all over the shop on the ranking and it was impossible to figure out what we had achieved. Jürgen was pacing round telling people how well everything had gone, and how it was such a worthwhile session if it is ever rough in the summer. I give a half-hearted look at the timesheet and him and give up.

Surprise, surprise, the lake is shut during breakfast. A novice four has been blown over and had to be rescued. We end up doing the second session on the ergo.

the 1994 season

Between 1992 and 1996 Steve and I dominated the pairs event in a way that no one has before or since. It didn't mean that we were the best pair that had ever rowed; indeed, far from it. We had a big man's technique, a kind of bullying element to the boat, which meant the craft squirmed rather than flying straight. The further we got from Barcelona, the more it became apparent that we were going to struggle to recapture the fluidity of our final races at the Olympics. In retrospect, even in the late '90s we looked back on the Barcelona experience as carefree and loose.

It wasn't as if our opposition didn't know it. If anyone had to race us they could easily pick out the weaknesses in our technique and attack us accordingly. But they had to get past our armoury first, and we prided ourselves on that. Under Jürgen's careful eye we had created the most powerful combination in the world. Thanks to our weight training, we were able to generate huge quantities of boat speed for short periods of time. Against weaker opposition we could cruise alongside them for large chunks of the race at what felt like almost training speeds, before opening up the throttles and leaving them for dead. But against top-class opposition we weren't allowed the luxury of cruising for any period of time, and the danger of our technique was that we would actually use more energy than the opposition. A sprint was fine, but a 2000-metre rowing race is not a sprint.

In 1994 Cambridge recruited two of the German team to row in the Boat Race. In the wake of the 1993 race they were keen to capitalise on the disarray our defeat had caused the Oxford camp and they wanted to keep us on the back foot. The Germans' names were Holtzenbein and Streppelhof (I promise you) and they arrived in Cambridge in late 1993 to start their studies and the Boat Race preparation. Cut off from the rest of the German system, their international options were limited. They had little chance of returning to Germany for any length of time before the World Championships of 1994 to force their way into an eight in the late summer, so they hatched a plan to stay in the UK and compete in pairs competitions. It was logistically a perfect solution: they could forge a new partnership together and combine it with their studies at Cambridge, and they could return to Germany for short periods when required to impress the selectors with their efforts.

In the run-up to the Boat Race a reporter picked up on the story that two of the quickest pairs in the world were training in the country at the same time and wrote a piece on the upcoming clash. Steve and I weren't worried. We had beaten Holtzenbein and his previous partner in 1991 and 1992, and we couldn't see a way that they were going to be right up there; but even so, the event had been in the doldrums since the Games, and even we acknowledged that it needed fresh talent.

In the end, we raced at different events throughout the early part of the season and met only at Lucerne in Switzerland, the last event before the 1994 World Championships. Both pairs had reasonable runs to the final, and we went in knowing that they were in good shape but that we could definitely outsprint them if it came to it. I went through my usual pre-start routine of checking everything was tight and secure and that the race plan was straight in my head. There is no chat during a race, no chance to weigh the options; whatever Steve says, I do. I have to be very happy with what we have mapped out ahead of time. If there is a conflict of direction at the cutting face of a race, you are unlikely to win.

It is obvious from the first stroke that the Swiss pair are not over-impressed by our record. They attack us from the start and within a few strokes we can already tell they are ahead. A crew that isn't willing to play second fiddle to us is a new experience since 1992, and we are surprised by the ferocity of their challenge. It isn't a token effort either; any muppet can go fast for 1000 metres or so, but I can tell by the effort and strain in Steve's voice that they are well out in front. They have long since left my peripheral vision and I am trying to keep the rhythm as consistent as I can. Panic is a bad thing in a rowing boat and never more so than in the stroke seat. Panic makes the stroke rushed and short, both of which are killers to speed.

Steve is busy trying to keep an eye on what they are doing and how to counter it. There comes a decision in any race when you are not in front where you change your plan and start trying to challenge for the lead. This doesn't happen early. In fact, the first part of a rowing race is like the opening moves of a grand master chess game. The earliest you are ever going to change anything is 500 metres into the race, and that's only if the rowing is going really badly. The killer for us in Lucerne is that the boat feels good: it isn't rolling back and forth, the rhythm feels okay. All that is wrong is that the Germans have opened up a lead of two lengths or more at the halfway mark. We could leave them out there in the belief that they had put in too much too early, but many races are lost with the lead crew getting ahead and benefiting from such a psychological boost that they can get the best of tired legs and push themselves over the finish line. If you stop chasing the lead with any determination, you can start polishing your Silver medals.

At the halfway mark Steve calls for a big effort in both power and rate. Normally you could do one or the other, not both. Trying to push harder with the legs when you have already rowed what seems like flat out is difficult enough, and is normally sufficient to merit the extra effort on its own. The other option is the rate. You can increase the speed by raising not the power but the frequency of effort. Doing both together hurts badly, like taking a knife to cut a wound while applying salt with the other hand. But we had no option.

I row the 20 strokes after the 1000-metre marker, gritting my teeth, and then take a peek over my shoulder at where the Germans are. Not good. They still lead by maybe 10 metres or more. We have 850 metres left. Steve calls again and we dig in some more. This time, he adds that we are closing and doing well, vital encouragement for his strokeman. If you are going to put in the agony, you have to know it's worth it. Both pairs are stretching away from the field; it's clear it is a two-way battle.

Five hundred metres, less than two minutes, to go. Now I begin to get a view of them without turning my head. They can't be more than a length up. We need to row the last 500 two and a half seconds quicker than them to win. It's a big task. They are tired, they know we are after them, but they are far from finished. The pairs begin trading huge efforts. The rate is ratcheted up level by level until we are both above 40 strokes a minute. Less than 20 strokes to go and their stern comes level with me across the course, we are less than 12 feet down. Another ten big stokes, I tell myself, and it's over. I look straight down the course and concentrate my shattered body on doing the best I can for that ten. We get level. We are both well clear of the third pair. I look over and see them both for the first time since the start. They are shot, moving awkwardly and not timing it well, but the strokeman catches my eye and in a flash I see he's got something left. After all, we are level with five strokes left – it's still for the taking. There's no way he was stopping. Steve shouts for one last charge and I know we need it. I rationalise to myself that I can ignore pain for five strokes and start counting down. We take the lead with two strokes to go.

The pain is immense. It starts with the legs, the generators of so much of the power, but the arms are not far behind. Lungs and throat are burning from the friction of the air I have breathed for the last six minutes. The arches of my feet are in agony from the pressure that the rest of my body is generating through to the boat.

On the final stroke we cross the finishing line inches ahead. Celebration is beyond us. Both pairs collapse into the shells and lie motionless, slumped for a couple of minutes. I can just about raise a hand to salute them and get one in response from Peter Holtzenbein. No smiles, no cockiness, just a wave exchanged.

Steve begins to manoeuvre the pair towards the medal raft but I can barely use my arms to help. Eventually, we land and get out. I pause on all fours, not sure my legs can take the weight. My ears have popped and I'm hearing my own voice and groans loud in my head. The Germans are in a similar state; soft-spoken and downhearted, they shake our hands with a depressed look. The medals are handed out and

Never quite forgiven my mum for those shoes.

LEFT: In Atlanta with my sister Katy. Relief all around.

BELOW: 19th October 2002. As exciting and rewarding a day as I've ever had.

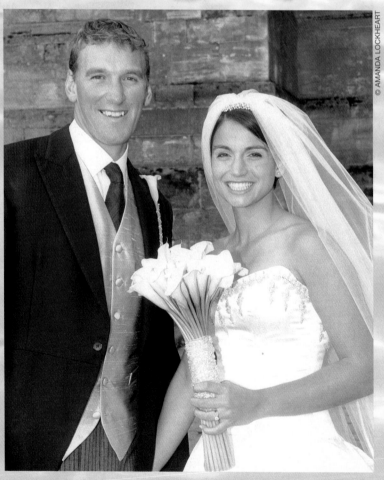

Boat Race 1991. Our strokesman Rupert in mid flow to Cambridge.

ABOVE: Guess which two were not pulling very hard?

BELOW: The last crew before the Redgrave era.
Martin Cross, Pete Mulkerrins and a short-haired Tim Foster.

Bad photo ideas no.62. 'Just slip these on lads. We'll crop out the flip-flops.'

ABOVE: Bronze in 1989 in the coxed four. Ahead of the East Germans but the Czech boat between us won silver.

BELOW: Olympic champion for the first time.

ABOVE: The Olympics in 1996 in ... hang on ... where was it?

BELOW: A lot happier than we look I promise.

ABOVE: 2002 – James is just saying 'You horse!'

BELOW: Bev and James, myself and Dee. Both weddings were a few days away.

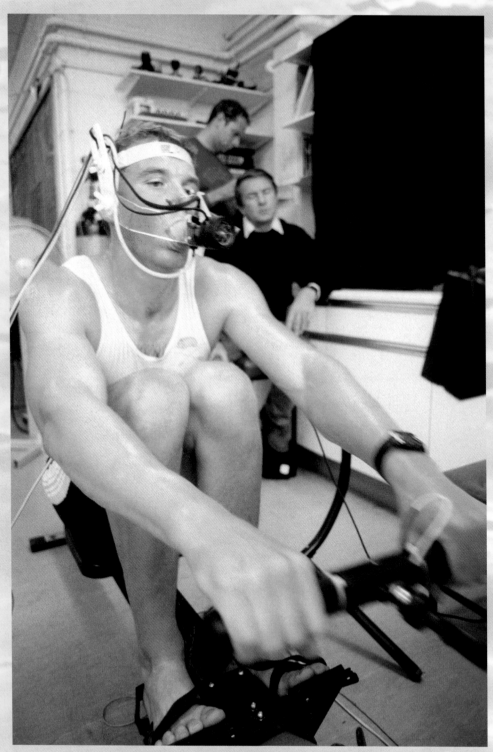

The horror of lab testing. Jurgen looks on impassively.

BELOW: The new Sir Steve.

What we hoped would be the final version. Alex Patridge (far left) has yet to find out he has a punctured lung.

Carrying the 2004 flame in London.

Athens 2004.

the fanfare sounds, though not the national anthem – this is just a seasonal race not the World Championships. The journalists press us for quotes and tell us we have broken the world record – a sizeable chunk of three seconds below our own record set three years before. A number of them say they think it won't be broken for a decade or more. They were nearly right: it was eight years, in fact, until I broke it with James Cracknell.

Paddling slowly back to the landing area, I begin to feel worse and worse. Normally exhaustion peaks after a few minutes, but I vomit half-heartedly over the side of the boat. By the time I get to the boating area the doctor is called and I'm fed rehydrating fluid from my water bottle. I am semi-comatose for the trip back to the airport, and Steve and I have a hushed debrief about the race. We both felt it went okay, especially winning in such a quick time. But we were rattled with how close the Germans got to beating us. A few metres shorter or a small slip on our long charge for home and it would have been very different. I say it feels like we have lost and Steve agrees.

We throw ourselves into the last ten weeks of training with a new zeal. We reason that the Germans must be feeling even worse. The 1994 World Championships are in the USA, which means a journey to Florida and a dry run for our pre-Atlanta base in Gainesville. But all is not well. The lake is huge and prone to a swell, which makes life difficult for a small boat such as a pair. The weather is stifling: both bright enough to burn and humid enough to make covering up a sweaty business. On our first training session on the lake the sweat is an inch deep in the bottom of the boat after 90 minutes. But the speed, as ever, is good. We do best in the competitive sessions against other boats in the group and are well set when we travel to Indianapolis for the World Championships.

After our last encounter we know there is only one pair to worry about – the Germans. But the Hollywood finish to the season is interrupted when we draw each other in the opening heat. Okay, we reason, if it has to be done, then bring it on. This time the script goes a different way. The Germans never lead us and we canter to an easy qualification. Morale soars.

We meet the Germans again in the semi, and again they never get going and we control the race from the start. But just before the final our great week begins to falter. In his last check over the boat, Jürgen spots a hairline crack in the rigger on my side. It's not large but you can't really tell with aluminium: it either holds together or breaks spectacularly. There is not much creaking and groaning. We could just about get it welded if we ask for a race delay, or we can leave it and risk it. Steve and Jürgen are unsure. I reason we have come this far and maybe the crack has been there for months unspotted. I suggest we just have to get on with it. The others agree eventually and we go out to race with as much courage in our equipment as we can muster.

• • •

The governing body of rowing (FISA) had for a number of years being fighting a battle against those who sought to jump the start. The start commands were predictable, being essentially 'Are you ready? Go!' in either English or French. This gave the crews a means to jump, as once the guy started, it was easy to predict when the 'Go' command would come. In 1994 FISA had unveiled a new policy whereby the starter would leave an indeterminate gap between the 'Ready?' and the 'Go'. Fair enough, you might think, but like swimmers teetering on the stands or sprinters twitching in their blocks, it was agony for us. Steve and I, in fact Steve (as he was in charge of timekeeping in the boat) made an utter hash of the warm-up. Concerned over the crack in the rigger, we were turning the boat gently and suddenly realised all our opposition was over 500 metres away by the start. We ditched the last parts of our warm-up and pegged it down to the start, arriving in a flurry of long-sleeve tops, water bottles and last-minute checks. We just had time to get ourselves together before the starter called us to order.

We jumped the start. Not by much; I'm pretty sure we weren't the first to move, but we were at the end of our first stroke when the guy said 'Go'. It's not catastrophic. You get a little orange board over your lane and you are out if you do it again, but I caught sight of the Germans having a little hushed meeting in next lane. There was only ever going to be one topic for them: 'Let's go for it and see if we can get a flyer.' They had no false start at that stage, so the worst that could happen would be that they would get one to match ours. We were caught in a cleft stick. Go with them and risk complete disqualification, or be safe and give them the initiative.

We have to wait. They time it brilliantly, not only taking a punt on when the starter is going to say 'Go', but committing everything to the moment they choose to launch. All the week's work of stuffing them in a box comes undone in forty-five seconds as we give them half a length, then nearly a full length. With the wind in their psychological sails, they take us to the cleaners in the first half, just as they had in Switzerland two months previously. Steve's calls take on the urgency of the chasing crew yet again, although this time we know it's going to hurt. I am trying not to predict what it is going to feel like later, and keep the legs driving on. They feel hollow with the disappointment of a naff start and I try to shake off the feeling that I am responsible for our situation.

A thousand to go and we are reeling them in just as we were before. The boat takes on a new energy. Steve is giving it large with 'We can do this' comments. Five hundred to go and we are catching them quickly. Suddenly it is beginning to depart from the Swiss script. Four hundred and we are over-lapping. Two fifty and we are just behind and then level. I'm gearing up for another hike in the rate, another push in the power, when it's over. Steve gives a triumphant 'Yes!' and I look over to see the Germans falling back quickly. In seconds we are clear water up. As before, the gaps in the race are big, but 200 metres is a long way if you are no longer going for it and they get pushed for the Silver by the Australians, who have rowed a steady race in lane two. We cross the line at 90 per cent pressure, whooping for joy. The relief is immense. Only we and the Germans know how close it was.

That afternoon in the food hall they called us over to their table for a drink. They were polite, friendly and surprisingly upbeat. We talked over the last ten weeks and the races we shared. We laughed over the implications of our false start and I asked if they felt they were going to win in the final today. Peter replied that there was only one moment, just before the 1000-metre mark, when they felt they had enough of a cushion against our sprint finish, but that it evaporated quickly, and from halfway on the signals were clear.

Just as we were preparing to leave, he suddenly said something extraordinary: 'We have been talking and we can't beat you. We are not going to do the pair again. Good luck in Atlanta. We are sure you can win.' Our biggest opposition, our toughest opponents ever, and they were clearing the road between us and the Olympics.

I got very drunk that night. I shot pool with the Aussie pair, Ron Walker and Rich Wearne. It was the first time I had ever shared more than one drink with the opposition. We got on well and compared notes about our coaches. Their coach Harold Jahrling was one of Jürgen's first superstars in East Germany. The evening passed in a haze of bad German accents. They were funny guys to begin with, and as the evening goes on, my jokes got funnier too.

the opposition

For a long time the opposition were hated. At school they were the enemy, challenged in secret crew whispers about what they wore, the way they warmed up or how they raced. If another school beat us, it was easy to hate them. They had been lucky or used a couple of breaks to their advantage. We had not had the same luck, or things would have been very different.

The chances for interaction with other crews were small. The regattas would be a maelstrom of travel, arrival and preparation, then the nerves of the race itself. This was followed by another rush of packing, loading and, if we were lucky, prize-giving. The much-advertised beer drinking seldom, if ever, materialised, and there was precious little chance to socialise with our competitors. There just didn't seem to be a time in the day when we weren't supposed to be doing anything else. What's more, an approach before we had finished would be seen to have ulterior motives – a chance to see the inside of our camp. It had not yet occurred to us that you learn all about a crew just by racing them.

The Junior Trials, which I attended in the summer terms of 1987 and 1988, were the nursery for every Olympic oarsmen for a generation or two. There the barriers had to come down; after all, we were changing our allegiance from our school to country and everyone saw how important that was. There were 40 or so candidates to be split between two teams: the superior Junior World Championship team and a 'B' team that would go to a European competition. The week was a fiesta of racing. We were usually in pairs, and after the first race you were unlikely to row with anyone from your school. We quickly learnt that harbouring any negative feeling against someone, just because you hated his guts a week ago, was never going to get you into the team. You had to make the most of the time between when your name was called and when they said 'Go'. It usually started with a nervous handshake, then you'd both look over your boat, which, like a horse in the pentathlon, had to be familiar to neither of you. There'd be a quick discussion over technique and tactics, and then off you went up the course. You'd have 1000 metres of warm-up on the way up, before racing for your sporting life back the other way.

You would have thought it would be a disaster. A push-me-pull-you of confusion and aggression. Sometimes it was, but often you found a surprising chemistry that took off. Pairs who had only met a few minutes before could often beat pairs who had rowed together for a season. Gradually a new dynamic emerged. If we went well together, we were friends, we had common ground. Gradually I found I was no longer just sitting with my schoolfriends at mealtimes.

When I got to the championship, however, all the old behaviour was back, this time between countries. We laughed at others' garish kit, even though our own tracksuits were a hideous glossy concoction. We pointed at the East European girls, who were bigger than us, and looked askance at the facial hair on blokes who were supposed to be under 18. The East Germans were a particular focus of our attention. At that time, they were a truly dominant team, collecting medals in every event and winning the Gold in almost all the women's races. But they also had an organisation that was fascinating. You never saw East German athletes on their own; they always moved around in crews or at least in groups. The coaches herded them everywhere, and interaction with other countries and athletes seemed to be frowned on. Some of our team got nods of hello, but for the most part it was nothing.

Every championship, junior or otherwise, finishes with a kit swap. About an hour after the eights race, the last event on the programme, everyone gathers by the boat racks in a fairly organic group and the trading begins. It's fun, a chance to swap with guys you have lost to and admire, or an attempt to persuade the really fit Scandinavian girls to get their kit off (it never works). It marks the end of hostilities and the beginning of the party. But the East Germans were never allowed to trade. Their coaches would carefully pack away their tracksuits and racing strip, almost as if to prevent it falling into other people's hands. A few got out. We wouldn't have hesitated to nick a top if the opportunity was there, but I never got that close. I had to make do with American, Aussie and Russian.

Even a couple of years later the East Germans were still a fascination for us. At Olympic level their athletes had names, records and medals up the whazzoo, but the interaction was still very limited. At one early regatta in 1989, my first international season in the senior men's team, I was picked to row in an eight. It was filled with Olympians from the Seoul Games, and to my mind they all had a hang-up about the East Germans. Tim Foster and I had rowed down the East German pair in our junior final the previous summer.

Though the tearing down of the Berlin Wall in November 1989 was only six months away, no one was predicting what was about to happen. It was a West German regatta and both Germanys were taking it seriously. The West German eight had won the Olympics in 1988 and the World Championships that same year, and had a strong crew again. The East Germans were determined to get back in the frame, and for the first regatta of the year at least had pooled the resources of both their Olympic Champion fours (coxed and coxless) into the eight. It was being built up into a national clash between the two Germanys and nobody was wondering about the little old Brits. We were a pretty eclectic bunch, some tall, a couple not much bigger than our coxswain. None of us trained full time, and but there was one cocky teenager who was giving it plenty of mouth about how we shouldn't be afraid of these turkeys.

I was arrogant off the water as well. At one point before we raced the final all the Easties were gathered waiting for their bus to their hotel. They had the most ridiculous '80s-style tracksuits – mostly black shiny nylon but with flashes of luminous yellow at the shoulders. We had all been laughing at them earlier on, and buoyed by a youthful exuberance, I swaggered out of our group and over to theirs. It sounds like a kind of *Grease* moment, with a face-off between the gangs, but it was more akin to one of those cartoons where the little helpless mouse is bounding around under the nose of a massive drooling guard dog. But I wasn't fazed. I wandered over and felt the quality of the day-glo strip on one of the shoulders above me between thumb and first two fingers and made a really exaggerated 'Mmm' noise. There was no reaction and certainly no laughter from them, and a kind of frozen silent horror from my own lot. I wandered away, trying to look as nonchalant as possible.

Some of our guys were apoplectic, horrified that I had dissed them so openly. I shrugged it off but realised at the same time that I had cocked up. I gave myself a rule from then on: 'Never give them an excuse to pull hard.' Any opposition was going to want to beat you anyway; but never give them a score to settle, an insult to return or a genuine hatred of you.

Despite the slight, we had a great row. Although we never threatened to challenge the West Germans for the lead, we stayed ahead of the East German legends whether they were pulling especially hard or not. It was the last season that many of them rowed – global events were about to deprive them of their chaperones and their kit.

If interaction with international opposition was concentrated into the kit swap, domestic relations focused on myriad connections between club and national allegiances. Domestic rowing has always been complicated. Like most amateur sports in the UK, rowing provided a haven for enthusiastic and committed volunteers. Their approach was to take a willing group of youngsters, add in a bit of water, a few boats and more than a few hours of freezing your bum off, and out of the recipe will eventually come some champions. Traditionally, the clubs have held the real power, forming squads of athletes long before the national team had the wherewithal to do it. The emphasis was on the Head of the River, Henley Royal Regatta and the Boat Race. But in the last 30 years, as the profile of international events has grown, the clubs have lost their pre-eminence, unable to compete for the attention of their best athletes when GB duties call.

Many clubs that dominated the rowing scene for decades at Henley or the National Championships now win in a

season what they used to in a weekend. For some, the dominance of the national crews is a crime, the unnecessary
erosion of the sport at its heart, the worst kind of profession-
alism. But for others it's progress, the price we have to pay
for medals at the Olympics. For the average aspiring international, it's a complication. There is no academy, no one place
you can go where the route to medals is assured. Instead
everyone has to nail their colours to one particular club
mast. There are still club events, and whether you are a
World Champion or a raw novice, you must have an affilia-
tion. In March, around Boat Race time, comes the Head of
the River, one of the biggest sports events the capital puts on.
One weekend 420 men's eights from all over the country and
some from Europe have a big time trial from Chiswick Bridge
to Putney. For most it's a rite of passage, the last event of the
winter and the herald of the summer sprints. For the
national team, split up between their home clubs, it can be
war, plain and simple.

When I left school and ended up at Leander it was
because it was an obvious choice of club, a brand leader over
the decades, if not always dominant. It was the home of so
many of the Olympic team that I had watched on television,
and ran a decent cadet programme for people like me who
aspired to international colours. But Leander attracts criticism, too. The old guard see it as predatory, taking the cream
of the talent and then bashing every other club with it. In the
early '90s the anti lobby thronged to Molesey Club. Where

the Leander group was headed by Steve and me, the Molesey group was led by our then-bitter rivals, the Searle brothers. We were not concerned by the challenge – we had the depth that Molesey could only dream of. We had two boats that were quicker than their best one, or so we thought. The Head of the River in March 1992 was the pits as far as club loyalties went. Both crews used the National Team base at Hammersmith for the last week of training, and it was like trying to jam the wrong ends of some magnets together. Practical jokes from one side were taken as insults by the other. We regularly walked in complete silence past athletes with whom, in a matter of months, we were going to compete against the rest of the world. The battle lines were drawn, the animosity intense. Leander lost. It wasn't convincing, it was a matter of a second or two, but we still lost. We had the advantage by starting the race first out of the long queue, and Molesey were in our eye line, looking back up the river. But try what we might, the ten-second starting gap stayed the same and we knew when we crossed the line a little over 4 miles later that the race was lost. The Molesey crew stayed to celebrate their win as we left for home.

International pairs were, in the main, treated with disdain. Both Steve and I are terrible with names and can seldom remember the combinations that we raced from season to season. As evidence, I submit Steve's inability to name the Australian combination that won a Silver medal behind us at the Olympics in 1996 when asked to do so on *A*

Question of Sport a few weeks later. We used nicknames for the good ones: Scratch and Sniff, or Slap and Tickle. I know the people we beat didn't like us. In fact, it's hard to dominate rowing and be liked. We never used to like the East Germans when they were on top; no one seemed to like the West German Hansa Dortmund eights when they were winning championship after championship. I guess we didn't care. We were happy to take respect if people expressed it, but Steve had been schooled too long in the 'I don't give a monkeys' camp. As his partner, I certainly wasn't going to do anything but follow his lead. It wasn't hard to go into a corner and tell ourselves we didn't need to like the opposition, but I watched other guys on the team jealously as they greeted old rowing adversaries as friends even if they were about to race them. Eventually I became disappointed that people seemed to keep their distance from us and that all we got was an uncommitted nod or smile.

At the World Championships in 1995 one of our old adversaries from the Slovenian pair, Iztok Cop, won the single scull. He wasn't the first rower (rowing being with one oar as opposed to sculling with two) to swap to the single and win, but it was still a pretty immense feat. At the team party on the Sunday night I ran into him and offered my congratulations on his race. He had paced it beautifully, keeping his boat in the pack as others charged to the front, and just at the last he had sprinted through to take the title. Even after all the years racing against one another, I had seldom talked to him, and he spent a few minutes telling me not how happy he was about becoming World Champion in 1995, but how he and his partner should really have beaten us in the 1993 World Championships. Apparently, they felt that we were beatable, but his partner had broken his leg in the spring before the competition and they had lost a lot of training time. We had both had a few drinks, his English was okay and way better than my Slovenian, but I came away almost insulted. Sure, Steve and I had not been going as well as in 1992, but you should never tell someone they didn't deserve to win. Needless to say, we went back to the nodding arrangement again, we are still on that.

Outright offence given or taken between boats is really rare. Rowing is a sport where the majority of the battle is won and lost inside your own craft. If you get the best out of your own men and, of course, yourself, then you are likely to be at the top of your performance. People often ask if there is any psychology involved between the boats, and there is really very little. You might be careful around race time in what you say to anybody else about your training, but even if you are not, it won't make much difference. I find it hard to spot a crew in real difficulties, anyway. Arguing on the water might be a bad sign, but some crews just operate that way, and you would be foolish to write off competitors just because of that. Even on the start, when you might think it a great moment for some attempted psychological ploy, you would almost always fail. At that point any good boat is focused on the race. Trying to fake them over some tactics or your well-being is laughable. You are much more likely to lose focus yourself in mid-antic. The best psychology is played out during the race: good rowing from your opposition is the ultimate downer, so you try your best to hand that out.

After the melting of relations with the Aussie pair Rich and Rob in 1994 we were invited by them and their coach to go down to Sydney and train together. We were happy to accept. After all the negative experiences we had had between us and our opposition, it was a welcome break-through to be relaxed together. We were still cagey over certain things, though. It would have been impossible to discuss in detail our aspirations for the coming season and the Olympics in 1996 without some awkwardness. After all, we wanted to win and so did they. But all this remained unsaid. We trained alongside each other just as we would a squad pair at home. We mucked in and trained in the same boats, too, when we felt like a change. It was a revelation and we loved it. First of all, the climate in January was amazing: we were trading in three weeks of wind and cold for sun and warmth. They were also great hosts. We were billeted at the sports academy and given the run of the place. We could spend afternoons at the beach and were hosted on Rob's family yacht in Sydney Harbour for Australia Day. After a few days we forgot that we were going to race them in a few months. To this day Rich remains a good friend, and it was almost totally down to that period. It never seemed to get in the way of the racing either. Both boats knew the routine on the water: you wanted to beat them as much as ever, but once you crossed the line in first (you hoped), you wanted them to have done well. I think both pairs benefited from getting to know each other off the water, and it made the medal rostrum for the 1995 World Championships very friendly when we won the Gold and they the Silver.

When Steve and I formed a coxless four between 1997 and the Sydney Games in 2000, it was just as dominant as the pair had been, but less aloof. Partly it was a new outlook from Steve and myself, but also our new crewmates, Tim Foster and James Cracknell, were instinctively more outgoing towards the opposition. Tim had raced in the coxless fours for a good few years and knew a lot of the field. James also had some friends he kept up with from his junior days. As a crew, we were less antagonistic publicly, even if we were just as judgemental privately. Every crew used to do a warm-up jog before each race, and for most regatta courses there would be only a few options about where to go. The result was that the chances of running alongside or past your opposition were very high. Whenever we used to run past the German four, their strokeman would wave at us. The gesture was seldom returned, not only because none of us knew him that well, but also it was when you felt most aggressive and didn't want to show it. It used to become a well-worn joke that if he waved, we knew we would beat them. Sure enough, however many times he waved, we never lost to their boat.

The Italians were not wavers, however. All experienced guys, most of whom had been World Champions in the four back in 1994, they were our shadows for most of the run-up to the Olympics in Sydney in 2000. The first time I spoke to their strokeman Carlo Mornati on the medal stage at the World Championships in 1998, he totally took me by surprise.

The politics of the medal stage are complicated. There are any number of emotions going on: exhaustion all round because everyone has just rowed for six minutes give or take, and, if you've won, you can add in elation. If you have lost, you may be happy to have won a Silver, but you can also be destroyed by the experience if you are disappointed with your performance. What I realised early on is that, as a winner, you may be the last person the other medallists might want to see at that particular moment. So you have to take a lead from them if all they want to do is shake your hand then walk away. If they want to talk, then that's cool, but I know from my own experience, I seldom want to. So when I shook Carlo's hand he surprised me, first by talking with enthusiasm about our race together and saying we deserved to win, and second by doing it in a quasi-Aussie accent. I thought to begin with he was taking the piss, but it turned out he had studied in Australia for a year after the Games in Atlanta and came home with a twang. His friendship has been a slow burner. Started in the late '90s during our battles in the four, it has continued to grow, so much so that after the Championships in 2003 my wife and I spent a few days at his home in Como. My wife loves him – he is an Italian Adonis, a kind of olive-skinned Jude Law, so how could she not? I know he hates racing me and we don't talk too much about the Olympics in 2000, but he was smiling on all the photos with his medal round his neck.

Amazingly enough, I've never really talked to the opponent to whom I owe the most. His name is Adam Holland and he rowed in the American pair in the run-up to the 1996 Olympics in Atlanta. He was obsessed by Steve and me, apparently carrying a photo of us around in his wallet and showing it to anyone who cared to look. He was conscientious in his training and diet, and pinpoint accurate in his focus on beating us at the Olympics. This was surprising given that it was the first time many of those listening at his college had ever heard of us, this random British combination. For a long time one of them thought it was one person, some unfortunate bloke christened Pinsent N. Redgrave. She eventually found out it was two, but it was nevertheless the first time she heard my name. She would eventually become my wife.

relationships

R owing is not a solitary sport. The motivation may be personal, even selfish, but you can't go it alone. The stresses of training are such that you will always need people around you to work against or with, someone on the towpath to give you an idea of the way your rowing looks from the outside, and, ideally, someone at home you can bitch to when it all gets a bit intense. Even single scullers, the most introverted and self-obsessed of the rowing fraternity, are in no way alone.

When I was a junior athlete my parents took on the role of external sounding board. They would happily show up to regattas and races and cheer us on. But from my point of view, they were not great as impartial judges. They had never rowed, and though they were bursting with pride over my developing career, they could never be the first stop for advice. They were supportive in lots of other ways, though. They stumped up the necessary money when I was first chosen to compete for Great Britain at junior level, and when I decided to combine rowing with my first year after school, Dad sent me and my mother shopping for a car. Although it was never said openly, it was essentially rowing transport to get me to Henley for the weekend sessions, and it basically became my car.

My parents continued to follow my career and started planning their summers around the location of each year's championships. They've been there in the stands to see all but one of my Gold medal wins and now understand that following someone at a competition actually means hardly seeing them at all. In fact, I didn't appreciate how stressful it was for them for many years, but they've grown more experienced, as I have, and unless it's a really big race, they don't seem to get as nervous as they used to. If it's a big event, Dad gets agitated as the time of the race approaches and can't stop moving about. He has to make up errands, whereas Mum gets still and quiet. More than one person told me how when I was standing on the medal raft in Barcelona and my name was announced, Dad leapt up and shouted, 'That's my son!'

Throughout my college career I had always chosen rowing girls to go out with. It wasn't a narrow choice: a decent proportion of the student population had rowed, and within that group I had made good friends.

Like me, James Cracknell has been a serial monogamist. Unlike me, he always gets the interest from more than the granny section of the market. If ever your ego needs sapping, go with him to co-present awards at a girl's school. He seems to have an almost Beatlemania effect on girls. In the wake of the Olympics in Sydney we did a rowing challenge on the ergometer at a school in Marlow. There were ten of us versus ten guys from a gym in Leeds, and we had to row the massive distance of 100,000 metres. The mechanics of it were such that we each had to take about 20 strokes and then change with the next guy. The whole event took four hours or more and they shipped in a load of pupils to shout encouragement. Which they did, until the moment James stepped up and all the girls went ballistic. Fair enough for the first few rotations, but they kept it up for the entire challenge. I wouldn't have minded but the difference between him and even the cheers for Steve were stark. James doesn't trade on it, though, and he takes the female interest with a bemused shyness.

James met Beverly, a TV presenter, a few weeks after the Sydney Games and they were married in 2002, ten days before my wife and I. They had a baby in 2003.

As in so many things, Tim Foster was the black sheep when it came to women. With Tim it became hard being friends with his girlfriends because you were never sure how long they were going to last. Just when you thought you had heard the worst, Tim would top it, dating friends of his ex with an almost seamless regularity. On one occasion he persuaded his girlfriend he was saving money for a ring, and then drove up in a new car. He is shameless, if consistent.

There are many things that I owe to rowing – my ability to

earn money from the job I love and the respect that comes from being a successful sportsman. But nothing is more important than my wife.

In 1994, just after I left Oxford University, I was approached by the Women's Boat Club to see if I knew anyone who would be interested in doing some coaching. I knew I couldn't make time and, to be honest, I knew I wouldn't be a great coach. Coaching is a complex mixture of psychology, technique and bluff. Furthermore, I knew that just being good at something doesn't by right make you a good coach. Sure, I could do the basics, but I didn't want to misjudge the difficulty of guiding a full boat club over a period of six months of training. I knew of a sure-fire candidate, though.

Ben Hunt-Davis was a key figure in the men's team and was consistently making World Championship finals throughout the '90s. But finals in rowing don't bring in much bacon, and he was always in need of a way to afford the sportsman's dream of full-time training. He had a good eye for a boat and a hard-working personality that made him a sound if not expert coach. He threw himself into the minutiae of organising a training programme and enrolling other coaches to help out. The Women's Boat Club is really the poor cousin of the Men's Boat Club at Oxford. The men's race takes 95 per cent of the coverage for the Varsity races and shares little more than 5 per cent of the sponsorship with the women. Market forces are, of course, instrumental in deciding what event is worth covering, but the men were always able to afford things the women could only dream of. It's a situation that infuriated one particular undergraduate in Ben's squad in 1998 and she told him so. She had come to Oxford on a Rhodes Scholarship from Harvard and was appalled to see that Britain had no parallel with the ruling in the United States that guarantees equal funding for men's and women's sport.

I offered my services to Ben in the last two weeks before the Women's Boat Race to help out. It was always going to be a fun fortnight – the crews based themselves in Henley to prepare for the race there and lived in a big house together. Ben offered me the role of Finishing Coach for the reserves, which I accepted happily. It gave me a finite role on the same stretch of river where we trained throughout the year. It boiled down to ten afternoons or so. He also brought me in to decide on the last selection decision. The first boat had been set, but the bow seat for the reserves was being contested between two rowers. One was weaker but technically good, and the other was strong, determined and willing to speak her mind. Though she contests it, and because this is my book, I can definitely say that I didn't fancy her to begin with. Ben and I decided to put one Demetra Koutsoukos in the bow seat of the boat. There was another issue that kept me honest for that fortnight. I had an ex-girlfriend in the same crew.

The race was a disaster. Despite, or maybe because of my efforts, the Oxford second boat lost to Cambridge by a very reasonable distance. No one was more dejected than me, and it hurt me personally to think that I was so capable on the water but, it seemed, so incapable on the towpath. Both Oxford boats lost that afternoon, so the dinner afterwards was understandably downbeat. Most of the rowers and coaches planned a schedule of alcohol immersion to rid themselves of an incredibly disappointing afternoon. Demetra was wearing a fantastic red dress that was more flattering even than rowing Lycra, and was being flirtatious (again, my take on the situation, I hasten to add).

Sometime late in the evening, I was standing at the bar ordering a drink and 'Dee', as I was getting to know her, came up to talk. Before I could say anything gallant I arrogantly blurted out, 'This is never going to happen, Dee.' (I know, I know – classy.) She immediately snapped back that she was only getting a drink and it was a free world. I then offered to buy it for her. At the end of the evening I urged her to call, and after the regulation three days, she did.

Dee's parents had emigrated from Greece in the '60s to make their lives in Toronto. They gave her a work ethic that she used to great effect through the state school system and then on to Harvard. Awarded a Rhodes scholarship, she interrupted her medical training to study social science at Oxford.

She made an immediate impact with my friends. Mediterranean to look at, but North American by accent, she was fiercely independent of thought and word, and willing to argue passionately about all things between the British weather and the monarchy. My parents loved her straight-away, and soon I did as well.

In my world there were two types of women: those who row and those who don't. I had dated both types and usually found the non-rowers had difficulty understanding the commitment that the sport demanded. Endless racing seasons and very few weekends together, combined with a social life dominated by the sport and the people in it, make dating a rower a mixed blessing. We were pretty cheap dates, never usually managing to consume much alcohol, but we ate our weight in food, or so it seemed.

After a few months it became apparent, at least to Dee, that this relationship was something worth committing to. She changed her life, first to stay in Oxford, and then to stay in the UK. I was, as ever, chained to the rowing grindstone. I never questioned that, and she has never asked me to. To begin with, her giving up a medical career in the US, made me feel under intense pressure. I wasn't sure I would have done the same thing for her. We had a horrible Christmas one year when I nearly broke up with her. Not that there was anyone else, I was just scared by how much she seemed to feel for me.

Dad waded in at one point to tell her that the biggest mistake I could ever make was not to marry her. All this did was increase her frustration with me. Her parents were even less helpful. Her dad was adamant that she should return to Harvard and become a doctor. Her new career as a management consultant didn't cut much ice with him. At one point, fairly late in 1998, her mum came to visit. They were on the

Tube in London on the way to see the sights when the subject of the new boyfriend came up. At that time, Steve and I were on a poster campaign for a health insurance company and Dee was able to point me out and say, 'That's him, Mum!' It took her the best part of an hour to convince her that she was telling the truth.

By the time of the Sydney Olympics in 2000 we were on firmer ground. The Games gave me the excuse of rowing to avoid the 'm' word, and Dee was never going to argue with that. It was the only thing that year I was a chicken about. But for the first time at an Olympics, I wanted to be with her afterwards more than in the village. So we spent the second week of the Games in a hotel in Darling Harbour doing pretty much what came to mind.

It was great to have her there. The whole build-up had been so intense that afterwards I didn't know if I was coming or going. I was jumping around the hotel like a kangaroo some nights, then calling a halt to the evening at 10 p.m. the next. Watching other people win medals brought me to tears. I mislaid my own medal in a courtesy car for a few hours, and then lost for good my backpack containing my passport and ticket home. Throughout all this, Dee was there.

My life was in turmoil after Sydney, and she became a bedrock of sense and advice. Whenever she caught me having any 'Do they know who I am?' moments, she would pull me up and tell me just what a prat I was being. As life went back to a more predictable routine of rowing for another Games, it was obvious to me and everyone else that although rowing was important, it was no longer my first love. I proposed in the summer of 2001, but we had to wait until after the championships in 2002 to have a wedding and a honeymoon away from the rigours of the rowing calendar.

seville diary

Thursday, 19 February 2004
Seville, Spain
194 days to go till the Final

We were totally unprepared for D-Day being today. Stumbling out of the lift at a quarter to 12, running late for another outing in the four that has been our training vessel for the last three days, Jürgen called us into a meeting. To begin with I thought it was just for James and me, but then as Steve Williams, Toby Garbett, Josh West and Rick Dunn got up from the chairs in the TV area, I realised something was afoot.

Everyone knew that Jürgen had to make a decision about whether we were going to put our main effort into a four or a pair. The pair of myself and James Cracknell had been successful throughout 2001 and 2002, winning two World Championships and breaking the world record. But at the World Championships in 2003 the wheels came off and we finished fourth. Some people were now advocating staying in the pair no matter what, putting it down to a bad day and concentrating on putting it right at the Olympics. But men's rowing has failed to win a Gold medal for the first time since 1990 and that is weighing as heavily with Jürgen as with any of us. But he is also our crew coach and, not for the first time, there was a potential conflict. His solution is to keep us out of the decision-making process entirely; our job is to make the pair go as quickly as we can this winter and he will look after the rest. Everyone believed he would never show his hand until after the April trials, when a pecking order could be established, but he had other ideas.

When we sat down I still thought it might be a housekeeping-type of chat about the weekend sprints – these are the crews, this is the general idea, all that sort of nonsense. But then he opened with: 'We have to come to a decision, having looked at all the tests and the results from last year's World Championship.' At that moment I woke up pretty suddenly, realising that this was going to be anything but an ordinary housekeeping meeting. 'We definitely strengthen the four, and by that I mean we put Matt and James in it.' This was two massive sledgehammer blows for all of us – not only had he committed to axing the pair with James and me, but he was doing it now, not after the April trials as we had all thought would be the case.

But he was far from done. 'We go with Steve and Josh in the four, and Rick and Toby have the choice for this weekend between the pair and the second four.' The air drained out of the room as we all took in the significance of the last 20 seconds. Not only had he binned the pair, but he had called a halt to any further trialling in the four, at least that was how I saw it. A guilty burst of adrenalin swept through my system as I realised that I was going to the Games to defend our coxless four title, and then I took in the shock of what must be happening in the chairs around me. Four years of work and anticipation had been snatched away from Toby and Rick in that moment. They had trained and raced in a unit that was now history, and though they had been well beaten by Josh and Steve at trials throughout the winter, it would have been a brave man to have said that their challenge was over. Today Jürgen is indeed that brave man.

I dared not look around and Jürgen was getting uncomfortable with my fixed gaze as he came to the end of his short speech. He pressed Rick for an answer over their choice for the weekend, which was rather like the Devil asking whether you wanted aisle or window for the journey to hell. Then it was over, and we emerged from the meeting like rescued miners, squinting and dumbstruck, to go rowing again. The outing was surprisingly good, given the circumstances, and none of us really mentioned the fact that as far as the chief coach was concerned, this was the premier boat for GB rowing at the Olympics. I'm sure poor Josh and Steve had mixed feelings about their 'promotion' and their erstwhile crewmates' disposal, but they kept quiet. Steve asked me privately at the drinking fountain if I had known what was coming. I could faithfully answer that I had not.

The signs may have been there – Jürgen sending us out in the four and asking for every conceivable improvement; John West, who was coaching the old four, being so quiet that I now realise he must have known since last night; Jürgen missing the opportunity to go out with the organisers for a fantastic meal last night, and indeed his quiet brooding over the last few days in a place that usually sees him relaxed and happy. Poor Toby must rue his missed trial last week because of illness, or stopping on his 5-kilometre test, or missing sculling trials for a wedding. The bad result this week must have been the final straw for his chances, though none of us were to know it. Rick is equally downcast, saying that were we at home, he would simply have left and gone away for a few days. The sight of us paddling around and racing this weekend must be salt in the wound.

In all the shock I really haven't had time to think about the implications for us. The challenge against the Aussies in the pair is now no more, and though I have always said to the press that I didn't have a favourite option, not doing the pair will, I'm sure, hurt most on that front. I look forward to a day this week when we can begin treasuring the new combination and looking forward to the Olympic challenge. It has been hard to hide our excitement this week, however, and James and I were saying just last night that it is already the best four we have paddled in. It will need to be. But the boat has a long, *fluid rhythm that we had only fleetingly in the Sydney combination, and I hope it has more guns than the crews since then.*

Jürgen has yet again surprised us all, and as James said so accurately at tea this afternoon, 'I thought Clive Woodward was cut-throat till today.'

17

atlanta

In my book, Atlanta never really had the right ring for an Olympic city. What is it famous for? What is its landmark? What was its particular brand of Olympics going to be? I'm not sure anyone really had a clear idea, but they made the huge mistake of telling the world it was going to be the best Games ever. Oh dear, talk about raising expectations. For the athletes training for the Games it was fine, though. We may not have believed all the hype, but we had every reason to think that Atlanta was going to be a competent and enthusiastic host.

The Opening Ceremony was where it began to go wrong. Steve was once again selected to carry the flag. This was an unprecedented move and one that underlined the difference in his profile within the sports world and outside it. At home he was well known and respected, but in 1996 he was a long way from the iconic status that he has today. The flag bearer is decided by the team managers of all the Olympic sports at a meeting a few days before the opening. Each sport puts forward a candidate and, of course, logistics play a big part. The athlete needs to be in town for the opening. Track and field competitors arrive only in the second week and are at a distinct disadvantage. Nevertheless, for Steve to be chosen again was a massive boost for both of us. This time, I'm going too.

We all get changed into our marching gear in the late afternoon. The powers that be have decided to break with the jacket and tie tradition and go with shorts and a collared T-shirt. It's fine and, most importantly, cool. We all get bused down to the Atlanta Braves stadium, right next to the Olympic arena. There we are organised into seats to watch the first part of the ceremony on the big screens.

After an hour or so of dancing schoolkids and speeches, the parade of nations begins. Greece, as traditional hosts, lead us off, and after that it's alphabetical. Gradually the volunteers begin gathering up the nations and taking them out. But pretty soon it begins to go awry. There are big gaps in the parade. The announcer says 'Austria!' and no Austrian appears over the top of the stadium ramp. There's an embarrassed pause and then here they come, looking slightly Morecambe and Wise, as if someone had just shoved them all on from the side. I begin to notice how long it takes for countries to leave their seats before they appear on screen. It's not long. The problem is that as the parade is eight people wide, you can get through even the biggest nations with hundreds of athletes in a couple of minutes, and the smaller ones take only seconds. Trying to extricate the nations from their seats in the baseball stadium is not nearly fast enough. It's like trying to get all the passengers off a plane – everybody has to wait in long lines while someone else finds their bag or camera.

By the time we are getting up, the situation is becoming comical, the gaps are appearing more and more often on the screen, and some countries are coming in with no semblance of order. One of the volunteers calls for the British flag carrier, and Steve is ushered forward. Normally, there is a careful protocol for the Opening Ceremony: British Olympic bigwigs get to go behind the flag carrier; then the women athletes, smallest at the front and to the outside; men are at the rear, with the tallest at the very back. That way there is a maximum chance of everybody getting an opportunity to wave and say 'Hello, Mum!' at a camera. But this time there is a real sense of panic in the volunteers. The tail-enders from Ghana have long since disappeared around the corner and an order has come down from some stressed lovey in a box someplace: 'Get them athletes in!' Our *chef de mission*, Simon Clegg, is trying to maintain some semblance of British order about who goes where, but it's no good. Then one of the volunteers says, 'British flag carrier get going, run! Keep the gaps down!' and team GB takes off like a flock of geese. Pretty soon everyone realises that the bigwigs are never going to manage to run the 800 metres or so across to the stadium and that the protocol is shot to hell. Time it right, everybody thinks, and I have a decent chance of being right behind the flag carrier, and right on primetime television. A cluster forms around Steve who is now moving at a fair pace himself, and then that group gets swallowed up by a sea of strapping hockey players, swimmers and rowers, all with the glint of fame in their eye.

After a minute I give up the chase. I suddenly realise I don't want to be sprinting anywhere a day before our opening heat and start a more sedate jog. When I see one of the rowing coaches I walk with him. Jonny Searle joins us and we take our sweet time over it, ignoring the volunteers who are all trying to chivvy us along. As it turns out, we are not all that far behind the group on the ramp, but Team GB makes a shambolic entrance with a big, heaving group at the front. Jonny, the coach and I are above all the pushing and shoving, right at the back, ambling around Lane One, a decent gap off the back of the Brits and only a fraction ahead of the girl carrying the Guatemala banner.

After assembling in the middle, I find Steve and we watch together as Muhammad Ali appears to light the torch. Everyone at once screams 'Ali!' in welcome. I notice how he is shaking as he reaches up with the torch. Steve turns and says, 'Okay, I'm ready, are you?' and I know straight away what he means. We weave our way through the nations to where we know we will be let out, and then slip under the human cordon and across the track while the ceremony reaches a climax. As the fireworks thunder over our heads, we get on the first bus back to the village and bed.

It was only next morning that we heard some of the other

stories from the Opening Ceremony. Garry Herbert, the coxswain who had steered the Searle brothers to victory in Barcelona and was steering the eight in Atlanta, had been trampled at the top of the ramp by the entrance to the stadium. Charged with adrenalin and the chance of being on TV, he had worked his way through the disorganised ranks to take up position behind Steve and had then paused to take in the amazing view as team GB were greeted by 60,000 people. Pushed from behind and sliding on the down slope, he had grazed his face. We were merciless in our piss-take of him, but only till we heard some of the other experiences. Some of the guys had seen the Polish *chef de mission* receiving treatment for a heart attack while he was in the middle of the stadium. None of us knew him and I don't want to risk a lawsuit, but you have to wonder about the 800-metre dash that preceded his attack. He died right there on the field. To their eternal shame, Atlanta never said anything about the chaos of the parade, and I even heard of some discussion afterwards about whether it was practical to commit so much time during the ceremony to the athletes. Thankfully, it has survived unchanged, and although it is unwieldy and long, the parade of nations is something I feel very strongly about.

Within a day or so we had other things to worry about – first of all, our heat out at Lanier. FISA, the governing body of rowing, had for the first time introduced seeded heats, which was a relief for the top crews in each event. You were guaranteed not to meet any more than one other seed in your first race, and, as top seeds, we were up against the sixth seeds Croatia. It wasn't a big deal on paper, and even if we had fallen in and swum over the finish line, we would have had another chance in the losers' pool, the *repêchage*. But without wanting to sound too much like a football manager, there are no easy races at the Olympics. With only one qualifying for the semi final I was tying myself in knots over who was going to do what. In reality, we had to do exactly what we had done in the previous hundred or so races between Atlanta and Barcelona. Namely, get off to a good start, take the race by the scruff of the neck and never give up the initiative. But in the British tent an hour before we went out it didn't seem that easy. I had drunk a decent quantity of water and sports drink to fight the effects of dehydration and was lying on the floor with my knees up. Steve was in a similarly relaxed pose, and had been since our warm-up row, but his knee was jiggling – a telltale sign of anxiety. I began to feel the butterflies grow into a general feeling of nausea. This is entirely normal for me, but one moment I was lying there, and the next I was depositing all the fluid I'd swallowed down the gap between the back wall and the floor of the tent. Steve didn't look worried. We both knew it wasn't a serious illness, but I promised myself that I would seriously rethink the food-and-drink strategy in time for the semi-final.

The race turned out to be as straightforward as we hoped, and we returned to the boat yard as semi-finalists. For the next race I at least managed not to vomit. This time we had an American pair with a bloke called Holland in the stroke seat. Yeah, that guy. It was obviously his moment to bring to fruition all the careful plans to beat Pinsent N. Redgrave and we never saw it coming. For the first half we were playing second fiddle to them as they leapt off down the course. I was getting a little concerned because I didn't feel we were going slowly, but we seemed unable to reel them in. Then, just at the 1000-metre mark, one of them shouted 'Fuck yeah'. And that was enough – it communicated so much to us. First, that they weren't really expecting to be there, they were pumped up and living off the adrenalin, and second, that we could burst their bubble. The second half of a rowing race is no place for adrenalin. You need to have got there in good shape. You have to be calculating and deter-mined about what you want the outcome of the race to be. You should be ready to attack if you are behind, and defend if you are leading. In either case, that means pain. We attacked them and soon found ourselves in the lead, and there were no more shouts of adrenalin or anything else from their boat. In fact, they were caught before the line by both the French and the Kiwis. We were rattled, though. We hadn't had anyone lead us in any meaningful sense since the German pair in the '94 season. It didn't help when it seemed as if the world's media had descended on Lanier with the explicit intention of interviewing Steve.

The level of interest took us by surprise. We were ushered into a hot tent and penned into a corner as dozens of tape recorders were thrust out towards us. 'How were we feeling?' 'Were we surprised by the American pair?' And 'What's wrong, Steve?' This last one was in response to Steve's demeanour, which was bordering on the murderous. Under the pressure of being on the verge of winning his fourth Olympic Gold medal, an unprecedented feat for a British sportsperson alive or dead, he had become fed up with being asked questions along the lines of 'Are you going to win?' He soon got up and left, the only time I ever saw him lose his cool at the Olympics. He decided to travel back to the main village to eat up some of the afternoon and to escape watching the awful NBC coverage.

Steve returned to the hotel in the evening and we had a drink in the garden after dinner. We had one last free day on the Friday before the biggest race in four years. Despite all our previous wins, there was a fly in the ointment. We had never raced the Australian pair of David Weightman and Robert Scott. They had beaten Rich Wearne and Rob Walker, the guys we had befriended and trained with. Seeded second, they had progressed smoothly through the competition and were now the only other unbeaten pair. On paper we had all the advantages: we were more experienced, more powerful, and had every right to be more confident, but we had a nagging worry that they were aiming to upset the favourites. We didn't talk too much about them directly, there is a limit to what you can learn just by looking at them, but it was obvious to us both that we were on an undulating road with our confidence. The boat was certainly going well enough to beat our regular opponents, and had we had a chance to race and dominate the Aussie pair the way we had raced the previous version, it might have felt different. The almost effortless speed that we had been able to conjure up at the Barcelona Games was a very distant memory.

Tensions were rising all around. That night, Steve wandered over to the four in the garden and mentioned that there was lots of post in the village for them. Jonny Searle replied that it might have been nice if he had brought it back with him and got a fairly tense reply about how Steve wasn't going to be their effing postman. Within seconds they were facing off to each other and Greg Searle and I were trying to calm our respective teammates, although I certainly wasn't going to step in between the two biggest sets of arms in the rowing world and get my nose broken. Sure enough, it all ended without violence, but the tension between the two boats (never good to begin with) ramped up even further. Not that it made much difference to either of us, but there would be precious little encouragement between the boats on finals day.

We were up long before dawn on the Saturday, and having experienced Atlanta's punishing heat, I was determined that I would have only water between waking and racing; I had eaten a decent amount the night before and was confident I had enough energy stored up. As I brushed my teeth I heard the TV go on. Steve was sitting on the end of his bed as I emerged from the bathroom. He looked at me with dread in his face. 'There's been a bomb.' Aghast, I sat down and we watched the descriptions of the explosion in Centennial Park loop around on the news. Within five minutes there was a statement from François Carrard, the director of the International Olympic Committee, to say that the Games would go on, that there had been no Olympic personnel injured and that Olympic security had not been breached. I remember him saying, 'As we speak, buses are rolling. The Games will go on as normal.' In an instant, Steve snapped off the TV and said, 'Okay, let's go.' Jürgen was downstairs as planned, with a car to take us to the lake, and as we arrived the volunteers were all saying the same thing – 'It's business as usual.' But it was hard to concentrate. Details were still trickling through, and although we tried to cut ourselves off from it, no one else seemed to be. Flags were at half-mast around the lake, and the atmosphere was far less excited than it had been even for the day of the heats.

We paddled as normal at first light and hid ourselves away in the tent that had served as sick bay and rest area during the week. Somehow it was a lot harder than it had been in Barcelona. I kept casting my mind back, trying to remember how I felt then. Certainly, this seemed to be ten times worse. Then it occurred to me that maybe in winning you just forget the feelings of nerves that you had before-hand. Perhaps I had been this bad before Barcelona, too. So I made myself a promise, as you do in that kind of situation.

Just like the drunk with his head down the toilet promising himself 'Never again', I told myself never to underestimate how hard it is to put everything – over four years of my life – on the line and go out to race. But at the same time I was persuading myself that you actually need the nerves. I always produced my best when under pressure, and the Olympics was when I really needed my best. On the few occasions when I have raced without nerves the results have not been good. So the battle goes on in your head – you need the nerves, but the thought of racing makes you want to run away and hide.

At last Jürgen came to rescue us for the warm-up. He was much more prescriptive than he had been in Barcelona, and we spent almost five minutes talking about the race. He highlighted again the dangers posed by both the French and the Australians, and stressed the importance of us rowing our own race. 'You are so strong, I'm sure no one can beat you,' was his well-used but nonetheless welcome sign-off. We both knew Jürgen well enough to recognise any signs of a lack of confidence and he certainly had none here.

We paddled off round the corner and, unlike in Barcelona, we had to pass the grandstands on the way to the start. A ripple of applause greeted us as we turned the corner and we received individual shouts of encouragement from the British fans as we drew level with them. Just as the noise died away, we both heard one of Steve's daughters shout, 'Come on, Daddy!' Steve told me later that it had him close to tears.

The warm-up is tense. We circle round a swimming line of buoys in the middle of the lake and can't help but stare at the opposition. It is not really possible to influence them at this stage in proceedings; any crew in an Olympic final is going to be up for a fight in any case. I try to avoid any howling mistakes, try not to look nervous and count down the minutes before the start. There is little room for communication between the two of us at this stage of a race. Steve runs through the warm-up routine in a measured voice that hides his nerves. I volunteer a tactical thought and reinforce a call that we both knew but, as usual, I zero in on something minute, something elemental to the process of the race. It is often something to do with rhythm, which I know is my responsibility alone. 'When we get to 300 metres gone then let it flow,' says Steve. 'Let them see how good you are. Remember what Jürgen told us – we are too strong for these muppets.' But we both know that they are not going to be rolling over and dying. If we give them an opportunity, they will take every advantage.

The last few minutes on the start are purgatory. Deprived of movement, your legs feel tired, and so it's common to see some guys slide up and down in a motionless boat just to re-enact the feeling. Some of the opposition breathe deeply, and across the water you can hear the last murmurings. Steve slides up behind me and in time-honoured fashion says, 'Let's have a really good row, Matt.' By this stage, I can only nod. I'm too dry in the mouth to offer a sensible reply.

By now FISA had got rid of the interminable 'Ready? ... Go!' gap routine and replaced it with a traffic light system that made false starts almost impossible. The starter calls out the crews' countries in turn, then says 'Attention!' The red light comes on and then the green. As the green lights up, a buzzer sounds but I never hear it. Both Steve and I can see the lights and at the moment it switches, we drive the legs down for the first stroke of nearly 250. Our first is seldom our best, and the smaller, lighter opposition take the lead by a fraction. But by five or ten we are flying, gathering the boat at the beginning of the stroke and letting all the adrenalin and training take over. After the last few days it is a relief to be into it.

We are in the lead at 500 and Steve is in control. Confidence is streaming from him, not just in what he says, but also in the way he says it. A tired bowman speaks through an open gasping mouth, rasping out commands when he can snatch the time from the body's demands for oxygen. But Steve is now growling through gritted teeth and his commands are clear and arrogant. We inch away from the field, making our intentions clear: 'We are going to win. If you chase us, you run the risk of blowing and losing any medal.' If it were another less well-known pair that was doing it, everybody would chase. But with us, they know it's not a bluff. We have the energy to carry it off.

At the halfway mark Steve would normally call for a big effort to open up a decisive lead, a killer punch. But he changes the call: 'We would normally be pushing here, but we are going to hold them without it.' It's not unknown for him to change the plan but it's a confident and inspiring call. It's a boost in another way. He would normally be fighting for breath but he manages a little speech, rather than the staccato orders. It's a 'We are too good' call and it feels great. We are in command of the race, clicking down the landmarks until we are Olympic Champions.

But the Aussies and the French aren't through yet. At 600 to go, they attack each other and us and the gap that was so comfortable becomes smaller. We raise the rate at 500 to go but they still come. We don't panic; it's not a crisis but we can't seem to stop their charge. Two-fifty and the noise kicks in from the right side of the course. Steve has to shout now rather than talk: 'Twenty left.' I count the strokes in my head. My lungs are burning now, legs aching, and the easy, arrogant confidence of the first half is gone. We know we can't lose now, but we are leading by only half a length. Then I turn my head to eyeball the distance to the massive finish tower and know we are there.

It is the last stroke and I can see the Aussies and the line in one glance. The finish is going to come for us before they will.

winning

Winning a race is a strange experience. Everybody thinks it must be ecstatic from start to finish. Of course, much of it is, but there should be a winners' manual somewhere because the range of emotions is extreme and coping with them can be odd, to say the least.

The first reaction is a starburst of joy. With experience you can judge the relative position of all the other boats in the race. With years of it you can tell the exact moment your own boat touches the finish line. The arm raised to punch the air, the shout of glee or roar of a score settled or favourite overturned, can all happen before your reign as winner is more than a second old.

But then your body has more important issues to deal with. The body is capable of amazing things as a normal adult, but train it for a few years and it can work for minutes on end without enough oxygen to sustain it properly. You can make your legs work harder than the internal mechanics of heart, lungs and blood are comfortable with. It's a perfectly natural state and one with which everybody is familiar. The run for the bus, the sharp incline in the path or the extra flight of stairs all produce it – a lactate burn. Your mouth gapes, your limbs burn and you need a rest to let the symptoms die back.

But in a rowing race there can be no rest. Rest is losing, simple as that. You need to get your opposition into the position where they can't match your speed, and the limiting factor is the pain. It won't happen in the first few seconds; even sprinting away from the blocks, your body doesn't register the pain problem for 20 seconds and then it only starts to really burn after 40. But after a minute, after two and most certainly after five, pain is a deciding factor. Deal with it better than your opponent and you are likely to win; force them into an unsustainable pace and they will slow. But even if you win, you get the burn.

It starts in the legs, mainly in the thighs, then the stomach, too, and the chest where the heart is racing at up to 200 beats a minute. Bending double in the boat doesn't make it go away but it feels natural to collapse down. Some guys lean back and tip their head back to suck in the air but I tend to lean forward. The pain fades from a peak after 20 seconds but it's far from over. The legs will ache and turn blue as the oxygen-starved blood courses through them; the soles of your feet ache as well after the pressure of all the power you can generate has been pressed down on them. At the end of the race some people remain motionless for minutes, but most prefer to move, even to slide up and down in an echo of the nerves at the start. Throats are parched, burnt by the hundreds of litres of air every minute that has been sucked through. But after a minute, you can usually manage a smile, or maybe turn to look your partner in the eye and know that you have done it.

Winning from the position of favourite is bitter-sweet, as it is tinged with relief. Underdogs are luckier as they have the unbridled pleasure of the unexpected. The jump-for-joy moments are usually reserved for them, as it's a mixture of surprise and happiness. The favourites are still happy, but it's less vociferous. Think of Cathy Freeman – a nation's hopes rested on her and all she could do when she won was crouch down and cry. It was relief that she felt more than anything.

Relief usually makes me tearful, if not an outright blubberer. Barcelona had me crying before the medal ceremony, and Atlanta was no different. We paddled back up the course in front of the stands and I had tears of relief flowing down my cheeks. I couldn't help but think of all the effort that had gone into this and how much I wanted it. A rush of memories of training and advice, people and places, filled my head. Tears are fine; you have the rest of your life to get used to being called a champion.

Paddle over to the medal raft and get out, if your legs will hold you. Embrace the crewmates; it's usually the only time you ever will, and it feels natural to do it. Exchange handshakes and a happy reaction to the race. Greet the opponents but don't be offended if you are the last people on earth they want to talk to right then. Ask only bland, inoffensive questions unless it's the last time you will ever race them. I have been burnt on the medal raft a couple of times by people who beat me and, trust me, you remember it the next time you line up against them.

The medal ceremony itself is the most eagerly anticipated event to do with winning the Olympics. Truth is, it passes in a blur. In Barcelona an Aussie official came over and insulted the Slovenians by calling them Romanian, and then turned to congratulate us. Then the magic moment came as he turned to the tray, lifted my Olympic Gold medal and placed it around my neck. I paused, eager to soak up the moment. The crowd were applauding my name, the sun was warm on my face and I could for evermore call myself Olympic Champion. Sure, it's a quirky, quiet corner of the Games; it's unlikely you are going to get a tickertape parade down Fifth Avenue, but you know that you are the best in the world. I haven't tried many recreational drugs in my time, but I'll bet few of them are as addictive as that feeling.

It can alter your life straight away. Of course, other people treat you differently; you are certainly marketable and, if you are lucky, you can make a career off the back of it. But it's how you view yourself that's most important. It may sound insecure and paranoid but years later I still get a kick out of what we did on those lakes against those other crews. It's not that I don't get a kick out of my friends, or a good movie, or hitting a golf ball straight, but it's just a different kind of kick. Nick Faldo was once asked what it felt like to win the Open and he replied, 'I can't tell you, you haven't done it.' Although I wouldn't say that to a reporter, it's very true. Try as I might, I can't put into words what winning feels like. Whenever I'm asked, I say that if I could accurately describe it, winning wouldn't be worth it. It has to be so awesome, so incredible, that it is worth four years of effort to achieve it.

After the final in Atlanta, Steve was called away for a dope test and I waited outside the hut for him to reappear. I listened to the race commentary for the coxless four and surprised myself with how much I wanted the British guys to do well. It was a turning point for me. After that, I never held negative feelings for another British boat. I suppose it was well past time. We held a press conference at the lake and then zoomed off downtown to do the now traditional stint on the BBC couch with Steve Rider. Then it was back to Gainesville for a celebratory dinner with our folks and their hosts. At the last minute, we realised we were being invited to a smart country club and had only rowing kit to wear. So it was that at about eight in the evening the Chattanooga Country Club allowed in two gentlemen with no ties, no jackets, in fact, no shoes either. We wore collared T-shirts, shorts and flip-flops; I know beaches where we would have been underdressed. The dining room paused as we entered but took up a polite chatter as we sat down covering our bare legs under the table. Three gin and tonics later and we were walking around showing off the medals. Our lack of dress was less important after they came out.

I accepted an offer to stay in the same house as my family that night and lay awake listening to my cousin snore. I was as tired, of course, but the longest sleepless stretches of my life have always been after Olympic finals.

It's perfectly normal for me to feel listless afterwards as well. You would imagine a long stretch of satisfied days as the Olympics reaches a climax in the second week. But life in the village seems dull after you have finished, and drinking the nights away loses its appeal after a hangover or three.

But the positive side far outweighs the negative. Beers are hard to pay for when you have won; interesting and interested people want to be around you, and provided you realise that it won't always be like this, then you should fill your boots. The party atmosphere in the village gathers pace so that the evening exodus of athletes for the bars downtown gets greater each night. Food in the village is available 24 hours a day, so the 3 a.m. munchie feeders gather momentum, too. The McDonalds is a mêlée of hungry partygoers until well past breakfast time.

With family on the outside of the fence, Steve never stays on in the village. It becomes hard to argue with a wife and children that you should stay on just to enjoy the atmosphere after months away from home and dozens of family weekends, events and holidays sacrificed to the rowing god. In Barcelona he spent a few days driving home across France. In Atlanta we went into the village to pack up and we shook hands at the door to the British block. There was a lot for me to be excited about, a second week full of happy nothingness awaited. I could hide away from as much of the media as I liked and could pretend I never got the messages that were piling up behind the desk at headquarters. But Steve's famous retirement speech was ringing in my ears ('If anyone ever sees me near a boat again they have my permission to shoot me') and we both believed that this was the end of our rowing together. Steve was in a fine mood. Buoyed by the small factor of winning his fourth Olympic Gold medal, he was less stressed than I had seen him in months, even years. He was taking his wife Ann and the kids to Disney World in Florida and he was looking forward to a break from the spotlight.

He said something meaningful and heartfelt, and not for the last time I fobbed him off with a crappy joke about Mickey Mouse. From the first time we rowed together as a pair we always had a fantastic relationship. Both of us were sensitive to the other's weaknesses and impressed by the other's strengths. Yet we never got emotional about it. I remember being really surprised and embarrassed by an interview in which I was asked if I loved Steve. I became all blokey and dodged the question, but of course I did. Not all the time, not even in a brotherly way, but you could never do what we did and not feel anything other than love for each other. There, I said it.

The second week was a predictable and enjoyable mix. I

missed out on some of the real highlights, like Garry Herbert, the Searles' cox, driving one of the trolley buses into the fence of the village and breaking his thumb. Poor Gaz started with a scraped face and finished with a broken digit.

I watched the men's 4x400 relay, the last meaningful event for Britain, in a sports bar downtown. Surrounded by Americans, I didn't cheer too loud for the Brits, but with mixed emotions I realised that Steve and I had become the only winners from Britain in Atlanta. On one hand, it was great for us to be singled out, but the jungle drums were already sounding at home. One of the few interviews I had done by that stage was on Radio 4, and I was asked to explain the disappointing British performance. Maybe it was not a fair question for me to answer, but at least it showed what the general mood was at home. There was going to be precious little celebrating going on.

Arriving at Heathrow was a small posse of medallists – Steve Backley, Roger Black and Ben Ainslie, the sailor. As we appeared in the Arrivals hall, there was an even smaller posse of cameras and journalists to greet us. We posed with medals up and then came, 'What does it feel like to be part of a disappointing British performance?' Fortunately, Roger stepped in before I could tell the guy where I wanted to stick my Gold medal, but the die was cast. Britain pretty much swept the Games under the carpet. The only upside was that in the corridors of power, sport and elite sport were now given higher priority when it came to handing out lottery money.

Personally, the lack of overall success didn't take the shine off our medals. Although it was nothing compared to four years later after the Sydney Games, I had more than my fair share of kudos and respect for winning at Atlanta. I was periodically recognised and seldom hassled and that was just fine by me. I didn't hate signing autographs, but I didn't relish it either. One night soon after getting back I was sitting in a restaurant with my girlfriend and my agent, Athole Still, and his wife Isobel. We were discussing the options for sponsorship for the upcoming four years without Steve, when the waiter arrived with a bottle of champagne. 'It's from the table in the corner,' he said. We all looked over to at least acknowledge the gift but they were playing it very cool and didn't look up or wave. Impressed, I reached down and pulled out the medal in its nice wooden box and asked the waiter to deliver it as a thank you. This time it was our turn to play it cool, and it was only as they were leaving that the couple came over to say congratulations and return the medal. They still didn't ask for an autograph – very classy indeed.

Steve and I saw each other a lot in the next few weeks. Appearances, whether paid or charity, always wanted us together and we had a great time. We never talked about the future and I was still convinced that Steve was enjoying the first few months of his retirement. His golf swing certainly needed work. It was only six weeks after getting home that I went to see Jürgen to talk about the future. We discussed the options: a four with the remnants of the Olympic four that had won Bronze; or, indeed, a pair with someone else. Jürgen mentioned that he had spoken to Steve about him carrying on and I was shocked. I genuinely had never believed any of the rumours in the press, or indeed the boat houses, about his keeping going. I went up into Jürgen's office and dialled Steve. 'Jürgen says you are going to carry on.' No messing with niceties. Straight down to business.

'Yeah, I'm thinking about it.' Typical understated Steve. That meant yes.

'Well, we're not doing the pair any more. We'd just be hanging around waiting to get beaten. I'm done with that.'

'Yeah, I agree. Although I'm still knackered, I want to take some more time off training. Jürgen has given me till the first of January. If I'm not back and committed then, he doesn't want to be involved.'

'When did you decide?' I asked.

'In Florida. I talked it over with Ann and she said I should do whatever I wanted.' Translation – he decided well before talking to her, and she knew trying to stop him would have been like trying to nail jelly to the ceiling.

I wasn't surprised that we hadn't talked about it, even though we had had many opportunities. I wasn't annoyed either. No one can force you into a four-year stretch of training. You have to be there first and foremost for your own reasons; you have to want to do it for yourself.

Evidently Steve was more hooked on winning than even I had realised.

poznań diary

Sunday, 9 May 2004
Poznań Regatta Course, Poland
113 days till the Final

We had a simple plan but the bare bones made for a bad night's sleep. In spite of the changes since the February line-up – Alex Partridge in for Josh West and Ed Coode covering for James while he recovers from a stress fracture – we have trained well in the last ten days. Nevertheless, I felt we were going into battle less prepared than at any stage in my career. We have never once talked about the German world record-holding crew or what to do if the wheels begin to come off. We seem to have a strong idea about what we want to happen and the way we want to row technically, but if I came up against a crew like us, I wouldn't be worried. The Germans don't seem to be either, paddling around the lake hardly glancing at us at all. We didn't scare anybody in the heat on Friday, but at least we won and got a day off yesterday. Every session counts, and even the morning paddle was a chance to learn something.

We had a great warm-up with some really excellent bursts. Alex was vocal throughout (a trait I am beginning to enjoy) and we got onto the start with a few minutes to spare. At that stage I was actually feeling good. The worries of the night had been replaced by a 'Come on, let's see how good you are' attitude to the Germans, which was exactly right.

The first ten strokes weren't as sweet as they could have been, but we weren't down on the Germans and we could already tell they weren't going to jump out into a lead. On the minute call there was a big power shove from the guys behind me and we started inching away. Six hundred, and we moved again and there was precious little response from the German boat. Halfway, and I was beginning to think they are going to attack soon, but they never did. We ran out winners by almost two seconds. Very happy indeed, although tried not to show it too much – don't want anyone thinking we didn't expect it. Sound of articles being rewritten as we passed the press box too!

Everyone quietly contented Jürgen, Alex and Steve Williams (very quietly). Ed Coode has done his chances no harm. He is not out of contention at all. James on the phone within a few minutes, which was great. He was genuinely excited by watching it. Desperate to get back in, though. He says he will be ready on Tuesday, which surprises me, but it would be good to have him back. The same smoothness with even more horsepower would be awesome indeed.

Haven't been this happy about a performance, both personal and crew since September 2002. Too long.

20

money

No one would row for the money. Steve Redgrave had to win four Olympic Gold medals before he broke even. Nearly 20 years of part-time work, along with sponging off his parents or his successful wife, ran up hefty debts. But he loved his rowing too much ever to ask whether it was worth it. The same could have been said for me, but I was lucky. I was able to join onto his financial coat-tails as soon as I started pairing with him.

At that time, however, the rest of the guys in the team were all rowing on borrowed time. Some, like me, were fresh out of school, kicking their heels till university or a proper job came along. We could afford to bum around for a few days each week, put in the hours that rowing needed under the old regime from Monday to Friday (which wasn't much – maybe an evening outing or two in London), and then be there at the weekend when both mornings were full-on. Some of the guys were already at university. Oxford, Cambridge and London were all well represented on the team because these places provided security by footing some of the bills. You would always see an Oxbridge van in the car park because those unable to afford a car could add the cost to the petrol bill for the Boat Race. A few oarsmen worked proper nine-to-fives, but it led to a quasi-nocturnal life, where they would have to get up before work to do some training, rush off from work to be in time for an evening session, and then give up their weekends, too. After a winter of that, anyone would be absolutely shattered.

There was a story about one of the blokes from the Olympic eight in 1988 who was working in Bedford and driving down to London to train twice a day, four or even five times a week. One morning he didn't show for the outing and everyone left the boat house after waiting for him for an hour or so. When he turned up the next morning, everyone had a go at him for missing the session the day before. But he swore blind he had been there, and recounted details of the session they had all done. However, it turned out that he was talking about the workout they had all done two days previously. After much argument and discussion, they worked out that he had gone to bed in Bedford after driving back from London, and had slept continuously for more than 18 hours. He woke up disorientated and tired, and finding it was still night, he went back to sleep. When he finally woke up, it was after 30 hours in his bed, but he hardly noticed the difference. It is no surprise that we weren't the model that other countries looked at when designing a sports system.

Before Atlanta there was precious little money around. Rowing was centrally funded by the government, but this went only so far. The chief coach was a salaried employee, there was a small office to run and the majority of the cash went on boats, oars and travelling to the championships each year. Athletes were very low on the financial pecking order; there was no way that they were going to be given a grant – there just wasn't enough to go round. In fact, quite the reverse. With the one exception of the Olympic Games, athletes were always asked to contribute to the costs of the trip. For a European regatta the 'athlete contribution' was in the order of £100, for a championship it might be up to five times that. These were people who, for the most part, were not well off, had few prospects of getting well-paid jobs while they rowed, and were essentially losing money by rowing in the first place. Some of the richer clubs might help out. My own club, Leander, was at the forefront of subsidising some of the up-and-comers, but everyone was aware of the financial uncertainty of a long rowing career.

The one concession that the Amateur Rowing Association made was that you were allowed to get commercial sponsorship. There had been a few sponsors involved in the team in the past, but as none of the athletes got the money, none of them gave a monkey's about the name on the side of the boat. As far as they were concerned, it all disappeared into the black hole that was the office at Hammersmith. You still had to get your cheque-book out at the airport before you flew anywhere and that hurt. But essentially, Steve changed the outlook for all of us. As part of a successful partnership with Andy Holmes, he was able to get sponsors interested. They had Leyland DAF for a few years running up to the Games in 1988, and they were the first guys to start getting money in from the sport. Steve had always joked that when he told people in 1983 or 1984 that he was rowing for a living they would ask whether he rowed for Oxford or Cambridge. The Boat Race swallowed up much of the going coverage and prestige for the sport. For a long time the race had been sponsored, and the two student Boat Clubs were the most professional outfits in the country. For the guys who rowed on the national team with a fraction of the funding and a lot more speed, it grated. They often dismissively referred to the Boat Race as the 'Tea Party'.

After the Games in 1988, Steve was able to command sponsorship of his own from MI Group, a financial services company with a rower on the payroll who got interested in the sport. Rumour had it they had access to thousands of well-connected individuals who were registered rowers. The group signed a relatively short-term deal with the Amateur Rowing Association to sponsor the whole team, as well as a four-year deal with Steve and his boat. For Steve and his partner (it was always assumed that he would do a pair) it meant sharing about £20,000 each year. It wasn't much, even in those days, but compared to the rest of the team, it was a different league.

In 1990, when I started pairing with Steve, I had a stilted conversation with him about money. He agreed that as his partner and a member of the sponsored boat I would get some of the cash. He offered £6000, and I readily agreed. As a student and the happy possessor of my mum's car, it was a fortune. Rent in Oxford was about £250, and it was the same again a month for food and petrol together. Throw in a student grant that everyone else was surviving on exclusively, and I was rich. I was able to go out shopping for a car ostensibly to return my mum's to her. In fact I wanted a car that wasn't a Peugeot diesel and, rather predictably, bought a Peugeot GTI. The insurance was crippling, but it was worth it. In my mum's car I had driven from Oxford to Henley with my knee jammed between the wheel and the window winder and my head cocked over to avoid the roof. Now I could drive the same journey, still with my knee jammed and head cocked, but much quicker. It was only a very quick tin can, but I loved it.

Every now and then Steve's agent, Athole Still, would get in contact with a job for both of us. It usually entailed a small-time photo shoot for a company doing a local promotion. The pay would be in hundreds rather than thousands. Steve would get the lion's share, but that was fine. Although Athole soon agreed to act as my agent as well, in national terms I was almost completely unmarketable. A few hundred pounds for a day's work was welcome petrol or beer money.

But even before the 1992 Olympics, I was becoming better known to the dedicated rowing audience. I started to receive requests from clubs and schools to do speeches at their annual dinners or awards. I happily agreed, and can vividly remember driving down to London from Oxford (quickly but uncomfortably) to do my very first one at Thames Rowing Club. Paranoid that they would find me unprofessional, I had written it all out in longhand and basically planned to read it out. It was pretty much the story of my arrival in a pair with the most famous British rower of all time. I kept it simple, a few rowing stories and a hopeful sign-off about what I wanted to happen in Barcelona.

I was very nervous and arose to the expectant silence of about a hundred rowing boys and assorted teachers and parents. But in spite of being the sweatiest guest speaker they had ever had, it went really well. I got laughs, well at least smiles, over things I had never expected, and after a while I left the script to include other stories and experiences. Reading the speech would have taken about ten minutes, but I was on my feet for close to 20. Relieved and elated by the end, I drove home on a high. From then on I began to format a kind of rowing dinner speech. I would try new topics or stories and if they worked they stayed for the next one. I'm definitely not saying I was the funniest guy to hit the dinner circuit since Bob Hope, but I reckon I delivered more value than some suit from Severn Valley Rowing Group. Besides, Bob Hope didn't do many rowing club dinners.

One or two offered to pay, but I never asked for anything more than a bit of petrol money. One dinner in Birmingham insisted on more than that and I drove home with the warmth of a hundred quid inside my dinner jacket. Slowly, I learnt interesting and useful lessons: a drunk crowd is actually a hard one to please; school audiences are cynical but fun; and, above all, taking your time over what you want to say always works. After the Olympics in Barcelona I had enough material to talk to a rowing crowd for half an hour. So I honed my turn into 'The ten golden rules of rowing in a pair with Steve Redgrave'. It premiered at Steve's home club in Marlow at their annual dinner. Both Steve and Ann were there and it brought the house down. It was all simple stuff: don't argue with him; don't pull harder than him; think caddy not golfer; and each one illustrated with a little story that you would really have to be a rower to get. Best of all, it took the piss out of him and all he could say afterwards was 'It's all true!'

Coming home from the Barcelona Games in 1992 changed everything for us financially. Athole was now able to start charging thousands for us to go together to corporate functions or photo shoots. In fact, he insisted that the days of turning out for hundreds were gone for good. Steve and I were happy to get the big gigs, but concerned that he was turning away work for smaller amounts that, added together, would make a big impact on our incomes. Athole was adamant about our worth, however, and was confident that we could sign a commercial sponsorship deal with a company that would provide a steady and guaranteed income over the four-year period up to the next Olympics in Atlanta. It was a necessity for us. The MI Group had been taken over in 1990, and the new management, although still paying the contracted money, had shown little interest in us or what we were achieving.

The deal came to an end in 1992, and we were on the market again. As a known entity with a good track record, we thought we would be an attractive prospect. We had been World Champions in 1991 and Olympic Champions in 1992, and we were committed to the Games in Atlanta. Easy. Well, not exactly. Like any agent, Athole confidently talked up his conversations with lots of different companies, but the line coming back was always the same: 'I'm in favour but I have to clear it with the board,' or 'The guy who actually has to make the decision is away until next week.' We were learning the hard way that few people were willing to say no to our faces.

It was only after a TV appearance by Steve, in which he said he was going to retire if he didn't get a sponsor, that a company called Manulife Financial came forward. They were another financial services company doing pensions and investments, but seemed keen on us and the concept of the sponsorship. They planned to use us mainly internally for their own staff motivation and client relations. Athole was pushing for a four-year deal worth a guaranteed £250,000, and he was keen for bonuses to be written in for race wins. Steve offered that we split the money 50:50, and, once again, I nearly took his hand off. It meant, as the back of my envelope informed me, that after both Athole and Steve had taken their cuts my share would be £25,000 a year. There would be even more if we won some races. I started getting car magazines.

I blew most of my first year's money on a lovely Jeep Cherokee, but during the second year of the deal I bought my first house, a two-bedroom terrace in Henley, and began portioning off some of the sponsorship each month to buy it back from the building society.

The speeches were going great, too. Steve and I appeared periodically for Manulife to talk about training and winning at the Games in 1992. We would take our medals along and sign autographs if people wanted. We split the time slot up between us, taking a subject each, and handing back and forth. It worked really well. Neither of us needed lots of notes, and we became good at reading the audience effectively. We could couch our rowing topics in terms of business as well, so our day-to-day motivation was a big theme, as well as goal-setting, teamwork and performance under pressure. We started doing speeches for other companies, too, and got a good reputation on the corporate circuit.

Corporate speeches are funny animals. Imagine you work in a business that has an annual conference to sum up the year past and give the troops the messages for the next 12 months. Everyone gets bored to tears by the MD standing there talking to them about the results or projections, so the organisers go out to look for an external speaker. It might be a business guru, an astronaut or an explorer. But sport, and especially team sport, has business parallels that don't need too much explaining. From our point of view, we could just leave the audience to do some of the work, and crucially, it was never about standing there lecturing people about how to run their lives. The balance was clear enough: laughs and stories to give people a flavour of life at the Olympics, and enough motivational stuff to keep the MD happy.

We were comfortably the best-paid rowers in the country, and because of that attracted jealousy from some of the other guys in the team. But the sport was being rewarded as a whole for our performances, and rowing was now considered one of our best Olympic events. Most members of the team were complimentary and encouraging.

Halfway between the two Olympics, Manulife was taken over by Canada Life. Our sponsorship was never in doubt but a change of emphasis took place. Canada Life were more proactive with our appearances, as stipulated in the original contract. Regional offices of Canada Life began approaching gyms and boat clubs to host evenings where we would speak. The local guy from Canada Life would put up hoardings and give a little intro with a soft sell for his pensions, and then one or both of us would do our thing. It was a great success. They felt they were getting their money's worth out of the deal, we got the feeling the sponsor was really interested, and the club got a good night's bar take.

Returning from Atlanta, one of the first stops we made was at the head office of Canada Life. They had a five-storey place with a large atrium in the middle, and as we arrived the whole workforce was out on the balconies to cheer us. We gave a little thank-you speech and then walked around the different floors. Everyone seemed to have postcards of us pinned up and mouse mats picturing the pair. It was a really wonderful welcome and great to feel that so many people got a personal kick out of what we had done.

There were also lots of good causes clamouring for our attention in the wake of the Atlanta Games in 1996. Schools, boat clubs and especially charities sent letters almost daily to ask for signatures, T-shirts for auction or appearances or speeches at events. It became almost impossible to corral them into order. We had both been involved with a sporting charity called SPARKS since 1993. Originally set up by Jimmy Hill, it raises money for medical research into children's diseases. They had been really appreciative of our efforts and made it easy for us to be involved. They organised golf days, to which we were simply invited for free and expected to give nothing but time. It was both fun and deserving, and neither of us wanted to get too heavily involved with a lot else. We both took the stance that if you were going to lend your name to something, then you had better put time in. Nothing put me off more than letters saying 'We really don't want you to do anything'.

They were the easy ones to refuse, but how do you deal with a multitude of small local, even personal, charities? Can you really make a choice between giving time to one or another? Of course, the best answer is to work hard for a few causes that you care most deeply about and refuse the others, but that's easy to say. Deciding who to help remains a hard part of the recognition that the Olympics brought us. We also had to consider how much time in total we were going to give to stuff outside rowing. We train for about 320 days a year. Typically, we are contracted to give 20 days a year to our sponsor, and spend about another ten on other corporate events. Already that accounts for 10 per cent of our preparation time. Add in a dozen charity days or speeches for schools, and you are getting quite disrupted. Of course, you try to minimise the effect on training, but try making polite conversation at dinner at 11 o'clock at night knowing that you have to be on the river a hundred miles away at eight the next morning.

Money changed for everybody in rowing after Atlanta. Part of the fallout of such a poor performance in the Games overall was that lottery money started coming on line. In fact, rowing had done comparatively well in Atlanta; our Gold medal, a Bronze from the four and a sixth place officially put us ahead of every other sport. Although we were never going to get more than the big sports, such as swimming and athletics, we were able to fight our corner, and, for the first time individual athletes were given grants. Almost overnight the number of people training full time increased. It wasn't a gravy train, however. You had to prove that you were capable of winning medals to get really good grants, and if you failed to produce as an individual or as a sport, you could expect to fall back down the pecking order.

At first Steve and I thought that we were going to need this new support. Once again new sponsorship was slow coming forward and it was only a fortuitous conversation with the BBC's Steve Rider that gave us a much-needed break. He put us onto Lombard, who used to sponsor the Rally of Great Britain and were now looking for something else in sport. Athole's policy of holding our price high paid dividends; we went for a meeting at their head office to establish that they were definitely interested and then left him to do the negotiations over the next month. The bargaining chip we had was that Steve had not yet gone public on continuing his career. He was playing a cagey game with the public and the media, who were still replaying the 'shoot me' quote. We knew that we could start any sponsorship off with a bang by announcing that, yes, Steve was carrying on and that we would both be sponsored by Lombard. They liked the whole package and Athole did an amazing job of negotiating the deal. Including bonuses, it was worth £1 million over four years. For the first time, international rowing in the UK commanded a higher price than the Boat Race, and once again I was more than happy with the envelope scribblings. My eye began to glance more seriously at the property pages of the *Henley Standard*

Although the contract was still technically at the lawyer's offices, we signed a dummy version in front of 40 or 50 journalists at the press conference. It was reported live by Radio

5 and we got on most of the news channels for that day. Then we had a photo call on the river in a four-man boat with Steve way up one end, and me down the other. The inference to the rowing world was clear – there were two seats up for grabs here.

21

the four

If Steve and I had sat down in September 1996 and discussed it, I think the two names we would have put on our wish list for a new four would have been James Cracknell and Tim Foster. After the Games in Atlanta, none of the crews that raced there showed any inclination to carry on unchanged. Steve and I had gone public about our wish to be in a four; the four from the Games itself of Jonny and Greg Searle, Rupert Obholzer and Tim had run its course. It had been a great run from them – Bronze in the 1994 World Championships, Silver in the 1995 competition and a Bronze at Atlanta – but Rupert had to commit more time to his career as a doctor. Greg was unsure to begin with, but then announced that he wanted to pursue the single scull. Jonny was a solicitor and had sacrificed much of his time for the Games; if he wanted to stay as a lawyer, he also had to go back to the grindstone.

Of the other boats, there was James's partner Bobby

Thatcher, from the ill-fated double in Atlanta, and a handful of guys from the eight that had finished seventh. There was talent there, as would be proved by the eight at Sydney 2000, but in 1997 the pecking order was pretty clear. Tim was a smaller athlete than most, being just over 6 ft 2 inches and weighing under 14 stone, but he had an ability that went way beyond his statistics. You could watch him in the gym and your eye would hardly pause at this guy; he was middle of the group in most of the rowing machine tests and below that on any of the weight-lifting exercises. But in a boat the picture changed. He had a fluid style and accuracy with his oar that maximised his contribution to the boat speed. Although smaller and less powerful off the water, he more than punched his weight on it. His long hair and laid-back attitude tended to give people the impression that he didn't care about his rowing or his ranking in the team, but make no mistake, he was as driven as any of us. Though he was perennially late and deliberately slow in getting down to the work, he had a hidden core that passionately wanted success.

James Cracknell was different in another way. Initially, he had progressed well from the junior team in 1990 into the ranks of the senior group. But despite an obvious drive and competitive edge, he had missed out for a combination of reasons. Injured (by me of all people) in a rugby game in 1992, he had eventually been offered the position of spare man for the team that went to Barcelona. He refused, preferring to bide his time until he could be part of the team proper. He was, to use the vernacular of the team at the time, 'stitched up' for many seasons after that. Consistently outperforming the members of the four, he was just as reliably ignored when it came to selection time. The powers that be, and Jürgen, who was as much in control of this as anyone, decided that a medallist crew like the four should be given a degree of independence and protection from challengers. This would help it concentrate on beating the foreign competition. James could certainly be accused of being unscientific in his approach to training at that stage, and his hunger and drive occasionally led him to overtrain, but there were many of us in the group who thought he deserved a shot at least once in that four years. Whether a crew that wins medals but not Golds deserves protection is another issue. It certainly wouldn't happen now.

Whatever our preferences, we were in no position to chose who we rowed with. The sport operates an open-door selection policy each year. The winter season begins with a long-distance trial on the water in single sculls. If you make the grade, you get invited to the next one in December. Add in some tests on the rowing machine and you can already begin to cut the number down. By the time you get into the New Year there are about 30 still in the running. The previous year's results might cut you some slack, and illness or injury might too, but nobody gets into the team without enough evidence to persuade the chief coach that he deserved to be there. The fact that the chief coach was Jürgen, our crew coach, made life interesting for Steve and me. On the positive side, it meant that we would be involved, even in a minor way, in the organisation of the training schedules and foreign camps for the squad. But on the negative side, Jürgen had to go out of his way to be seen to be fair over what he asked us and everyone else to do. We lost training time with him because of his other duties as chief coach, and even though people thought we could influence him over selection of our four, they were wrong. He might sometimes ask for your opinion but you'd be a fool to think you were the only one he was asking or, indeed, that he would heed what you said.

What was clear to us was that we had to prove to the squad that we were the first pair in the pecking order and get our names on the first two seats in the four. If we did that, then we could sit back and watch the scrap to decide the other two. In the spring trials of 1997 that's pretty much what we did. A six-abreast format meant that the top six pairs could race off, and we finished a small but controlled distance ahead of Cracknell and Thatcher, with Foster and Obholzer in third. In the following few days we trialled both Tim and Bobby Foster off against each other by doing a pairs race with Pinsent and Foster versus Cracknell and Thatcher, then, straight afterwards, a second race of Pinsent and Thatcher versus Cracknell and Foster. It's a cruelly tiring format, and some would say far from accurate, but the difference was marked. Tim was considerably faster than Bobby in the pairs in either combination, and by lunchtime Jürgen had seen enough to form the first attempt of a four. The only problem was that Steve had just gone down with appendicitis and we had to wait for him to recover before we could start our assault on the fours event.

I had a tense conversation with both James and Tim over money. Obviously the four was going to be sponsored by Lombard, but there was no golden hello from us. The financial set-up was that the Lombard money would be split by Steve and myself, and only if James and Tim couldn't get enough support from the lottery would we offer to spread it around. Looking back, it seems odd that we didn't pay out; after all, Steve had when I joined him in a pair in 1990. But the lottery grants were coming on line and James and Tim had both done enough throughout the winter to deserve top-end money from that source. Even though we would eventually get Lombard to support Tim and James on a smaller scale, and they were on a better financial footing because of being in the four than outside it, I would handle it differently today.

When we did eventually get together in Henley all fully fit it started well. We seemed to have a good relationship between us and enjoyed the mileage that had been set. Even though we were all in it for different reasons, there was a unity about the four from the start. For Steve it was the vehicle by which he wanted to extend his already huge career; if he wasn't going to regret his comeback, then this had to go well. For Tim it was a chance to win the Olympic title in the fours that had so far eluded him. For James it was the best chance he had of proving that he was way better than his international record testified so far. For me, to be honest, it was a relief to be out of a pair for the first time in six international campaigns. Had Steve retired and I had gone on to form another pair, it would have been difficult for it to have had the same degree of excitement that I now felt getting into the new four.

But despite the talent, power and enthusiasm, we had to sort out several issues. On several fronts, Steve and I had to adapt the way we thought about our rowing. The first lesson was that we could take nothing for granted about what we expected to happen. Of course, the nucleus of the team of Steve, myself and Jürgen had been together for six years. We could have simply plugged James and Tim into the equation and hoped for the best, but we wanted them to be proper, equal members of the team. Every rowing session is followed by a quick debrief. This is usually led by Jürgen, but the floor is open to anyone in the crew to add their thoughts. Both James and Tim were good at offering new angles on technique and training that might help us improve. Tim, especially, with his long career in the coxless four, was a key asset in getting the best from the four in the early months. We also spent a lot of time talking about things that Steve and I did automatically. How did we want to race? Who was going to organise the crew on the water by making the calls that change the speed or the rate?

It was all up for grabs, and Jürgen did his part by seating the four in an unusual format. In a traditional crew the rowers sit on alternate sides with one strokesider behind a bowsider and so on. But Jürgen shook this up by putting bowsiders Steve and Tim together in a tandem in the middle of the four. I was in the stern stroking and James was in the bow. This seemed like a good plan for a number of reasons. First, it drew Tim into the crew and got away from the idea that this four was just the Redgrave-Pinsent combination with a couple of freeloaders stuck on the front. Second, the four benefited a lot from Tim having more control over the rhythm. I was stroking so that it started with me, but Tim added his fluidity and length, as opposed to Steve, who was more power and oomph. It's a technical point, but I think it affected the mindset of the four immensely. Moving Steve back one seat also freed him up to make the calls when we raced. From the three seat (right behind me) he could still have done it, but from two he had to shout less and could control the crew better.

When we race there are responsibilities that can be shared and others that are all your own. Everyone had to do the rowing, of course, and whatever anyone thought from the outside, we all had to do our share. With a tired or weak member, a boat will only go as fast as he allows it to go. Another stronger, fresher guy cannot cover for him. In a four or, indeed, an eight, it is vital that the crew trust each other all to commit to the race in the same way. Starting a race and trying to be too economical while somebody else is hammering along will tire the hammerer out really quickly. In a pair, you can feel what your partner is doing and match your effort to his. At least then you tire and push on together. In the four, initially, it was hard to tell what everyone else was doing.

My particular responsibility was stroking the boat. Stroke is the glory seat, the centre-forward of rowing. Essentially, stroke sets a rhythm for everyone else to follow. This is one of the ingredients that turns a good crew into a great one, and is made up of the power phase, when the oar is in the water, and the recovery, when you slide up and take another stroke. Get it wrong and it feels like a Benny Hill chase. But get it right and everything happens more slowly and deliberately; everything, that is, but the boat's speed. Good rhythm means your energy lasts longer and you preserve a sprint finish; with a bad rhythm, energy runs away from you and the crew slows down just when it should be charging for the line. During a race I had to concentrate hard on it, using a combination of blind luck and experience. Sometimes it would work beautifully, other times it would be poor. But we were on a very steep learning curve and we all had some slack in the post-Olympic season in 1997.

Tim was behind me, backing up the rhythm with his long, slick rowing. If I began to make mistakes or row short (as is my tendency when I get tired), he'd be perfectly positioned to give me a verbal nudge: 'Stay long' or 'Keep the hands moving' would be more than enough. He was just as likely to shout encouragement when it was going well, so I never felt he was sitting behind me and judging what I was doing.

James in the bow seat was a long way from the action and

it would have been easy for him to have felt cut off. His challenge was to be quick and sharp so that the boat felt light for the rest of us. If you have a bowman who is too slow in his movements, it gives the crew a lethargic and inefficient feeling.

Steve had two jobs on top of the rowing. The first was steering the crew. Normally in a rowing boat each oarsman has a pair of trainers attached into the boat. They don't move, they just provide a really firm anchor for the power. But one of Steve's pivoted. He could swivel his right foot about 45 degrees; attached to the top of this shoe were the wires that controlled the rudder way back in the stern. If he moved his toe out to the right, the boat would start drifting that way too, and vice versa. Anyone who has steered any type of boat will know that it reacts slowly, so to say that Steve had extra responsibility on his plate would seriously understate the situation. He had to row his heart out, estimate where we were pointing in the lane (and, by the way, Tim and I are blocking his view), and move his foot to make a slow-reacting rudder move. Oh, and he was calling, too, remember? This means that he had to execute the plan as we had all arranged and change it as the race demanded. He had to keep a sharp eye out for five other boats, establish whether any one of them posed a threat and, if so, how we should counter it. The fact that he could pull this off was just one of the reasons that Steve was respected inside the rowing community and, indeed, inside his own crews way before the public cottoned on. Simply put, he was a master of the sport.

Immediately after the Olympic Games is a good time to start any challenge with gusto. Lots of guys take time away, some for as much as year or two. Some even retire, especially if they've just won the biggest event in the calendar. So the rowing world goes quiet for a season, younger talent moves up and the standards are unlikely to leap ahead. For us, it was a perfect opportunity to get established as a force within the fours. The Olympic Champions, Australia, were definitely not coming out for the season, and the World Champions, Italy, were changing their boat radically. We could climb the ranking ladder fairly quietly, and we did, winning European races in the early summer before stamping our authority on the event properly at the World Championships in France by taking the Gold medal. Even the death of Princess Diana in the racing week couldn't stop us. Although we asked to move the race from the day of our final to the Sunday, we were given a straight choice by the organisers: race on the Saturday, the same day as the funeral, or don't race at all. So while the nation mourned, we went out to win our first World Championship. We wore black tribute ribbons on our vests and flew the Union flag at half mast but, to be honest, until the race was all over we had little thought for what was going on at home.

It was a happy conclusion to an eventful year. James and Tim could call themselves World Champions to anyone who would listen, and Steve and I could say with confidence that we were going to Sydney in a four. The pair, in international terms at least, was history. But the next few years would not be so easy.

22
henley

Just as the Lucerne race in 1994, when Steve and I broke the world record, was a watershed moment for the pair, we were now heading for a critical moment in the four. It would not happen in Lucerne or, indeed, any of the international races that we had that season. It would happen at Henley.

Henley, or Henley Royal Regatta as it should properly be known, is first and foremost my home water. The early summer months see a transformation of the fields and banks of the river, which we know so well as a rural idyll, into a tented village to rival any in the sports world. There are no permanent fixtures. Everything is built from scratch each year. The river that can flood and surge all winter runs calm and clear in summer, and the regatta authorities put in a huge series of booms and piles to demarcate the racing course. Although the overall distance is similar to that in an international race, the course is divided by landmarks and waypoints that are traditional rather than metric.

There is no halfway mark, just a point called 'Fawley'. 'The Barrier' is about a third of the distance and the final charge is punctuated by 'The Hole in the Wall', and the 'Progress Boards'. The only logic is that it has always been like this, and it is all the better for it. To row at Henley is a goal for any oarsman (and, more recently, oarswomen) because of the history. It also allows the chance to row in front of a crowd that is bigger than any other race bar the Olympics.

Henley has no sponsors, no television coverage, but more than 100 years of tradition to work from. It runs two boat races in a straight knockout fashion over five days up to the first weekend in July. It has become part of the English Season and, as such, attracts thousands who know nothing about rowing. But they don't need to: the atmosphere, whether you are in the Enclosure or dabbling your toes in the river at the start, is enticing. Some come just to be seen, some come to drink until they can't see, but most see a race or two.

My first trip to the regatta was in 1986. I'd been rowing for two years, and the highlight was the chance to see Steve and Andy row past. It was an early round and it wasn't a race so much as a procession, but the bars emptied and the stands filled to see the famous duo cruise past. They had no trouble that day or, indeed, that week, but every now and then Henley throws up a clash of epic proportions. The finest are the best British against the best foreigners. But the latter know that the regatta is not the place to challenge. Why travel to their water, their crowd to try to knock them off their perch? Why not wait a week or two and do it on neutral water with no tricky stream to worry about? But the draw of the biggest regatta in the world is strong, and the results of that can be awesome.

Steve and Andy had a battle against the Russian Pimenovs in 1987. After an unheard-of incident, the race had to be rowed for a second time after a canoe drifted into the course and under the British boat. The following year there was an upset when the Australian then-World Champions were beaten by the British eight by 2 metres or so. The single sculls have often seen the two best in the world sort out their differences. In 1998, we would join the party.

The winter of 1997/8 had been eventful. Steve was diagnosed with diabetes at the end of the year, and although he was depressed and discouraged about his health, his specialist told him that there was no reason for his rowing to suffer. He had no choice about going public. Depressingly, there was a reporter waiting for him at home when he travelled back from the appointment. He had already told Jürgen, who had promised his support whatever the specialist said. The rest of the crew knew within a few days. I understood how much it hurt him; Steve had always prided himself on being fit and healthy. In 1992 he had had to submit to a series of pills when colitis interrupted our run in to Barcelona. But now he was eight years older, and diabetes and exercise seemed a harder combination to juggle. Though he never confided in me directly, the feeling within the crew was that this might be the end. He had suffered really badly during the winter camps with the new, longer rowing machine pieces and everyone could see that the big guy was far from his best.

He took a long break at Christmas to go skiing with his wife and children. I think it was there that he decided he wasn't going to let the illness be a factor in his rowing. It was part of his extraordinary stubbornness: if the rowing world couldn't beat him, he certainly wasn't going to let diabetes do so. He then began a long period of experimentation with injections of insulin (that every serious diabetic knows well), in combination with the exercise regime that only an Olympic athlete could consider. He learnt fast and, to his credit, I never saw him suffer a low blood sugar episode during training or racing. In the spring of 1998, however, another problem was to upset our progress.

I arrived at the club just about bang on eight in the morning, when it was normal to find the guys in the throes of preparation. Steve may still have been on the road behind me, James would be stretching and Tim would normally be getting changed. But not that day. The crew was gathered in the lobby of the club, Jürgen was in one of the chairs and Steve and James were both sitting on the floor. Jürgen then started an impromptu meeting.

'I have heard from a rowing journalist that Tim is in hospital.' All our minds were working overtime to figure out what the hell was going on. 'He has cut his hand.' Jürgen was measuring his tone and choosing his words with ease –

he had clearly practised this speech. Into the short silence that followed, James volunteered that he had been invited by Tim to a party in Oxford the night before. He had left for home just after midnight. His last sight of Tim, he 'was dancing with a vodka bottle'. While we waited, James then rang Luka Grubor, another squad member who lived with Tim, to get some more details. He learnt that they had been in casualty all night waiting for Tim to be seen and stitched up. It appeared he put his hand through a window. His thumb was badly cut and, at the very least, it would be weeks before he could row again. It looked like a career-threatening injury.

I was furious, boiling with an indignant, selfish anger that was worried less about Tim and his hand and more about what the stupid accident would do to the four. If you had to pick someone to have a drunken incident, it would be Tim, I reasoned. He had always prided himself on his natural ability and, what's more, gone out of his way to be different from the rest of the crew. Where James would have been happy to toe a line that Jürgen set, Tim would flout it.

Steve and Jürgen were always pragmatic. 'Okay, we see what comes up,' was Jürgen's classic response to any kind of crisis. If it mushroomed into something bigger, he would deal with it when necessary. He sent us off for the morning's training in the gym. But the unity had been punctured – how could we concentrate on training when one of us was in hospital? How could I focus on the exercises when I wanted to add to Tim's injuries?

By lunchtime the situation had clarified a little. Tim had got in contact with Jürgen to fill him in. He was drunk, he said, he cut his hand. He now had an appointment to see a hand specialist to get a better idea of how bad it was and how long he would be out. By this time I had calmed down. I reasoned that he never set out to injure himself and we couldn't live our lives in cotton wool. Both James and I rode motorbikes, Steve went skiing with his family around Christmas for a few days ('Just staying on the nursery slopes'), so none of us could honestly say that we insulated ourselves from every risk.

Tim came to see us all within two days to talk through the situation. He was embarrassed, contrite even, but we didn't let him off lightly. None of us, Jürgen included, were more than passingly sympathetic. We wanted him to get better, we wanted him to get back in the boat and help us win an Olympic Gold medal. But right now we wanted him to feel bad. It was obvious that he did.

Jürgen had to consider alternatives for Tim's seat. It was not easy – he was breaking up formations further down the team to feed the top boat; but the pecking order was clear. The four was the top priority and everything came second to that. We tried Simon Dennis from the eight, who was young and enthusiastic, but in the end settled for Luka Grubor, Tim's friend. Luka was originally from Croatia and had a sharp brain on his wide shoulders, but he did a good impression of a dullard. He moved slowly out of the boat, although he had an athletic ability in it. He fitted in better than Simon, and though it felt far from natural, we decided to race in Germany with him a few weeks later.

The trip was a disaster, with the crew disjointed and upset by the events at home. The opposition never give us a quiet race. Harried and under pressure, we didn't have the experience as a combination to deal with it. Although Luka couldn't be blamed individually, we missed Tim's control and sangfroid tremendously. In the final race of the weekend we finished fourth – the lowest position that Steve had come for more than a decade. Thankfully, during the trip we got good news about Tim. Although the cut would take time to heal, it had missed the crucial tendons. The prognosis was good.

The loss of the race in Munich sent a little message round the rowing world, however. If ever there was a moment to beat us, this was it. When the entries were announced for the fours event at Henley there were suddenly some very big names in the draw. We, as World Champions, were in, as were the Lightweight World Champions from Denmark. But most dramatic of all was the entry of the Australian four who had won in Atlanta. Like most Aussie rowers, they had taken a year out after the Olympics, but now the challenge from them was clear: if you want to come into our event, you are going to have to deal with us. We got Tim back on board in the middle of June with just a few weeks to go to the regatta. Irrespective of the draw, we knew we would have to be on top form to win. We hoped that the system would set up a race between the Danes and the Aussies for the Saturday on one side, and we would have a clearer run against the lesser club crews on the other. But our prayers weren't answered: the Danes got the clear run at the final, while we had a Saturday showdown with the Aussies. It would be World Champions versus Olympic Champions.

In addition to the home crowd and the river we know so well, we have another inherent advantage at Henley, and that is our club, Leander. Standing in the angle between the Henley town bridge and the river itself, the club is hugely proud of its history and its contribution to British rowing. It has the atmosphere of a gentlemen's club, with a smart balcony restaurant and a members' bar festooned with photos of crews winning Henley medals and Olympic medals stretching back to the 18th century. But look closer and the memorabilia is not all ancient. There are blades from the 1992 Games and, indeed, the flag that flew at the medal ceremony for the 1996 coxless pairs. Go past the doors that say 'Athletes only' and you can find the gym that hosts so much of our most painful training. The carpet is clean enough, but there are no trophy cabinets here. The business side of the club is dedicated to future winners rather than the past. There are towns with streets named after Steve Redgrave, but here at his club, the place that witnessed more of his career than anywhere else, there is no Redgrave Bar or Wing.

At regatta time, the club plays host to its members and their guests. There are 2000 members and many of them come only once a year. Then the club becomes a haven for the ultimate one-uppers. 'I'll see your Steward's Badge and raise you a Leander ticket,' kind of thing. In fact, the Pimms is just as expensive inside the club as in the Stewards' Enclosure, but the security at the gate gives it a wholly different taste.

Tucked away for once inside our own club, we await the time to set out for our races with the usual mix of nerves and excitement. Even against nominal opposition, Henley can be frightening. There's always the chance of making a fool of yourself if you hit the wooden booms or, indeed, the island. But it's mainly the crowd. Whether knowledgeable or inebriated, they know good rowing when they see it. Our time in the shed before we leave is commonly interrupted by autograph requests or guided tours of the boats, as Uncle Geoffrey (who used to row at the highest level) impresses his guests by calling Redgrave 'Steve' to his face. Mr Redgrave never lets on that he has no idea who the man is; he is on the verge of telling him to get stuffed, but we are all saving our energy for the racing.

Outside, the river was in spate. Not with winter rainfall, but with almost every craft moored on the Thames. The Thames is enshrined in law as a 'riverine path', with the same rules of access as a public footpath. The regatta can't shut it for a week, any more than the inhabitants of Richmond can shut Heathrow. So every punt, canoe, longboat, narrow boat, barge and cruiser descends on the stretch for a few days. The river police try their best to control the mayhem, but the rules are there to be stretched by every Captain Birdseye and gin palace around. Speed limits are nominal and steering seems optional.

As we push off to the applause of the Leander faithful, it's as if we have to manoeuvre a felled redwood across the busy M25. Fortunately, the races on Saturdays are separated by enough time to allow us to row down the course in reverse past the enclosures. The press box on the finish line might yield a 'Good luck' or two (even the rowing journos are biased at Henley), and then we pass the judges' box, from where we get furtive smiles of support. Then the ripple begins as we paddle past the crowds already filling the stands and deck-chairs. It's not uproar, just applause, but it chills our spines and sets our hearts racing. The shouts are too numerous to hear clearly, but the smell of the river, the canvas and the lawns cuts through the nerves. As we paddle down towards the start, the smells change, lawns are traded for the trees at the end of the enclosures, then beer and barbecues appear by Remenham Farm. The cheers and applause from here are usually fickle. Against domestic opposition we get some flak, jeers or warnings. But now that we are up against the Australians, it is different. A brave soul tries an 'Aussie, Aussie, Aussie' chant, but it goes unanswered. Today, of all days, we will get roared on from start to finish.

The boat is wobbly in the disturbed water of the river, pushed left and right as we try to get some kind of warm-up done. The claps and shouts from the nearby boats are ignored as we go through our routine, ready to take on the biggest reputation in the world of the coxless fours. We get glimpses of the opposition, who like us, wear shades to shield their eyes and emotions from the outside world. They look good – athletic and lithe. They row longer than us, with deliberately less power. They sweep the boat rather than drive it, and they have won everything going in rowing, doing it their way. We prefer to dominate races with our power, and plan to do the same to them – get them on the back foot as early as we can and keep them there. We have the power to get ahead early, but know they have the rhythm to come back if we let them.

Side by side, 20 feet apart, we are attached to the start and await the arrival of the magnificent, cigar-shaped umpire's launch, which also carries three timekeepers and four people from each camp. You are not allowed to shout from the launch and it becomes a sort of floating Royal Box: all decorum on the outside, but partisan cheers straining to get out on the inside. Today we have the inside station, closer to the crowd and with less stream to battle against. If it were winter, they'd have no chance in the middle, but in midsummer the advantage is slight. The inside station won't win the race for us this time.

A hush falls on the informal crowd at the start as the umpire stands to give us instructions. 'Leander and Melbourne, when I see that you are straight and ready I will start you like this.' He raises his flag to demonstrate the falling motion. 'Attention. Go... Get ready please.'

A final check. Oar in the water properly, seat exactly where you want it, mind clear but for the simplest of tactics – crush them.

'Attention!' The external sounds fall away, the vision tunnels onto the man with the flag. The first glimpse of movement and you are released.

'Go!'

My brain turns the volume back up and I am barraged from all sides. The blades bite the water, the boat lunges away for the first stroke. In an instant, the crowd go from polite silence to cacophony. Some may be cheering for the opposition, but we can't tell and don't care. The driver forces the umpire's boat into gear and the engine roars into life. Even with a 5 litre monster in its belly, it can't keep with us from the standstill, but after ten strokes or so it's there, keeping the umpire and all the coaches right with the action.

As planned, we take an early lead, and by the end of the island we have about half a length. As we hit our rhythm, we start to believe that the changing of the guard is happening right in front of us. Surely they can't win the race from back there? It's not as if we are going to win by five lengths, but if ever there is a moment to go flat out, it's the first minute, and they can't stay with us. But another minute later the story is different. We are into our rhythm, but we can't shake them. We have all the trump cards: the inside station, the crowd sensing a home win and the years of experience on this river. But coming up to halfway, we are no more than three-quarters of a length up. It has taken us three minutes to get 15 feet further ahead.

They start to attack in the second half but we don't panic. We can all watch their moves as they call them, and we can all see them look around to judge the distances. There are no records to be set, no minor medals to worry about. This is winner goes to the final, loser goes home.

We get within earshot of the enclosures and the noise of the crowd is overwhelming. Steve has to bark out his orders to be heard As we enter the final stages, there are hundreds of people hanging over the riverbank, closer to the wet end of my oar than I am. Here the crowd is nearer to you than anywhere else in rowing, and it sounds like a jet in full throttle.

Now the Aussies are running out of time. They have kept up the challenge, made us work for it, but they are not getting by. Not for the last time in the fours history, we are going to be narrow winners, doing enough to win without rowing ourselves out trying to open up a margin. With a couple of strokes left, the occasion gets the better of me. Excited at the prospect of winning, I take a hand off the oar to punch the air. In a pair this would be catastrophic, unbalancing the boat to the extent that you would certainly confuse your partner. In an eight, it just feels heavy for the seven other guys who are still doing their fair share. In a four it's dangerous but not foolhardy; it's arrogant but never going to lose us the race. The rest of the crew don't care. Jürgen gives me a serious chat afterwards but can't stop himself smiling throughout. The chairman of the regatta is not so amused: it's unsporting and a bad example to set in the showpiece race of the day. I don't care. It's been a very long time since I've beaten any Olympic Champions and it feels good.

lucerne diary

Sunday, 20 June 2004
Lucerne, Switzerland
63 days till the Final

Woke up early as usual for a race day and was surprised to find that, despite the size of the event, I was not as nervous as I expected to be. Given our crappy season so far, I was really gagging to get out there and prove that we could beat the Canadian World Champions. At last we had our best crew of myself, James, Alex Partridge and Steve Williams, and all were fit. Weather was terrible with showers blowing through, periodically soaking us on the warm-up paddle. Back to the hotel for breakfast and a short sleep, then down at about 12. We had a good plan to beat Canada and were adamant that we should not let them get away from us at the start. If they tried to take the lead in the middle, we'd punch past them if necessary when we got into the last quarter.

We started pretty well, and even led for a while. My biggest mistake was not setting the same rhythm that we had in the semi. We could have moved away here. I guess we were just happy not to be behind, which was a stupid mentality. In the middle they pushed past us, and into the last 700 we were maybe two men down. But I had no doubts we would get past them. I was aware that the Yanks were up with the race over in lane one but pretty much ignored them.

We started sprinting back at the Canadians and moved pretty well to begin with but then stuck. It was only when I looked at them in the last 200 that I realised that neither of us was going to win. The Americans had gone straight past us. Given that the Canadians had beaten them in the heats and we had beaten them in the semi, both with ease, I can't help feeling it is a strange result. Maybe they had a good lane, maybe we got too carried away with racing Canada, but it can't happen again.

In the final evaluation, we were poor because we didn't row our plan and I am more to blame than the others for that. We consequently lost to Canada and our plan didn't factor on the USA at all. But at least we are a long way beyond where we were in Munich, when, without James, we came fifth. The Canadians are very beatable but we have to have the confidence to get our own race done long before we start looking at the others. We were all disappointed, of course, but I've been here before.

Three Gold medals at the Olympics and I've never won at Lucerne in Olympic year. Was hoping that it was going to change in 2004!

the 2000 season

The shower is usually a place of sanctuary, a time to feel the aches of training recede and to change gear out of rowing mode and return to normal life. But it wasn't like that in September 1999. After training the streams of hot water were washing away the tears. I was away from home and, for the first time, I didn't like it. It wasn't as if I didn't have lots of things to be excited about. The four had gone from strength to strength.

The championship win in Canada 1999 was our best performance yet, and despite the loss of Tim to a back injury early in the season, we found a worthy replacement in Ed Coode. Unlike the experience with Luka in 1998, the change hardly affected us. We dominated throughout the season. Tim was now treated differently, too. Far from being castigated, he was sent off to the surgeon with our heartfelt sympathies. No one wanted him gone and we couldn't wait for him to get better. His back needed treatment of the most serious kind, otherwise he risked having no future in rowing.

I almost literally ran off the medal podium at the World Championship in 1999 to go to a friend's wedding in Maine. Dee was waiting with a rental car and air tickets, and after a three-hour dash I was watching our friends getting hitched under a starlit sky. At three in the morning I was dancing with my girlfriend. I was in culture shock, thinking, 'Did I really win a World Championship Gold medal today?' I couldn't have got further away from the rowing world or, indeed, the pressures of the run-up to the Olympics, and it was with a heavy heart that we whiled away the last few days.

The rowing year started with a camp in Brisbane on the Gold Coast, where the team would be based right before the Games, and I was scheduled to meet the group in Singapore on their outward leg. Dee was joining a consultancy firm in Toronto, and for the foreseeable future we were going to be apart. Though the prospects were good of her moving to London within the company, it could be months before we saw each other again. For the first time in my life there was something way more important than rowing and it hurt so much to be apart from her. We agreed that when the time came we would just go our separate ways without too many painful goodbyes. As I sat on the edge of the bed, she kissed my forehead and walked out to catch a plane to Canada. She told me she cried most of the way there, and I arrived with the group in Australia with a heavy heart.

On the face of it, the four was in good shape. We had been World Champions three years in succession, had taken the scalps of the Aussies at Henley, and were deserving favourites approaching the calendar year of the Olympics. But there were flies in the ointment. For one thing, we had a running battle with Steve's health. Though he was a master at concealing most of it from us, there are few places to hide during a really hard camp, and we could see that he was far from his consistent best. During the early '90s, when he was in the pair with me, I never saw him at the back of any group. Even if the exercises and disciplines were far from his forte, he was driven by pride. But throughout the four years running up to Sydney he had to be more choosy. There were cycling sessions where he was way off the pace of the group within minutes of leaving for a three-hour ride, and even in the boat, I could tell that there were times when he wasn't blasting away as normal. Racing was different, though, and I could never have said that I didn't trust him to be at his best. If ever you wanted a guy in your boat for the Olympics, it would have been him. But with Tim coming back from his injury, and Ed having been crowned World Champion in Canada, we could all do the maths that five people didn't sit comfortably in a coxless four. The added complication was that both Tim and Ed were bowsiders, the same as Steve. If he fell back off the pace in any way, then he was likely to be caught in the battle to decide who sat where. If he wasn't at his best, it wasn't a choice so much between Ed and Tim, but more Tim, Ed and Steve.

In charge of this, as ever, was Jürgen. He handled it really well throughout the camp in Australia. He called a crew meeting and told us that no one was safe. None of the seats had anyone's name on them. He was the man in charge, he said, and he would pick the best crew to win the Gold medal in the fours. This was a more important principle than it might at first seem. There was already a rumour that he might hedge his bets. What about picking a slightly slower version of the four, knowing that it might well win anyway, and putting the balance in the pair and trying to win a medal there, too? For the chief coach this might have been tempting when the funding for the sport depended on the quantity of medals across lots of events. But at the same time it would be really scary if you found yourself in a detuned Gold medal shot. But he put that one straight to rest, saying that no matter what, he would put the fastest four out.

The real problem is that there is no single test you can do to determine whether one rower is faster than another You can gather data from a rowing machine test for fitness, the weights room for strength and the single scull for natural ability (at least in a sculling boat), but a boat and crew work in complex ways. We could run a version of the American selection procedure, where everybody comes together and is given a ranking following one-off races. Under that system, if you miss the sudden-death competition through being ill or injured, then it's thanks and goodbye, we'll send you a post-card from the Games. But British rowing doesn't have talent to burn; we can't afford to leave good people behind, so almost automatically we have to have a degree of human subjectivity involved. Enter the chief coach. It's his responsibility to decide ultimately who goes where in which boat and who stays behind. Jürgen was generally a master at it, overseeing the most abundant period of British men's rowing ever. His detractors say that Steve's boats would have won even if we had a ham sandwich in charge of the team, and that any other medals were won in spite of, not because of, his system.

The Gold Coast was proving a superb base. The British Olympic Association had done a great job of making contacts and contracts locally to provide facilities for almost all the team for the month or so before Sydney was due to kick off. We were given access to a rowing lake that had hardly seen rowers before, and we were all to stay in a luxury beachside resort with a golf course. We were looking forward to going back to the Gold Coast to put the last finishing touches to our campaign.

But exactly who were the four going to be? James and I as strokesiders were getting used to having conversations on the subject and I reckoned that he had a favourite between Ed and Tim. I urged him not to tell me, though, as I was keen to get through the process without trying to second-guess Jürgen.

But Tim was now forcing the pace hard. Normally a decent distance behind Ed in the gym, he was making it a big priority to get stronger. When we got home, however, Ed had a great run in the single sculling trials and finished ahead of Tim. If the first three months of training proved anything, it showed that Steve was out of the picture, not behind, though, but ahead. He could sense the danger, and just as Red Rum was taken to the National to give him a sniff of the air, the old warhorse Redgrave was smelling the Olympic waters. He didn't win everything; in fact, he finished first on very few of the winter tests, but he had a different air about him.

I was getting myself into the shape of my life and putting the finishing touch to a winter that I knew was incredibly important. If this four was going to carry on being dominant then it needed the best strokeman in the world. I was turning myself into that person. Steve helped enormously in the process by telling any press who would listen that I was the best oarsman around and had been for some time. It did wonders for my self-confidence, and I was able to answer the old question, 'How does it feel to be in Steve's shadow all the time?' a little better. I had been very lucky to be paired with Steve. It had given me access to sponsors and the media interviews you need to keep the sponsors happy. As a result of the pairing, I had been the youngest full-time rower the UK had ever produced. It wasn't because I was good; it was because I was good enough to row with Steve.

But now the partnership, within the coxless pair at least, was well past its sell-by date. Since the Atlanta Games, we had only really rowed the pair domestically for trials and we both knew it wasn't a priority. But just because we didn't put too much emphasis on it, didn't mean others took the same line. We were, of course, still reigning Olympic Champions, and everyone wants to beat them. The April trials were a low point for our old pairing. We knew it was coming as well. James and Tim had been partnered up, as in previous years, and were going really well. They had stuffed us by ten seconds on one piece over 2000 metres right before the racing week. If that wasn't enough, Greg Searle and Ed were busy trying to keep up to their pace. Ed, especially, couldn't afford to give Tim an easy win over him.

The trials were a disaster for us. Off the pace and dejected with our speed, we had to focus on defending our position in the pack, fending off challenges from the guys in the lower half of the team. We finished third, five seconds off James and Tim and a decent margin behind Ed and Greg, who were second. I have seldom set out for a race knowing that we were not going to win, but that was one occasion. Jürgen was amazingly positive afterwards, urging us to keep our heads up and speak positively to the press that had gathered to witness the demolition. I was genuinely pleased for James and Tim, but knew we were going to get a hammering in the press. Sure enough, in the car on the way home Radio 5 carried a piece about Redgrave managing to finish only third in the trials. I tried to persuade myself it was going to be good for us in the long run.

In a sense, the result didn't help Ed at all. On a warm April morning Jürgen asked all of us to meet in one of the rooms at Leander. He took each of us in turn, talking about what kind of winter we had had. Mine was easy (I like to think): a good series of land-based tests and an undisputed role in the stroke seat. The verdict on James was similar, with the notable addition of a win at the trials. As for Steve, he was never going to be left out. He had been much more consistent than during some previous winters, and we needed his power. Tim had really raised his game, finishing his winter with a flourish at the pairs trial. Ed was a World Champion, but was now going to be asked to row a pair with Greg Searle. Jürgen had told Ed beforehand what was going to happen, and I don't think any of us were too surprised by the coach's decision. He gave us the usual spiel about crews can change, no one's seat is safe, but we all knew the deal. We each shook Ed's hand and within ten minutes the prospective Olympic four was out on the water back to its 1997/8 line-up.

In May I had my first Olympic Games dream. I don't normally dream about rowing; people and places, certainly, but racing hardly ever. From my experiences of the last two Games I knew it was normal, just my body's way of telling me that it, too, knew this season was different. I dreamt we won. Then I woke up with the best, calmest feeling, knowing that it had all been worth it. I then had to face the crushing reality that I had to go to training again for at least another three months before I could fulfil the dream.

If dreaming of the Olympics is my stage one, then being officially selected is stage two. There are no short cuts to being asked to represent Great Britain at the Games, and Jürgen is far too meticulous to allow a system that permits anything other than the best combinations to go. The process starts early, with a water race over 7 kilometres in single sculls in December. If you do well enough, you get an invite to the next round in February, this time in coxless pairs. If you get high up the finish order there, you get an invite to the final trials in April, which is run on a more regular regatta format. The last trial carries the most weight because it establishes the final pecking order down through the whole team. Finish in the top nine pairs in a World Championship year, and you are in the picture for the team. For the Olympics, it has to be top seven.

But the selection is still far from over. The top pair might be home free, but exactly who sits where in the coxless four or the eight takes a few exploratory races. Add in the gym tests we do – 2000-metre races in November and March and a horrendous 5000 in January – and the season becomes a bit of a decathlon. It's important not only to have really good results, but also to avoid shockers. If you miss one test because of illness or injury, that's okay, but you know most of the guys vying for your seat won't.

We had all done well enough to get selected in 2000, because during the winter Jürgen had already turned the microscope on us all to solve the five-into-four puzzle. But he wanted to select the whole team at once to give an extra sense of unity, so he was going to wait until after Lucerne to announce the final line-up. Lucerne is the centre of international rowing for a week each year. If Henley is the mecca to be visited once a lifetime, Lucerne is the Grand Central Station. Every year it holds the prestigious position of the last European race of the summer calendar. Taking place about ten weeks before the annual World Championships, it attracts the highest-quality field of the year up to that point. Win there, and you become favourites for the Gold medal; lose, and you have other things to focus on rather than learning the words to the national anthem. All the countries are there. The Americans attend in force, as do Canadians, and the Australians make it the focus of their trip to Europe.

On paper we were in good shape. The season was ticking along just fine. We had been untroubled by the European opposition so far. It was an emotional week, with everybody fully expecting it to be Steve's last dash down the enclosures. Lucerne comes hard on the heels of the Henley Regatta, and in all probability we were asking too much. But what the hell, we thought. We have done it before and won at both events, so why not now?

But we struggled right from the start, losing our opening race to the New Zealand four with a really jaded performance. That knocked us back with the sharp realisation that if we didn't have enough energy, we had precious little time to do anything about it. The boat felt lethargic and listless – we all knew we wanted to win and knew exactly how to do it, but to me it felt as if we had several sacks of coal in the boat some-where. Stroking the four was usually easy – I just did what came naturally and the boat would take off like there was a team of huskies attached to it. But not that weekend. By the time we had limped into the final, the other fours had smelt trouble on us like a bad cologne, and the Italians, for starters, were keen to grab the middle of the podium for a change. A couple of years being 'bridesmaids' had got their backs up, and if they got half a chance to change it, then they were going to grab it with hands, feet, legs and teeth.

As it turned out, the race just developed in front of us, with the Italians shooting away from the start. Their only realistic challengers were the Kiwis and the Aussies. We were a distant fourth, a massive six seconds behind. We couldn't even muster a sprint finish, which was for us a point of honour. We could all feel the energy draining from us and I, for one, spent good portions of the race just wish-ing it was all over.

Thoroughly disgusted with ourselves, we had to go through the indignity of getting out of the boat to get a prize, not for our woeful fourth, but for points winner over the season. The fact that the Italians, Aussies and Kiwis hadn't been at the early regattas made it a poisoned chalice. But we also had to face the press. James was desolate, downcast and a silent picture of defeat. Tim was able to raise a smile and a handshake for the medallists, but you could see the anger and regret seething in Steve. He knew more than anyone what it meant. The press didn't hold back, some of the old rowing journos would be less harsh than others, but the line was pretty much the same 'Was this weekend the end of the road for Redgrave's Odyssey?'

It made it all the more ludicrous that we were almost immediately selected and confirmed as the British four for the Games. It wasn't as if anything else was going to happen. The best guys were in the crew and that was that. But it didn't lessen our own critical approach to the training that remained before Sydney. After two days away with family and girlfriends (God knows what that was like for them), we had a chance to vent the anger and disappointment.

Jürgen started the meeting with a typical summation. 'I'm sorry too,' he said, 'maybe we did too much in the two weeks before. We won't change the training now, we are too bloody strong for those guys, I tell you. We get it right with the best technique and the best preparation and then we shock everybody in Sydney.' He finished his take on the situation and opened it up for a general discussion.

To a man, we disagreed with his whole 'we overtrained' line. No one wanted to take an easy option and pretend that everything would be okay. Tim attacked our lack of technical approach and brought up a hit list of things that he wanted to change in the boat. He added that he thought we were overweight and couldn't afford to be. As the heaviest and fattest guy in the crew, I took this on board with a wince, but quickly realised he was right. James gave the bowman's view on the race and targeted the poor length of the stroke as a primary cause for us losing. Steve got in with a renewed mantra of every session counting, that we had only a few weeks left to train and that if we turned it on, we could beat the other boats with ease. He also added that the losing margin was in some ways a good thing; we weren't squeezed out of the race in a blanket finish, so we knew something had gone awry with the boat during the race in Switzerland. If we were all of the opinion that the boat was going really well and that we had simply lost to a better boat (or three of them), then we might have felt in deep trouble.

Left to go last, I couldn't add any more. I rather lamely agreed with the trends we wanted to impose and reinforced a couple of them. It didn't seem to worry anyone that we didn't really establish exactly what went wrong. But that is sport. The exact ingredients for success and failure are always a bit of a mystery. We all seemed happier to leave them untouched and stick with what we knew.

We left for a punishing altitude training camp within a few days, but had already had time to establish a new routine. From now on Tim and Steve were never late, and James was much more conscious of his moods and how they affected the rest of us. I devoted more time to a diet less reliant on sugar and took a pride in losing a few kilos. But on the water the whole crew was transformed. The paddling took on an almost parade ring quality, with all four of us devoting a much higher degree of energy and concentration to every stroke. We all wanted to be able to look back at Lucerne and see it as a successful kick up the backside.

Up in the Austrian mountains, we kept the momentum going magnificently. In a three-week-long period of training we didn't miss a beat for illness or injury, attacking the work with a hunger that surprised even Jürgen. Normally, he would have to kick us round the lake for the last few rowing laps each day, but not now. There were even occasions when he would have to call us in to stop us from overdoing it. The reaction to losing wasn't to bury our heads in the sand or even to rush around for a few days trying to put a few things right. We had been stung into action and it lasted the entire intervening time until we had a chance to race those guys again.

At the high-altitude camp, we had the lake, the hotel where we ate and the hut where we stayed. There was not much else, apart from a few horses and lots of rocks. In Jürgen's words, we were building the engine, using the lake to groove in mileage of almost winter quantities. We were doing weights as well, before gradually changing gear to do the more racy stuff. We finished with a full 2000-metre lung-bursting charge down the track. It didn't hurt so much as sear, and the only comfort was knowing that it marked the end of the ordeal that was high-altitude training.

If stage two of the Olympics is getting the letter to say you are going, then next in the line is actually leaving home for the last time before the Games. We got two days at home, just enough time to get used to the hum of the washing machine and food that wasn't Austrian, and then it was time to leave for Heathrow. I found myself going round the house at the last minute, collecting up the final few items for the bag and deciding what I had forgotten: razor, flip-flops, oh yes, and passport. Over it all hung the nagging thought that the next time I saw my bed I would either be Olympic Champion again or I wouldn't; the next time I came over the bridge into Henley, there would either be a banner above the road or nothing. It would be weeks at least before I could say I was nervous, but way down inside, my stomach certainly knew the stakes were high.

The Gold Coast camp was even better than we imagined. We all enjoyed the rooms and the food, but the Olympic Association had added a layer of Britishness that included an athletes' lounge, an army of volunteers and Internet access. It was a happy place to be. Some sports were there in force, some came and went on to their own bases in Australia, but it was the first meaningful taste of the Team GB atmosphere that was to prove so beneficial for us all.

They had set up outfitting for the team in a primary school near the swimming centre. It was a massive operation. There were pallets of boxes and endless rows of cartons, all flown in to equip us. It was staffed by local volunteers and British tailors from M & S. You got loads of kit: tracksuits, waterproofs, T-shirts, shorts, long sleeved tops, all in addition to the formal suits and rowing suits. But the crowning glory was the Opening Ceremony outfit. Now I know it's got to look good on television. I know it has to be relaxed and informal. I would be the last person to want to spend four hours in a suit, but we now looked like extras from HMS *Pinafore*. The outfit consisted of a blue-and-white long-sleeved, a shiny tanktop and bell-bottom white trousers that reminded me of my dad's old navy whites. Blue plimsolls rounded the whole ensemble off nicely. At the Opening Ceremony it might look okay in a group, but some poor lemon had to carry the flag in this get-up. Oh yes, and that was going to be me.

The flag bearer isn't really told he or she is in the running. It's an emotive issue for lots of people, and the last thing you'd want is a massive anticlimax right before you go to the Olympics. It's decided behind closed doors between the team managers of all the sports that GB sends. Rowing chose me – sure, Steve was more experienced, but he had carried it twice before and he didn't want to do it again. We also knew that rowing getting the honour once more would be pushing it; hockey had a claim, as well as track and field, and I'm sure sailing would have put somebody forward, but rowing won out, no doubt a reward for being the only Gold medal sport from Atlanta. The press release predictably said that I was delighted, honoured and surprised, but it was all true.

However, I was also pissed off I had to march in this crappy uniform. Steve had a fantastic picture of himself carrying the flag in Barcelona wearing a classic dark suit. All I could imagine was having photos of me looking like a 6-foot-6-inch Benny Hill. So I nipped into the town centre and got the trousers altered from bell bottoms to straight. It wasn't a radical transformation, so no one noticed, but it made me feel better about the moment I would step out in front of the world.

25

sydney

The last few days of the pre-Olympic camp were positive and enjoyable. The boat was going really well, and we were performing strongly against the other boats in the team, too. We weren't destroying them, but we were proving every two days or so that we were not five seconds behind where we had been in Lucerne. Steve was rampant in his approach, eating up sessions like in the good old days. On the water he was adamant that we let nothing get past his quality control, which, allied with Tim's, made it a pretty high bar to get over every day.

But away from the lake we were enjoying the atmosphere of the beach town, if not the beach itself. The only thing that we got serious about down there was a golf game against the two javelin guys, Mick Hill and Steve Backley. Both keen and proficient golfers, they laid down a challenge and we battled it out in fine style on the course that surrounded the hotel. Even though the match was tight, and Team Rowing played some of the best golf of our lives, the conversation in our buggy was all rowing. The javelin boys, too, were only partially concentrating, and you'd turn to the tee box to find one of them frozen in mid-hip turn, arm extended back behind them, rehearsing throws to beat Jan Zelezny. The match turned only on the 18th, when Redgrave choked and drove into the water and I missed a putt from 12 feet to force a play-off. As we walked back to the hotel in the tropical evening gloom, we all knew that it was going to be down to business very soon.

Experienced hands that we were, we set off for Sydney trying to keep it all low-key. We got the maximum relaxation possible on the various legs of the journey – bus, plane and then bus again to the village. There was just a momentary blip in the heart-rate when we saw a two-page spread in one of the Aussie papers that gave predictions for every medal in all the events. We were down for the Gold, Australia the Silver. We got another jolt as the plane gave us a glimpse of the Harbour with the Olympic rings on the bridge. Two hours later, we couldn't help but get excited when we saw the flat.

We are in with the eight and the pair. There are two apartments rolled into one and every bedroom is split in half by a cheap dividing wall. As ever, Steve and I are sharing, and dragging bags behind us, we find the door together. I open it and find a space some 5 metres long, but only 2 metres wide. At the far end are French doors obscured by curtains, which I immediately throw back. And then we both see it – Stadium

Australia, less than a mile away and not one building between it and our balcony. There is a big, open expanse of grass between us and the fence, and then the immense shadow of the stadium begins. I grab the bed by the doors, keen to keep the view to myself. Later in the evening I spent half an hour on the balcony staring at the torch, as yet unlit.

We work hard to establish a village routine. Early races mean early starts and the alarm goes off at four each morning. The food hall is a few hundred metres up the hill and close to the buses, which even at five in the morning run routes out to the rowing lake. The water is dark and cold before dawn each day, but the rising sun gives it a ripple and a light that needs dark glasses to take in properly. The stands are massive, with row after row of empty seats, and even the huge press and VIP stand on the other side are dwarfed by them.

Once again, and not for the last time, we ramp up the quality of the training. It's not about energy now. In fact, all the sprint stuff is done. Now it is more like dressage, running over the routines and the drills and, a priority for us, looking the part of Gold medallists. The crews that beat us in Lucerne are quiet and polite, asking the traditional rowing niceties. How was altitude? How are the rooms in the village for you guys? They don't expect, and don't receive, the truth. 'We are going to beat you,' your inner voice screams as you paddle past, but the sport is great for your inner control – let the rowing do the talking. For lunch we are still at the course, just finishing up the second row of the morning before a quick snack in the food tent and home to the village. We can sleep in the afternoons if we want, and it helps pass the time. One of the skills of the Olympics is passing time.

The Opening Ceremony helps, too, a last diversion before the racing begins. Each crew makes its own choice about whether to go. This four is in no doubt – their strokeman is carrying the flag and there is no way they are going to miss it. We get changed in the flat into our sailor suits and walk over to the huge gymnastics arena that will host us during the wait until the parade. Spirits are high within the British group, but the hanging around in the arena seems to kill it somewhat. All the different countries begin showing off. The Kiwis do a *haka*, which draws a huge round of applause, the Aussies do their 'Ozzy, Ozzy, Ozzy' chant, which gets slightly less, and when the Yanks try a 'USA, USA!' chant they get booed. We rack our brains to see if we can contribute, but are saved when they begin taking countries out to start the parade.

They are well ahead of themselves, so the lessons of Atlanta seem to have been learnt. The queue of nations snakes gently around the curve of the stadium, and then suddenly I notice the point where I am to get the flag. There is a huge collection of them by the side of the path and as we approach I get sweaty palms just thinking about it. I am given a white leather holster to put over my shoulder, but as soon as I receive the flag, I know I will follow Steve's tradition. The pole is of lightweight aluminium and I could hold it all day. I drop the holster into a pocket and turn back to face about 200 Brits who have decided to march. The hockey girls are in the front row and want photos, but I run back into the group swirling the flag over everybody's heads. The momentum is reinstated and we start chanting and trying to initiate a Mexican wave. Everybody stoops over in the count of '5 ... 4 ... 3 ... 2 ... 1' and then jumps up, hands high over our heads, on 'Go'. Now all the other countries are getting booed if they don't follow our example. As we disappear down the tunnel that goes under the main stand, one of the spectators above us shouts, 'Go GB! Stuff those Aussies!' and we all cheer back.

As we turn the last corner, I can see the entrance and the massive stand on the far side of the stadium. Goosebumps all over me now as I step under the last concrete ceiling and wait. The rows form up behind me and the last few from Ghana disappear up the 100-metre straight. A guy with a headset says, 'Great Britain, go!' and I lead out the team. I walk at what I think is a decent pace without wanting to march too rigidly. I have my left arm out ramrod straight to my side to magnify the 'I'm not using the girly holster' effect, but it may be lost in the 'I'm wearing a sailor suit' effect. It has gone very quiet behind me and for a second I think they have let me go out all on my own but in fact the team are there, it's just the cheers that are drowning out the British excitement.

About halfway down the first straight I relax and start thinking to myself, 'This is the only time you will ever get to do this, so enjoy it!' And I do. Another guy in a headset tries getting me to speed up, but there's just no way I'm rushing this. After 300 metres we turn off the track into the infield and I have a long walk on my own down the centre line towards the as yet unlit flame. Then it's up a few steps and then, damn it all, they want the flag back. Almost reluctantly I hand it over and watch until they put it in the racks with all the others. Above me somewhere my parents, sister and Dee are all shouting to get my attention, but I don't hear them. I know they have seen my proudest moment, and that is what counts.

Back within the British group in the centre of the field, we all become spectators rather than participants. We are stunned by the roar as Australia make their entrance, and the four of us exchange glances. We know that we will be dealing with different Australian crews if this happens at the lake. They make our excitement look like a funeral march. They are all jumping about and throwing little kangaroos into the crowd. It's epic. A bit later and the cheers get louder still when Cathy Freeman steps out to light the flame.

Steve gets his traditional 'Okay, let's get on with it' mood towards the end, and all four of us turn our attention to the racing rather than the awesome fireworks. Back in bed later that night I reverse the way I sleep on the bed so that by twitching the curtain with my foot I can get a view of the Olympic flame.

We always predicted that we would be seeded fourth. It doesn't seem to affect the crew too much, but Jürgen is wound right up. Almost unbeaten for four years and then one slip-up before the Games and we plummet down the rankings. The seeds are split across three heats. As fourth seeds we get drawn with the third seeds, who are Australia. We all know what this means. There are three places up for grabs in the semi-finals from our race, but we have much higher standards. Only a good win will get our campaign on track again. Lose, and we haven't got time to change anything. It's a good test of our last ten weeks, either it's worked or it hasn't.

Early that Sunday morning in the food hall I make a mistake. Jürgen is looking over the four of us while he has his first coffee. Steve is munching cereal and checking his blood sugar. Tim and James are both eating toast and fruit, and I sit patiently. There is not a thing in front of me apart from a bottle of water.

'Come on Massew,' Jürgen encourages. 'Eat something.'

'I'll be fine, Jürgen. Honestly.'

'No, you need to eat,' he presses. The others are looking at me now, and the last thing I want is to cause some issue at this point. I relent and fetch a bowl of cereal. But my stomach is churning and I have to force it down mouthful by mouthful.

All the way to the lake the feelings of nausea grow. I know exactly what it is. 'It's just the nerves,' I tell myself. 'Nerves are good. You need them to get up for any race.' This is a well-worn mantra for when I'm under stress. We start preparing for a warm-up paddle but the nausea doesn't dissipate. At long last we go afloat. This is normally the time when I feel more in control; the lake is quiet and I can use the activity to channel the aggression. The paddle always starts in the same way, Tim and I sitting motionless while Steve and James paddle the boat together. Within seconds, I know what's going to happen.

'Okay, let's get it over with,' I whisper to myself. I lean forward to hang my head over the water and, without more than two contractions, park my cereal in the lake. No one says a word. James and Steve paddle on seamlessly and I have time to sip and swill some water before it is stern pair's turn. James told me weeks later that it was a pivotal moment for him – he had never seen me nervous before a heat, much less throw up, and from then on he knew the Australians wouldn't trouble us. He has always had an endearing and inspiring confidence in my abilities, and he knew that when I was as nervous as this, it would get the very best out of me.

Indeed, the Aussies didn't trouble us. We went out with as much Lucerne fire in our bellies as we could muster and attacked the heat and the opposition as if there were medals at stake that day. We launched away from the others and could afford to cruise in the last part of the race, concentrating not on the opposition behind us, but on sending a message to the towpath and the other heat winners: 'Lucerne was a blip. We are back. We are as good as we ever have been.' We earned ourselves a few hours after the race to relax and enjoy the press attention, and then it was back to the flat in the village.

The time in the village went in a kind of waltz. Slow, slow, quick, quick, slow. Slow, the time between getting up and getting out onto the water up in Penrith. Slow, the time between the sessions, when we cast our eyes around the opposition and the boat yard, knowing that the most important day of our lives was approaching. Quick, the journey back, as we dozed in the warmth of the bus, and quick, the early afternoon in front of the television with all the guys laughing at the coverage. Then slow, the nightly meeting with Jürgen to get the pattern for the next day sorted and talk about the semi. Then, last and slowest of all, the few hours before sleep, alone with your thoughts, even in crowded, noisy rooms.

The semi was a less advantageous draw. The Italians eluded us, so we had only one chance to beat them. Instead, we got the Kiwis. They had still beaten us in Lucerne, but were less of a threat for the Gold medal. Once again, we had a great row. There was no repeat of the breakfast nonsense, Jürgen now accepting that having an empty stomach and less nausea was better than the alternative. By now, we were all very conscious of the clock running down to the final. After the first heat we had had three whole days before racing again, but this time there was only one. There was little time for relaxation: the Italians had qualified in fine style on the far side of the draw, dealing with the Aussies on the way, so on paper it was us against them. We started the last episode of nervous routine until the final. During some moments I was sure there would be no problem whatsoever, in others the chill hand of insecurity gripped my belly and I had to fight it off. Even for an experienced athlete, the last days are always a challenge. It never gets easy, and nor should it. Anyone who says they don't get nervous is either a liar or not very good.

Our final pre-race meeting was a classic. On Friday night we headed for Jürgen's tidy room to talk tactics for the last time. We filed in for the occasion early and twitchy. We had all been spending the last afternoon in the village trying to relax, but for the meeting there was no hiding the nerves. James looked taut, ready to snap if someone let off a banger. Steve was drawn too, his plan of just having fun at the Olympics had run slap into the final. We perched on the bed and the chairs in the room, no one sitting with their back resting on anything. We were all leaning forward, hands fidgeting between our knees.

It was too late to make any dramatic changes, but it was important that if we were unhappy with anything in the plan we used in the first two races, we should get it out now. No one was, and we moved on to talking more generally about the race and the opposition. Jürgen fancied the Italians to be our main threat, with an early charge from the Aussies.

'I'm sure the Italians will come hard at us in the middle,' he ventured. 'They are hard guys, but we have more than they do. If they put their nose in front, we don't panic. We are strong. We focus on long strokes. Don't go crazy getting the lead back from them we might be fighting someone else at the end. But I'm sure you can win.' The old classics were in there, too. He complimented all of us in turn, telling us what our jobs were and how best to do them. There was no dialogue and, indeed, little eye contact between the four of us; most of us either looked at the coach or at the floor.

Steve took over and talked about how much he and, indeed, all of us had put in to reach this point. We all deserved to think of ourselves as favourites and we should extend what we had done in the first two races to eclipse the others. 'We will win this, I've got no doubt at all in my mind.' We all offered similar heart-felt sentiments and realised that the last day before the Olympic final was over. There was nothing left to say or do.

On his way back to the flat James called in at the Team GB headquarters to ask a question and caught Steve Rider saying to the nation 'There are only 16 hours left till the event of the Games for Britain.' Back at home our famous day had been trailed and built up and we had missed it all. James left feeling even more nervous than before.

Upstairs on the balcony I got a call from Dee, who had been at the lake all week to witness the progression from nervous contenders to favourites for the Gold medal. She was staying with some of the other girlfriends in a flat by the harbour. She kept it short, realising that I was in a mono-syllabic mood. She told me that she loved me and that she wanted me to have the race of my life. I knew I would have to.

26

the final

By the time I left the bathroom, Steve had already left the flat. I picked up my rucksack and walked out into the hallway. I got a quick glimpse of Tim on the couch getting treatment on his back from one of the squad physios, Mark Edgar. Neither of them saw me, and I went down to the street level. It was chilly outside; it would be hours before the sun rose, so I was glad I had chosen the waterproofs to insulate me. I walked up the road that had been so lively during the previous days, but at this time in the morning my only company was a security quad bike puttering gently along. I went past the Canadian block, which, like ours, was festooned with flags and laundry, and then up to the huge food hall. James, Steve and Jürgen were clustered near the door, the only eaters in the huge space. There were a few staff beginning to lay out the trays of food, but across the acres of tables and chairs they seemed miles away.

I wasn't going to make any diet mistakes again. Jürgen

could have held a flame to my wrist and I wouldn't have eaten a thing. I had been preparing my body for years for this day, and knowing I would reject any food that morning, I had eaten nothing but carbohydrates for two days solid. Breakfast, lunch and dinner had been cereal, bread, pasta, rice and potatoes. Next to no sugar and certainly no meat. I didn't want any question about my energy reserves for the final, and I knew that after 48 hours of carbs it would be no problem to miss breakfast. I hadn't eaten for hours but the nerves gave my stomach a feeling as if I had just swallowed lead pellets. Watching the others eat just made it worse.

As we sit there, conversation is limited. Jürgen might try an 'Okay, Massew?' but he's lucky to get more than a thin smile and a nod from me. After 20 minutes or so we troop out to the road and then up to a separate gate behind the food hall. No one is taking any chances with the buses today. We have been allocated one of the Team GB minibuses. It's a little faster but no more comfortable. As we rumble out on the dual carriageway through the dark, my thoughts turn to the magnitude of the day. I can't avoid the fact that everything has been about today; all the sessions on the rowing machines, all the freezing mornings on the river, it will all be in vain if we don't win. I try to put myself in the opposition's boat. Sure, they won in Lucerne, but we have been impressive here in Sydney. In the heat we toasted the Aussies, and the semi finished the Kiwis as far as Gold medals were concerned. But you mustn't be too arrogant, and it's a brave man who can banish every negative thought from his head. Then I think about the other guys in the bus. Steve, already a legend, but battling his body and his age to make Olympic history. If he can do this, so can I. He needs support, not a quivering wreck of a strokeman. James, who so desperately wants to win that he would sacrifice everything in his life to do it, so burned by his previous Olympic experiences that he has out-trained all of us in his quest. Tim, who has had health issues with his back and his hand, probably knows this is his last Games. Staring out into the darkness I promise myself that no matter what, I won't make mistakes because of nerves. I vow that I will stroke my boat better than the other strokemen will theirs. I am going to be the aggressor; my nerves are going to make me a lion.

Just before six we unload in the car park behind the massive grandstand that will soon hold thousands of spectators. We pass through the security checkpoint to have our bags checked and for an instant the volunteers try a cheery greeting.

'Jeez, you guys are here early!' James is lost in his headphones and the rest of us ignore them. Only then do they realise what we are here to do.

'Sorry, guys. Have a good day.'

As we get into the boat park, we split up. Jürgen goes to check the boat, James and Steve to the rest tent and Tim to the warm-up area to stretch. I sit in the changing room for a few minutes, carefully folding my waterproofs back into my bag. It would take seconds if I wanted it to, but I need to kill time. Any little job is good for the nerves, even if it takes only a few seconds. As I emerge, the first signs of dawn are creeping into the sky: it won't be long now before sun-up. There are other people around – the bus from the village must have pulled in. Danes, Kiwis and Americans are all emerging from the gloom. We gather by the boat and quickly run over what we want to do.

'Okay eight k, two laps. Just a few bursts. Steve?' Jürgen asks. I don't know why. It's exactly the same paddle with which we have started each day for a week or more. We lift the boat off the rack and down to the water. The nerves can be assuaged for a while; the comforting predictable routines of the session take over. An early paddle is normally about stretching and waking up, but today it's more about calming down. As we spin around at the top end of the lake and set off down towards the finish, we can't help but drive the boat harder than normal. Apart from everything else, the adrenalin is flowing, but you also want to demonstrate to the other guys that you are up for this. The boat slices down the lane in silence, with only Steve's quiet commands telling us when to stop. Then we hear them.

'Go on, GB!'

'You can do it, GB!'

'Yeah, Redgrave!'

People are in the stands already, and though none of us turns to look, we can tell there are dozens of them. As we cross the finish line there is even a smattering of applause from the stand. As we turn the boat to head back up for the second lap, we see the flags. The railing right on the finish line is a solid mass of Union Jacks and St George crosses; the faithful few are leaping about in the Australian dawn, delighted that they get to show their support to us first. Rowing, unlike cricket, has no Barmy Army, no fans who follow the sport abroad without knowing someone in the team, but that day we sprouted them.

Steve clears his throat, 'Okay, we'll do a few bursts this lap, back stops, ready, go.' We glide away back into the silence of the lake to do our warm-up. As we return in the race direction the fans are ready for us. Every 500 metres or so, the session calls for a burst of 12 strokes at full power. The first one might be only 20 strokes a minute, but by the time we get to the last two we are at race speeds, ripping through the water with a sense of release. The last few are absolute beauties – four guys at the peak of their game, primed on the morning of their Olympic final. As we start the last effort down towards the finish line, the Brits go crazy. There are more of them this lap and they all want to make themselves heard. Across the water I realise that no matter what, I am going to cry today, and if I'm not careful it's going to be right now. Hours later I found out that everyone was feeling the same way, happy to hide the beginnings of tears behind their shades.

We have finished the outing and given our bodies and our brains a taste of what to expect today. Sweat is just beginning to soak through our shirts as we paddle gently back around to the dock. The boating area is alive now; crews for today's finals are all out and about doing their warm-ups, and all tomorrow's eights finalists are here as well, going through their own routines before heading back to the village. We cut a swathe through the mêlée with the boat lifted up high before gathering by the rack to talk.

'Any problems?' Jürgen enquires.

Shakes of the head all round. I haven't heard a word from James all morning, and even Tim, normally the most vocal in a post-outing chat, is dumb. We all retire to the tent for the hardest hours of any Olympics. Tim has another appointment with Mark to free up his back and give him the confidence to twist in the directions that rowing demands. James lies out on his back, legs jiggling too quickly to be following any rhythm from his personal stereo. Steve has no music, no book – he sits and lies on a stretching mat in the corner. We don't speak to each other, but there is lots of communication.

Everyone is on the verge of a massive physical effort and all the pain that goes with it, but we also need emotional courage. You can't win without taking risks, and being who we are means that anything less than a win is a disaster. Though we don't know it, the British audience at home has built this race into the must-see event of the Games. Millions are planning to end their Friday night with a few minutes in front of the television to watch. It's not quite big screens in Piccadilly Circus, but for rowing it's the biggest event in our careers. If we lose, the disappointment will be huge. But that has no bearing on us in that little tent in Sydney. We are all concentrating on the minutiae of the race, the simplest of things that we know will enable us to win. But as practiced and hardened as we are, our minds are under attack from doubts and nerves like a ship caught and creaking in polar ice. It was months later that Steve told me he would periodically disappear from the tent to find quiet, lonely places in the boat yard to weep.

Ninety minutes before we take to the water the racing begins. The commentary is broadcast into the boating area and we follow each final down the track. The men's single scull is won by the Kiwi, Waddell (good news, I think, he was favourite), the women's by the Belarusian, by a hundredth of a second. The roar of the crowd is impressive even from this distance, but more taxing on our nerves are the medal ceremonies.

'First and Olympic Champion ... *Premier et Champion Olympique* ... Rob Waddell!' Massive roar. Then a pause as the medal is hung round his neck.

'Please rise for the National Anthem of New Zealand. *Levez-vous s'il vous plaît pour l'hymne nationale de La Nouvelle-Zélande.*' Another pause, then the anthem, which raises goose bumps on all of us as we desperately try to think of something other than our own ceremony.

An hour before we boat and we can begin a more structured routine. Check the water bottle is full, get into our race kit, pack away anything we won't need till afterwards. We begin stretching and make numerous trips to the toilet. It's a chance to have final words with the others, nothing complicated, just a reaffirmation of what we are there for.

I talk hurriedly to Steve. There is no trace of pressure as he hardens his lips into a tight line.

'Make sure the calls are loud in the last 250,' I say. I am worried about losing stuff in the cacophony of the crowd.

'I will. You think James is okay?' I look over to see if there are any worrying signs. He's jiggling about like a puppet, headphones jammed in his ears, eyes lunging around the tent as if he is trapped in a corner.

'Yeah, he's good.' It's too late to do anything even if he isn't and all the outward signs are normal. James just does this.

At last Steve glances at his watch and then looks around purposefully. 'Okay, it's time.' We gather by the boat, which is now the right way up on two slings. Jürgen has been over it time after time, checking that nuts are tight and there are no signs of problems.

'Okay,' he starts, 'I think we had a good meeting last night. I'm sure we all thought a lot about the race overnight, and I don't want to say too much more. We keep it very simple – the race is definitely ours to win, we have the strength and the power to do it, I know it. We talked about the Italians last night and I'm sure they will give it a good go, but don't let them rush us from our plan. Maybe they come at a thousand, maybe earlier, but we are ready, and when Steve calls, then we go. We don't go crazy early on but if we make our own rhythm, then I'm sure we'll get it right. I think everybody is happy with the plan?' Nods all round. 'Then we go, unless there is anything else?' Normally someone would chip in to add to the moment but there is no need. Everyone is keen to get on with it.

We plod out on a short jog, more to keep with the routine than to warm up. We decide to run along the grass bank by the lakeside and we get a view of what awaits us. The lake is a brilliant blue in the bright morning sunshine, lapping gently against the stark white of the pebbles on the shore. The emerald green of the grass is visible only on our side of the bank because of the thousands of people who are hiding it on the far side. We expected the stands to be full. They were even for the semi-finals, but now the whole far bank is packed. As we turn back towards the boat, the coxless pairs come past. Greg Searle and Ed Coode are leading the race. None of us shout because we pretty much realise it makes no difference – they would never hear us. As they draw level with us, the French pair makes a suicidal charge at the Brits. Rating above 40, as if it's the last 20 strokes of the race, they overtake Greg and Ed. Surely it can't last, but their bravery has taken the rest by surprise. With the line in sight, the Aussies try to respond, and the Americans sprint, too. The British are caught in the race for the medals and we are disappointed to see them finish fourth. The French, exhausted beyond even the normal limits of rowing races, nearly fall in but they know they have won.

A thought occurs to me: 'What if the Italians do that to us?'

We get back to the boat and take it down to the water. Our opposition are all around us now and we studiously avoid each other. Jürgen sends us off with a last, almost traditional, 'Have a good row.'

The warm-up paddle is a release from the worst of the situation in the tent. Like a submarine rising from the depths, we can begin to get some sense out of our limbs. We rip into the few strong bits of paddling that we have on the way up to the start, and then turn to point down the course. A quick glance over the shoulder tells me yet again what I knew to be true when I first saw an international course – 2000 metres is a hell of a long way. From here, the massive stands are just colourful ribbons jammed between the azure water and the green of the trees behind. The lines of buoys marking the lanes all converge on the furthest point like the light from a prism. After another couple of bursts we are nearing the end of the warm-up. The other boats are circling now like sharks, punctuating the silence with their breathing as they practise their starts. I concentrate on the strokemen – 'No way I'm getting beaten by him ... Look at the size of his legs. My arms are bigger' – but it doesn't wash. I know we will need everything to win. We finish the last practice start, then paddle gently towards the start installation, where we turn to offer our stern to the stake boat boy.

All the other boats are attaching too, and with a few minutes left, the starter turns on his microphone.

'I am arming the system now.' He presses the button that controls the 'clogs', and with a rush of bubbles six yellow holders – one for each boat – pop up onto the surface right on the bows. A quick wiggle from all the fours and the bows are wedged in, holding each boat exactly straight. At the moment the light goes green, the 'clogs' will dive under the water releasing the bows as they go.

'Two minutes.'

A last chance to check everything. Water bottles are jettisoned onto the bank, rigger nuts squeezed to check they won't rattle (I have a small spanner in case there's a problem). The mind goes crazy, thoughts rush past like a mountain torrent: 'This is it! ... Think of winning ... Watch the Kiwis ... Don't choke!' I calm myself one last time. 'Okay, I am good at this. They are not stronger than us, concentrate on the job of stroking, and everything will be okay.'

'United States of America ... ready?' The call-over begins and we slide into our start positions: knees up, seat forward, oar in the water. 'Slovenia ... ready?' Steve has a last look round, his steerman's instinct demanding one final check, but the clog is doing its job of keeping the boat straight. 'Australia ... ready? Great Britain ... ready?' A last chance to call in a problem but there's nothing wrong. 'Italy ... ready? New Zealand ... ready?'

The last few seconds of the preparation tick away. My heart is racing.

'Attention!' It's the last word the starter utters. The start itself is the light going green and the buzzer. The red light comes on. I stare at it and as it goes out the race starts.

As usual, our first stroke is longer and slower than the others, the dead weight that we have is a disadvantage here. But it's a good first stroke and we attack the next few with venom. We don't fall behind, as we would normally do in the opening ten.

'Great start!' my brain cheers. Years later Carlo Mornati, the strokeman of the Italian boat, told me he was thinking the exact same thing about his crew. But when he looked over at us he was surprised to see us already ahead.

We get to 15 strokes and the first of Steve's calls. 'RHYTHM!' He doesn't have time or breath for much more, but we all know what it means. We lower the rate a little from the high 40s down to 40 or so in order to begin our transfer into a pace that we can sustain. We can all see we are in the lead, it's not much, a few feet maybe, but your peripheral vision can work wonders at times like this.

We are rowing really well, long and yet aggressive, the perfect combination. We are getting into the driving seat for the race, becoming the focus for everyone else in it. A minute gone and Steve makes another call: 'One minute ... NOW!' The rate has been stable the last 30 seconds and it's time to take it down to race pace. It should be about 38. A few seconds later he calls again 'Thirty-eight ... good.' He has the only display in the boat, a small, lightweight piece of electronics that uses a magnet under his seat to tell him the rate.

Some strokemen have the display for themselves, but I don't want to be shouting anything. We begin to stretch the lead, 6 feet turns to 10 then 12 then 20. On the television the blue bows of our boat are showing clearly on the screen: James is rowing out the front of the race.

Five hundred metres comes in a flash. We are just over a second up, good news. There has been no surprise sprint from anyone to grab the lead from us – yet. The calls are few and far between, a good sign. If Steve is jabbering all the time, it's not going to plan.

'Seven fifty ... good!' We are going to win this by a long way, we are nearly three-quarters of a length up. I'm the only one now who can look over and see anything other than open water beside us. The Aussies are in second and we have loads more power than them. The pain is a constant background now: two minutes in and your body is searching for oxygen, mouths are open, throats being rasped by the rush of air. Our legs are pumping down each stroke at 90 per cent of what we could ever do, but the brain is icy cool. Messages of stress and agony are put somewhere else for a few minutes, the brain replies – keep going, this is good, deal with it.

The Italians make an effort just before 1000. I smile to myself. 'Just on schedule, fellas.' We know this was coming and the plan is to let them have a go up to the halfway mark, keeping our powder dry, and then to attack right back. Nothing drains your effort quicker than seeing a push work to begin with, and then the opposition take it all back.

I am biding my time, building up a store of energy and working out the angles from the markers behind us on the shore. It must be five strokes at most. They are within half a length and clearly ahead of Australia now.

'Thousand ... Now!' Steve growls out the command and it adds extra urgency to the moment. We all know what this means – finish them off.

I attack the next stroke and the response is good – to begin with. We take a few feet out of them, but after ten strokes we stop moving ahead. It stays there for another spell and we are at a tactical crossroads. We have maybe 800 metres left and we can try another attack now, or we can run off a bit more of the distance and then start a sprint for home. Steve is the only one who makes the call and we all have to wait for what he chooses. Whatever he calls, we do, no argument.

In fact, the Italians make the decision for us. The bowman looks over at us and calls something to his crew. They are about to come at us. 'Ready....now!' is our response. No problem, it's just another chance to do what we should have done at halfway. But the result is similar – with a few strong strokes we move ahead, then there is a stalemate for a few more, then danger as they start moving back on us again. It's as if we are attached by a rubber band – we stretch it, then they contract it again.

My heart is racing, maybe up at 190 beats a minute. It's as severe a test as I have been through in years. It is all pain from the neck down, muscles driving, stretching, reaching and working. But there is a pocket of calm inside, a mental calculation that is ticking over, ready to send out more commands. Another gear maybe, but the legs are not happy about it. More importantly, it tells me I'm okay, I'm in charge, this is going to be fine.

We are getting to the last 500, the sprint for home. The Slovenians go for the draw first, pushing the rate and their boat up to challenge for a medal. They haven't got the legs or the time to get to us, but the Aussies respond and the race begins to concertina up again. We start hiking our own rate. Thirty eight goes to 40, to 41 and then to 42. Each step is accompanied by a dose of fire from our legs and a spreading ache from our bellies up across our chests. After nearly five minutes of rowing I am already on the edge of what I can manage and the final charge has only just begun.

Two fifty to go and the Italians are still right there. They are sprinting flat out, their bowman calling every few strokes. If we are going to give up the lead, it's here. Sometimes the brain makes the last 30 strokes into a challenge that even with a Gold medal as a reward you can't face. But we are not breaking, we won't let them take our prize away. I begin counting the strokes in, five more good ones, five more good ones. With ten strokes to go the noise is unbelievable: the stands on the far side are echoed by the boating side as we come past our families in the reserved section.

Last ten strokes. The Italians are closing again, either

because we are wilting or they have found something left. Steve makes his last call: 'In the water!' It's a reminder that despite the rate being flat out, despite the body being on the edge of collapse, it's important to hold the form and the technique. One good stroke is worth two bad ones, and the most important facet of the stroke now is what happens in the water. It must be driving the boat across the line. I turn my head to the left so that I can see both the Italians and the bank at the same time. The rest of the opposition is academic now, they are too far back to feature. But the Italians are within striking distance. The finish tower is right by us now. I need to do is row out the last few strokes. But the body is folding, legs aching and cramping, the drive has left them.

Head lolling to the left, eyes still confirming I am just ahead of Carlo in the corresponding seat in the Italian boat, I take the last stroke.

silvretta diary

Friday, 30 July 2004
Mountain training camp, Silvretta, Austria
23 days till the Final

Thinking back to the beginning of this camp, it is hard to recon-
cile where we are now. A few days before we left the UK, Alex
Partridge was diagnosed with a punctured lung. It wasn't just
a question of him being off training for a while, it was Games
Over. It hurt us all to see his dreams shattered, the youngest
and most excited of the line-up reduced to hospital out-patient
and holiday-maker. He can't even fly to see us compete – he
just has to spend his summer being 'normal'. Alex ushered Ed
into the crew with an aplomb and grace that will never be
forgotten. He could have left well alone, gone away and tried
to forget what might have been. But he didn't: he stayed first
to cheer us on at Henley, then talked to Ed about what he
thought the three seat role should be. He then sent us away to

Austria with a letter. It was full of compliments, encouragement and advice, along with quotes from his favourite films. But it also communicated his desire to win. He told us never to forget what it meant to be where we were and how much others, him included, would love to be with us.

For days, I was shell-shocked by the speed of his departure and missed his voice behind me in the boat. I was beginning to think along the lines of 'How the hell are we going to win now?' or 'A Silver is going to be a good result from here'. But then I caught myself: 'This is likely to be my last chance,' I thought. 'Why the hell am I giving the oppo a break, folding up shop long before the races have even started?' So in bed one night in Henley, with my wife pretending to be asleep next to me, I made a promise to myself that I would never give up on a race or a chance for Gold.

I'm sure the others had their own battles before we left for Austria, but when we had our first crew meeting we all agreed that Silver wasn't good enough, that Gold was our only option. It set up the camp beautifully because it is actually easier to aspire to the best rather than hedge our bets. James can be as perfectionist as he likes, Stevie as reticent and Ed can make serious plans to erase his fourth place from Sydney. Every session became a mission, and although we started gradually, we climbed the rankings in the team throughout.

The eight and quad outperformed us at the start, but we never lost drive and our finish was spectacular. It always ends with a 2-kilometre race, which at altitude is a challenge for mind and body. We had a blinder, finishing in 6 minutes and 6 seconds, the fastest fours time GB has ever produced up here. Quicker than the Bronze-medal boat from Atlanta, quicker than the Sydney winners, and quicker than the four of the last three years. Of course, the conditions were good, but we got a real buzz out of it. James was tired and coughing badly, but even he was impressed, Stevie too, but all of us noted how hard he pushed himself in the bow seat.

For the first time almost the entire summer I feel at peace with it all. We have more to do in France, important boxes to tick, but we are almost there, and after all we have been through I don't feel short of time. To be honest, it feels as quick and deft as any combination that we have put out all summer. I feel we are real Gold-medal contenders again, and it makes me remember the crushing pressure that this entails for the whole of the Olympic racing week. Sydney was far from pleasant in that regard and the media are going to be all over us again this time. Maybe I should take a leaf from Steve Redgrave's book when he said a fortnight before it all began in Australia that he just wanted to enjoy it.

28

media

Rowing was never a big concern of the media. There are a handful of papers with rowing correspondents, who are wheeled out to cover the Boat Race and small international events, and that's about it. For many years the World Championships got a short recorded slot on BBC *Grandstand*, pretty much showing the Redgrave race from start to finish and clips from other British boats that did well. But by the mid-'90s, the inexorable winning habit that Steve had going could no longer be ignored. Although he was operating in a sport that had no tradition of being big news, he had already won three Olympic Gold medals and was still going strong. The real turning point, however, was when we won in Atlanta in 1996.

Feature writers, who up until then had covered us only periodically, began to ask for more time and more often. All writers are treated the same: set a date to come watch us train and, if they want, they can bring a bike to follow the first session alongside Jürgen on the towpath. Then, after a break for us to change, we will sit down with them over breakfast and conduct an interview over the top of the large jugs of squash that are our staple method of rehydration (I've lost count of the number of mentions they get). The vast majority will want a photo, and this can never be one that someone else has taken. So you get bored to tears of the same old set-ups down by the river and in the boat house. I don't envy a sports photographer his life of trying desperately to be in the right place at the right time on a cold touchline somewhere, or trying to instil some bored rower with an incentive to smile. Before Atlanta we were getting through five interviews a week, and most were well-researched and a pleasure to do, the reporters revelling in the access and honesty that they so rarely get from other sports. We would seldom dodge a question, and never spin them a line for our own ends. The relationship was straightforward: they were taking the time to cover us and would be treated openly, and in return we and our sponsors get into the paper.

But after Atlanta the policy had to change. The run-up to Sydney was awash with all sorts of people, some of whom didn't cover sport regularly, and some who hadn't even bothered to do the least amount of research. I don't mind those who don't know or understand rowing. It is, after all, a pretty quirky corner of the sports world. But it was annoying when I had to give them information that it would have been easy for them to research themselves. Steve was also getting increasingly bored and frustrated with being singled out for the same 'Are you going to win your fifth Gold medal?' question each time. The best interviews are always from those people who take the time to get to know all of us and the issues involved, and can then come up with some original and fresh questions.

Doing television shows was another kettle of fish entirely. First of all, you get a car sent to pick you up. This impressed me hugely to begin with, and I would feel like a top executive, sitting in the back using my mobile phone. The novelty didn't last, and after a year or two I got used to bracing myself for when the car was late or had the wrong address, and the interminable waiting around that television seems to demand.

There were continued appearances on *Question of Sport*, and after Atlanta I was asked to go on *They Think It's All Over*. This show make no pretence of caring who wins as long as it is entertaining, so they let both teams know the questions beforehand. They even go to the extent of supplying material to those who are not professional comedians. Essentially, you are given a couple of simple gags for each of your rounds and head out into the auditorium quaking in your boots about who has to say what and when. When the picture comes up, the line that sounded so funny and quick in the meeting room dies on your lips and its backside in front of a live studio audience. In fairness, the professionals, such as Jonathan Ross, have their fair share of duds too, but they plough on regardless, whereas the poor sportspeople disappear down below the desk. The quickest and funniest parts of the programme come from the interaction between the team leaders and, the host Nick Hancock, and there is nothing to do but sit quiet and be the butt of most of the jokes. Some people hate doing the show, and there are loads who refuse to go on, but I have enjoyed most of my trips, only once asking the producers to cut a joke that I thought was out of line. It concerned my wife, and as soon Jonathan Ross mentioned it, he reassured me it would come out of the final edit.

There is no space for smut at *Sports Review of the Year* (despite Gary Lineker's recent efforts), and it remains one of the most enjoyable and well-attended evenings of the sports calendar. It is always a thrill to be recognised for a successful year and to find so many of your heroes in one place, all so obviously getting the same thrill.

Steve and I had spent years in the cheap seats at the back, but after Atlanta front-row seats were assured. Nevertheless, when Steve won in 2000, it was no surprise that he started his victor's speech with 'I've been coming here for 20 years' and a sardonic smile.

It was all pretty far from our minds on the warm waters of the lake in Sydney, however, though from anybody's point of view the competition over the BBC's silver camera that year had ended right there and then. I spent a moment arms aloft and mouth wide in ecstatic celebration, echoed by James at bow. But the look on Steve and Tim in the same photo is one of exhaustion. Within seconds I reached down to undo the straps anchoring my feet into the boat and headed for Steve. It was not planned, and on the way I virtually climbed over a still-seated Tim in a most ungainly fashion. I don't remember saying anything to Steve as I got to him, but there was no need. He was beyond words in exhaustion and emotion, and the embrace we shared is captured in one of my favourite photos (and one of the few that my wife allows) up in our house. After a few moments, my first conscious thought was that I was really uncomfortable and that Steve must be, too. I was kneeling on the deck of the boat with the majority of my weight on one knee, resting on Steve in a hug and there was only one way to get out of the situation. With hippo-like grace, I rolled into the lake and only when under the water found the ache in my legs a barrier to breaking the surface again. I managed one kick and then had to hang on to the stern before hauling myself back into the stroke seat.

The BBC were there in force, with the normal commentary team of Garry Herbert and Daniel Topolski augmented by Steve Rider. Normally cooped up in a studio in downtown Sydney, Steve had been given orders to present the day's sport from the media raft just after the finish tower. He had interviewed everyone he could get his hands on before the race and was now interested in us, the winners. But Steve Redgrave had other ideas, and despite the pleas of the marshals on the water, he turned the boat to face up the lake towards the spectators. 'The media can wait. They weren't here at six this morning to wish us good luck and these guys were. We'll paddle up this side first.'

Pandemonium broke out as the Brits in the stands ran down to the water to cheer us back up the course. A few days later I even met one guy who broke his leg in the rush to the water's edge. But he didn't mind, 'It was worth it.' We got applause from the whole stands and manic cheering and chanting from the Brits. Once we started along the stand, there were always more people further along, waving us to get up to them for a photo and a flag wave, so we ended up paddling the best part of 800 metres back up the course. By the time we turned, the medal ceremony for the previous event was well under way and we were getting short of time, so we paddled back in one go.

Back at the finish line the BBC were getting desperate for some appearance by us on live television. They had got hold of Jürgen to say a few words, and he was only interrupted by us arriving to hug him. Steve Rider tried talking us through a semblance of the race but we couldn't get much sense out. Steve told him that he thought the race was won within 200 metres. We knew that no one was ever going to get past us in the last thousand of a race, and pretty much the only way that they were going to get in front of us before a thousand was to hammer off the start and get a lead. Once no one took that tack, then, he said, he had every confidence we would win.

Steve Rider then asked me a question about Steve's impact and reputation after the final and I got a chance to say in public what everyone in rowing in general and British rowing in particular knew. He had already been a legend for many years, a standard-bearer for our sport in more than the literal sense, and he was by a margin the greatest Olympian we in Britain have ever produced. You could make an argument for putting him in the running for the greatest Olympian ever from any country. By this time the organisers were getting nervous about the timetable for the medal ceremony, and one of them, the same one who had been madly ushering us into the media raft just moments before, came over to get us to go back in the boat.

'Great Britain, I need you to go to the medal raft now, please.'

'They'll wait for us, I promise you.' Exhausted and sweaty, I felt I couldn't rush anything.

'Well, I don't know about that.' The official was fighting his corner now and getting an earful from the radio.

'How many medal ceremonies have you been to?' Steve the diplomat wades in to finish any discussion.

We spent a few more minutes with all four of us talking about the race, and then paddled the boat the few metres round to the medal podium. Getting out, we had an embrace between the four of us, the first and to my knowledge the last we ever had. The Aussies had beaten back the Slovenians to secure the Bronze and seemed happy enough as they shook our hands, and Carlo Mornati and his Italian crew were saying they had had a great race.

We line up, as tradition dictates, with the Gold medallists in the middle.

'Victory Ceremony for men's coxless four. Medals will be presented by Her Royal Highness Princess Anne.' She steps forward, smiling. The announcer continues: 'Gold Medallists and Olympic Champions ... [it sounds pretty sweet even now] ... Great Britain.' There is applause from round the finish area; we raise our hands above our heads and take it all in. The Princess Royal steps forward to present each of us with our medal and for a moment I wonder if I should kiss her rather than shake her hand. Decide against it pretty quickly, not for any protocol reason, but because she would get smudged with a sweat and lake water mixture that might ruin the moment. I settle for a handshake and then the magic moment as the ribbon goes round my neck.

'*Levez-vous pour l'hymne nationale de Grande Bretagne.* Please rise for the national anthem of Great Britain.'

James has a union flag around his neck and sings the anthem proudly, Tim sings but *sotto* voce and Steve and I, as has become our custom, are stiff-lipped and silent. The finishing of the anthem signals the end of the formalities, so, being the last event of the day, we are not pushed off the medal raft by the next race. We all split up to find our families in the stands in front of us, hopping barefoot across the hot road. I find my group jubilant but exhausted. My dad, in particular, is sitting with his chin resting on his arms on the railing. No one can get enough words out to describe what

has happened, and with other supporters and friends wanting to shake my hand, I get stopped from spending time with
my parents and Dee. It won't be the last time.

After a few minutes we gather back at the boat to pose
for more photos before rowing it round the back to the boat
area. Members of the team appear from nowhere – managers,
boatmen, coaches and medics – to lend a hand for the boat or
for shaking. There is one face that I don't recognise, but
before he speaks I know what he is.

'Are you Matthew Pinsent?'

'Yes, I am.'

'You have been randomly selected for dope testing. I am
your chaperone and you have one hour to report to the
medical area. Sign here.'

It is not a shock. One from every medal boat will be tested
and it might as well be me. We gather up our bags and start
walking over towards the stand again. The media are waiting
in their tent, and though their deadlines are not nearly as
tight as when we raced in Atlanta, they will be hungry for
quotes. It is a slow business getting there. Steve is stopped
almost every step by friends and enemies within the rowing
world keen to pay their respects to the man who has
achieved the ultimate. We agree that we will call by the
stands again on the way to have a little more time with our
families, and I rush into the rows of seats. This time it is
quieter and I can catch up a little more with them. More to
the point, we make plans to see each other in Sydney when

we get through and I take Dee with me. She has no car to drive anywhere and I've spent months depriving us of time together. Now, for once, she comes with me.

The media tent is packed. There must be 150 people in there. The Beeb are well represented, as are the broadsheets. But the front row is made up of all the tabloid guys – the *Sun*, the *Mirror*, the *News of the World* and the *Star*. They are all there to put rowing on their back pages. But the red-tops always came with a health warning: 'Careful, don't get too close! Keep your wits about you!' But the questions are coming from everywhere but the front row. First the obvious: 'How do you feel?' 'Did you ever think you would lose?' 'What did you say to each other?'

Then a surprise. 'Did you realise that 7 million people watched at home?'

We look at each other in shock. Seven million? But we haven't time to take it in. The questions keep coming, all good-natured. I take the opportunity to put a few things right about Steve that were said after the Lucerne race that we lost. In particular, the *Sunday Times* wrote that Steve was risking a Gold medal chance because of his selfish desire, and that maybe age was going to beat him. I merely asked that the *Sunday Times* admit that they were wrong. I firmly defend the principle that any journalist can write pretty much anything; but if they are wrong, they have to say that, too.

My hour to do the drugs test was running out and we started wrapping up. Just as we got up to leave, the front row rose almost en masse and approached. Oh, here we go, I thought.

'We have been trying to come up with a better British sporting moment than the one we have just seen and we have to go back to the 1966 World Cup and that was English. Can you sign our timesheets?' The hardest lot to please, and all they wanted was a memento. Truly, we had the world at our feet.

With a few minutes to spare, I checked in at the medical area and began the formalities of a dope test. There are no corners you can cut, and nor would you want to, but they need a minimum of about 200 millilitres of your urine, which, after a hard race in a hot place, is asking a lot. Luckily, I was able to get enough out and within 20 minutes or so I could get into a shower. The medal stayed on. By the time I was out and with Dee again, they were herding the four of us into a van to take us to the main media centre in Sydney.

The journey was a pleasure, all four of us savouring the memories of the hardest week together, and we were able at last to laugh at the pressure we were under. We could all call anyone we liked in the UK, but all my family were in Sydney, so I didn't bother.

There are more media accredited at an Olympics than there are athletes, many more, and most of them hang out in a massive building called the International Broadcast Centre or IBC. We had to wait for all of us to get security clearance and then we were ushered into the various arms of the BBC that were covering the Games. We all sat in on a Radio 5 interview, and then walked along to find the television part. Behind the scenes one of the researchers came up to thank us.

'Thanks guys, that was absolutely superb. You wouldn't believe how many events we have worked on and gone absolutely huge on with the build-up, only for it to end in failure. To have gone as big as we did on you guys and then for you to actually win was special.'

We went through to the studio to do a live chat on the sofa with Sue Barker and Steve Rider. They put a montage on the screen of our three races and the backing track was Green Day's 'Time of Your Lives'. Cut to us looking shocked at how tight our victory looked on the screen. In the boat it just wasn't an issue, but suddenly seeing what everyone else had watched, we could understand why it looked like we might lose. We answered the usual questions with a relaxed attitude and the usual humour between us, cutting into each other's answers to poke fun. As we finished, Steve Rider mentioned that it had been seven hours since the race and we were amazed. Seven hours! All we had done is talk about the race.

After the BBC there were other foreign channels that wanted us, but we were running out of enthusiasm. We pretty much decided to split up – Steve to Darling Harbour to be with his wife and kids, James to the village, Tim to his parents in the Blue Mountains and Dee and I to Paddington near Bondi. You might think that at a time like this we would have stuck together to celebrate but, for a while at least, we had had enough of each other. To tell the truth, we always planned that we would at some stage get together, just the four of us, and get really, really drunk. We tried a few weeks later when we were at home to find a night for a celebration, but when we got the diaries out we couldn't find a date for four months, so we gave up. We have been to countless functions together, some of them specifically to celebrate our win, but just the four of us? No.

There's a curry house that has said if we take our medals in, they will serve as much beer and curry as we can take. One day, one day.

29

a new pair

Even following Steve home from the airport that morning, it was hard to realise just what we had landed into. The press and public had been all over the airport to welcome the whole team home, especially Steve. There had been a quiet rumour that Steve was going to be knighted in the terminal as a returning hero, but his wife had organised a brand-new Jag for him to soften the regal no-show. I was being chauffeur-driven separately to his house when we passed into Marlow Bottom. The schoolkids were just going back into lessons. They had all watched the television news and timed a street welcome, complete with banners, to see the big man back into his home town. His house, for almost the last time, was relatively quiet, with mountains of post and invites to get through. He had good people around him, not least his family, who were going to keep him rooted in normality. But it would have been an exciting and exhilarating time for anyone. Things would never be the same again.

We shared a cup of tea and then walked out to my car, a sponsor's loan that had been dropped off at his house a few days earlier. He tried to say goodbye in a way that summed up what we both were thinking, but I wouldn't take him seriously. We both knew that whatever he said in the press about being unsure over retirement, he would now most certainly call it a day. His rowing career had run its course and he had squeezed every possible performance out of it from the early '80s until the turn of the millennium. Though none of us placed much importance in coming out at the top, he was achieving it. Driving home that day, I knew that another Olympics was almost certainly on my agenda, but it would be without Steve. That held no particular fear for me. You could even say that I was relishing the challenge of a new combination. What it would be was still up in the air.

James was always going to carry on. He went back to training within three weeks of getting home on the basis that he had never taken a long break from rowing and wasn't going to start now. Tim was most certainly taking a break, not least because of his back, and though I never had a direct conversation with him, I heard on the grapevine that he wanted time to take stock and figure out how he and rowing were going to carry on. There was Ed Coode, of course, who, despite being despondent over his pairs performance with Greg in Sydney that had so nearly netted them a medal, was still keen to carry on. Jürgen was adamant that it shouldn't be a four. Just as he had been in agreement when we changed after Atlanta in 1996, he now felt that the four from Sydney was becoming so idolised and celebrated that any attempt by remnants from the crew was going to be under pressure right from the start.

James, I'm sure, worked out his favourite option straight away because he was now learning to change sides. In rowing you can either have your oar out to the right with your left hand on the end of the handle, or to the left with your right hand in control. It isn't really governed by your dexterity, however, and lots of people change sides. Steve had done it after the 1988 Games when he felt that the strength of the team was dominated by strokesiders. It took about two years before he became totally accustomed to it, but many believed he was better during his later bowside career than his original incarnation. James set about it with an eye for detail that only he could muster, brushing his teeth left-handed each day to train his brain in as many ways as he could. Try it, it's impressively hard, and an ample example of what he was up against. He also had to train his muscles to move in different ways. We both knew why he was doing it, and that was to row in a pair with me. Though we never talked about it after getting home, we were both happy with the concept and would try it at least as far as spring trials. If we could prove to be in the quickest British pair, then who knew what we could do?

But I was a long way off wanting to do any kind of training. Steve had taken a long break after Atlanta and I figured I could now, too. Jürgen said he wanted me back for the first camp of the calendar year in January and that was fine by me. It gave me 12 weeks of celebrating, enjoying the offers that came my way and doing the normal things that rowing precludes.

I did absolutely no exercise and enjoyed the feeling of fitness slipping away. If I had been retiring, I would have hated it, but I made the most of it, knowing that when I went back I would be training harder than I wanted to, so for a spell it was fantastic. I did a fitness test for a television programme in early December, nearly three months after the Games, and found that nearly 12 per cent of my endurance and strength had ebbed away. Levels of effort on the rowing machine that I could hold for an hour at the time of the Olympics were a struggle after five minutes. Suddenly it became a bit more of a worry. Losing 1 per cent a week was no joke.

The first camp was a horror show. It was in the Canary Islands on bikes, and the very first ride was about 100 minutes long. I held in the group for about 40, keeping my front wheel jammed up behind the wheel ahead, making the most of the hole in the air. But the hills were killing me. On a long, steady ascent the group kicked on and I was left behind, literally crying over my handlebars as my legs screamed their way uphill. Jürgen had parked his car at the top and was watching impassively as I ground past. No encouragement, no smile, just a quiet stare to see how I was faring. The first week was a training hell the like of which I have never known, but each day was better than the last, and after ten days I was finishing in the group rather than behind it.

The new pair was hard work to start with as well. James was having difficulty with the swap in mentality for bowside, and we had several sessions where we were passed by club-standard single scullers as we struggled with the boat and each other. Jürgen was confident that when we got it sorted technically, two of the best rowers in the world would make a good pair. We won the Spring Trials convincingly, beating the Coode-Searle combination from the Olympics, and with all three medal-winning pairs in temporary or permanent retirement, we were confident, too. Our agent Athole signed up Camelot to be our sponsor, with a deal worth nearly £1.4 million over the four years up until Athens. It all seemed to be falling into place.

As I lay there in the boat house, I reminded myself that it was James's idea in the first place. He had floated it at Henley Regatta and Jürgen had not batted it down out of hand, which he normally would with radical ideas. Two events at the same championships? It wasn't unheard of. Indeed, some of the Canadian women had doubled up at the same Olympics and come home with two Gold medals. But on the men's side it was a different story. Steve and Andy Holmes had tried several years in succession to win both coxed and coxless pairs in the same weekend. They had even tried it at the Olympics in Seoul, but never managed the double.

It was the second event that was the killer. If you were good enough even to consider it, you were probably capable of winning the first, but going out to race fresh opposition for the second race was the deal-breaker. Steve and Andy had the Abbagnale brothers in the coxed pairs, who were mighty opponents at the best of times, so trying to beat them with tired legs was a tough challenge. To incorporate lightweight rowing, the coxed pair had lost its Olympic status after 1992, and the event was now a shadow of what it had once been. Historically an arena for giants and legends, it had become a home for lower-ranked athletes from some of the bigger teams, who were hoping to get up the pecking order for the Olympic crews by the time the Games hove into view. It would have been a hollow challenge to have raced the coxed pair on its own, but there was a sting in the tail. Despite numerous requests, FISA, the international governing body, had refused to move the coxed pair to after the coxless. That put us in a dilemma. The coxed pair was supposed to be a bonus event after our main priority had been put to bed earlier in the weekend. But FISA were adamant: not only did they insist the coxed pair go first, but they were also unwilling to spread the races more than two hours apart.

We went into it with our eyes open. The season had gone really well and we were generating a dominance in the post-Olympic pairs field that impressed everybody. A Gold at the World Championship was seemingly a given. We took the coxed pair to training camp and split our training between the two boats, enjoying the added angle that Neil Chugani could give us as he lay prone in the bows of the slower boat.

The coxed pair was more like a rowing machine on water, more stable and more a test of power than the finesse demanded by the coxless. We loved it, doing as many of our water tests as we could in it.

We also designed a programme to take account of the two-hour gap between races. Steve Ingham, our physiologist, was keen on lots of angles. First, we had to refuel as best we could, which meant fluid and food (with a high glycaemic index, just so you know) straight after the first final, the coxed pair. Next was a walk to move the acid out of our muscles in a way that wasn't going to make us any more tired than we already would be. Then there would be an attempt to get our temperature down to help recovery. Steve Ingham suggested a wet towel soaked with ice water on our torsos. James couldn't handle that and downgraded it to a cold shower, which was fine enough. If you needed 30 minutes on the water before the coxless final, then that was almost as much as you had time to do. Jürgen was adamant that it was much more a mental battle than a physical one, so he built in a ten-minute rest to prepare for the second race.

I spent my ten minutes in the back of the boat house in the shade, cursing the remnants of the ice on my back and the sickly sweetness in my mouth. I had always been wary of biting off more than we could chew and now felt that the two-hour thing was a pretty large mouthful. The coxed pair had been fine. We just had to stay ahead of the Italian crew, whose weekend had been ruined anyway by us turning up.

They pushed us hard, and it was close at the finish, but we knew and they knew that we were always going to do that if we had another race coming.

When we went out for the coxless final we were already World Champions, but vulnerable because of it. The others knew it and flew out of the blocks, hoping that we would recognise our folly. If I had seen what trouble we were in, I might have given it up, but James kept us in the race, urging me and us through the field in the second half until it was just the Yugoslavians ahead of us. We dragged up the remains of our energy to challenge, and with ten strokes to go had just put our bows in front for the first time in the race. But the steering of the boat, which was my responsibility, had all gone south, and far from being in the centre of our lane, I had put James's oar over the lane buoys. It was entirely my fault that he hooked one within three strokes of the line. For a second I thought I had blown it for us. 'Well, it'll be a close Silver then,' was my reaction as we pounded the last three strokes across the line.

The photo finish took ages to come through, and it was only James's roar of victory that gave my muddled brain the idea that we had actually won. It was by the narrowest of margins – two one-hundredths of a second, about 2 inches – and we were awarded both Gold medals in ceremonies that ran back to back. It was a spectacular way to end our first year together, which had started with battling past slow scullers and had finished with a double Gold medal. But the best was still to come.

Rumours were flying around the rowing world that the Australian pair of Ginn and Tomkins were thinking about getting together again. They had made a big impact on the event throughout the '98 and '99 seasons, but an injury to Drew Ginn, the bowman, had thrown a spanner in the works before Sydney. The strokeman, Jimmy Tomkins, is a giant of the sport, and before Sydney he was being pushed at home as a likely three-times champion, a feat not achieved there since Dawn Fraser in the 1960s. He had to cobble a partnership together with a spare man called Long in time for the Sydney Games, and for a while they looked as if they could win. But the unpredictability of the French charge that we had witnessed from the bank at Penrith that day finished their chances of Gold, and Jimmy had to settle for a Bronze medal. After a year away from international rowing following the Games, the injury to Drew was in the past and they could re-form with a distinct target in mind – us.

We didn't have many weaknesses to pick out, but, unlike us, they had a superb length of stroke. The efficient application of their power through their long stroke gave them a cruise pace that was hard to match. We could outpower them, though, and that gave us an advantage at the start and in a sprint finish, but if we were anything but our very best, they would kill us in the middle of a race. We first came across them in Lucerne in the summer of 2002. We had two opportunities to judge ourselves against them and found ourselves a lot slower in both heat and final. It was a seemingly disastrous blow for an unbeaten combination after we had been so dominant for the first 18 months of our partnership. But we picked up the lessons, just as the four had in 2000 when we had lost at the same event in the run-up to Sydney. We went home, sucked up the pain and got to grips with what we felt we were doing wrong. Just as in the four, we knew we were stronger than the opposition: it was just a matter of applying ourselves to the water in a more efficient way. However fit and strong you are, the lake will suck your arms and legs dry if you try to bash it into submission. You have to respect the water and use it to lever the boat past and through it.

Using the bank of data that Jürgen was building up, we began crawling back up the rankings in the British team, and then in our own minds as well. But at the same time we knew that if we lost again the partnership was going to be on the back foot. We talked about it often, always in circumstances where we would not be overheard or judged by other members of the team. I was conscious that I needed to be mentally very tough around and with James, and that he relied on me to be that way, so even if I had worries in my head, I kept them to myself. The pair progressed, though, which goes to prove that the right mentality is not always blind faith or belief that you are on top of everything. A healthy respect and understanding, even a fear of losing, is not bad in some circumstances. We knew going into the 2002 World Championship in Seville that we could easily lose, and that if we rowed anything like we did in Lucerne, then we definitely would. Jürgen, for his part, was always confident without being blinded by how good we were; he urged us to be offensive and arrogant in the way that we rowed a race in training, sure that only a dominant performance would be good enough.

We had to wait for the final before racing the Australians. They progressed smoothly through the heat and semi on one side of the competition, as we did almost the same on the other. There were some people in our set-up who said that we looked better as we did so, but equally I got the distinct impression that there were others who doubted we were going to win. After years of dominating and being the lead boat within the British team, I could discern who was on my side in these things and who was, in fact, looking forward to seeing me get beaten. It didn't upset me. I had spent a decent number of years wanting to be the only winning crew on the team, so what goes around comes around.

The Aussies looked as confident as ever, making into a slice of Australia the bay that we shared with many of the pairs field. There was no mistaking the intention: the cupboard at the end of the boat house was festooned with green and gold stickers, and it became a staging post for most of the Aussie team, who left their bags there during work-outs. The press caught wind of the tension between us and built it up in the articles they were writing home. We genuinely wanted to win, of course, but I don't think we ever wanted them to do anything other than their best. It's pretty much an acid test of how much you respect or like your opposition: if you want to beat them at their best, then it's respect. If you want a sea monster to swallow their boat whole or wish every conceivable mistake on them personally, then I'm not sure respecting them is an accurate description. We always respected the Aussies, maybe even a little too much. James had been coached at school with videos of Jimmy rowing in the early '90s as a technical ideal, and I had certainly admired his abilities in the four from the safety of another event during my partnership with Steve. He said that he had a jokey agreement with Jimmy that they would always do different events, which worked fine while he did the pair with me and Jimmy stroked the Australian 'Oarsome Foursome' to several Gold medals. But now, for the first time, we were to meet head on.

Maybe the weather helped us. James certainly felt happier than on the day of the final when there was a strong tailwind, and we both knew that the race would be really fast. We also knew that we had to make a good start if we were to counter the pace that the Aussies could generate in the middle of the race. The warm-up was especially tense, and I, for one, was battling the contrasting voices inside my head. I knew that if I couldn't control the negative ones, then we would lose, and lose badly, and that I had to take a lead with the way I rowed, not least for the sake of the guy sitting behind me. A bowman cannot do much if his strokeman is out to lunch for a race, and if his calls start falling on deaf ears, then he might as well join him and order a salad.

By the time we got ourselves onto the start pontoon I was down to the very basic methods of coping with the nerves and the distinct possibility of losing. I was telling myself: 'Concentrate on the very simple ingredients that make you good, and if you row your best, they won't beat you. Allow them to dictate this race, and it's all over.'

But as we start the race, it is apparent that something different is happening. The boat is surging through the water with a ferocity that we have seldom achieved in very short training sprints, even at our most aggressive. It is a suicidal pace to maintain, but the start of any race is unnaturally quick, such is the premium of getting the lead. But just as our bodies are beginning the first notes of a painful overture, our brains are saying something else. Not only are we leading the race, we are moving steadily further out. What started as a few feet becomes half a length, and within a minute I am able to look across the lane to the untouched water ahead of every other boat in the race. Just as we are moving well, the Aussies are not, struggling to get second place from the South Africans and Croatians, with whom they had dealt so well earlier in the week.

'Let's finish them!' Now James seizes the advantage of a lead to put the Aussies in deep trouble. If we can get about a length and a half up, then our boat's wash could really upset the crews behind. The Aussies are getting into the danger area in the lane on our right and it's hardly a third of the race gone. The tailwind is helping to keep the rate high, pushing the boat along and allowing us to get the oars through the water with less power than normal. We jump to the call and dig a little deeper, telling ourselves that though it might hurt us, it is far, far harder for the opposition when someone is stretching out ahead of them. Drew, the bowman of the Australian pair, turns his head to the side to see exactly how far we are in front. We have now gone from his peripheral vision, and it gives me a burst of satisfied adrenalin to see him have to crane round to get to us.

At the halfway mark we are almost five seconds up, the furthest margin ahead I have ever been in any major race. We love the feeling. Now we can rely on winning the race and measure out our remaining energy so there can be absolutely no mistakes about running out. With 750 to go, the race is developing behind us as the South Africans make a desperate move to win a medal. It starts the sprint for home, and though we are far out ahead, the field starts closing. Five hundred to go and James begins our own sprint, calling the rate to go higher as we approach the line. But I'm not bothered one bit, and only go through the motions of increasing the speed of the boat. The field closes a little more as the three crews – the Australians, the Croatians and the South Africans – all chase two medals. But they are never going to catch us, even though the race closes significantly in the last section. We consider ourselves to be World Champions long before the line comes, a fine feeling, indeed.

Exhausted and relieved, I fall back in the boat so that my

torso is across James's legs. He is screaming at the world, the opposition and the sky.

'Yes! You horse, Matt, that was awesome. Those f******s were finished in the first half!' The remnants of the race are scattered across the lake: a dejected Australian pair, not sure if they have won a minor medal and not really caring; an elated South African pair, who have gone one better than their bronze in 2001. Then the crowd suck in their collective breath in an enormous sigh that we can hear right out in the middle of the course. To begin with, we assume it is a reaction to the fact that the Aussies have not medalled, and that a race so hyped as a one-on-one showdown has disappointed. It is only when we spot Jürgen on the raft and we paddle over to him that he tells us tearfully, 'Well done, boys, well done – 6.14!'

For me, it is a magical number. Not only a decent chunk faster than the world-record 6.18 that Steve and I had achieved in Switzerland eight years before, but the exact level that Jürgen had established as a Gold standard in the four-year span before the Games in Athens. We were only two years into our partnership and we had become World Champions, world record-holders, and could make a genuine claim to being the quickest pair ever. In a state of blissful shock, we climbed out of the boat to be interviewed. At least we made a better fist of it than we had in Sydney. Steve was there, right by the camera, and I jokingly referred to the fact that I had almost for the first time achieved something he had not. But I could see that he was genuinely moved by what we have achieved. 'I never doubted you for a minute,' he said.

As we carried the boat back up the concrete towards the boat house, Jimmy and Drew came over to shake our hands. They hid their disappointment well, and were genuine in their congratulations for us. But as I wandered about in the bay, gathering and packing our equipment away, one of the Norwegians came over. 'I just want you to know something,' he said. 'When you paddled back up to get your medals I was here in the bay when the Aussies came back in. Jimmy always looks like he doesn't give a shit whether he wins or he loses but, I tell you, Drew walked out to get changed and he just sat at the end there, sitting on the tool box, and cried his eyes out. For a guy who has won as much as he has, to care about it like that was one of the most amazing things I have ever seen.'

Losing hurts.

30
losing

The sun was beating down onto the lake, making the bushes in the distance shimmer. Even the roar of the planes taking off from nearby Milan airport was hushed by the heat. We were hot, too, sweat pouring off us as we raced down the track at the 2003 World Championships in Italy. There was a slight following wind, but that only helped when you were attached to the start pontoon. Once you are racing, it almost feels like rowing along in a confined space.

We were also rowing badly. The strokes were too short to be effective, especially for two big guys like James and me. We needed to sweep the boat along, get the oar in the water at full stretch and lever the hull past with all the languid power that two tall men can muster. But we were struggling with the length, and it set off a vicious circle – the speed of the boat was dying between each stroke, making it heavier and heavier to keep moving. At this point the body usually begins to tire; the breathing already laboured, as the heat scalds our throats; arms and hands cramp, so that the dextrous movements required to turn and place the oar become a battle.

The unity between us, so important in any rowing boat, was under attack. Both of us were now reverting to habits we hadn't displayed for weeks or months just because we were at the limit of what we could take. My habit was bending my arms too early in the stroke, not allowing my legs to take the lion's share of the work. It wasn't as if my legs felt fresh, far from it, but my arms felt even more leaden and droopy. And, of course, like so much in life, once one thing begins to run away, it takes everything with it.

Normally in a race the pain and effort is just background, a consistent wallpaper in a room where tactics might be furniture and technique the carpet. But in the situation we found ourselves in in Italy, it became all I could think about. My limbs screamed for relief and one thought began to crop up again and again. Stop. Stop rowing and all this will stop with it. Stop rowing and I can deal with the consequences later. I knew that the fall-out would be severe for the race and for the partnership, even for my career, but I didn't rationalise at that point. I just wanted to stop.

I can count on two hands the number of times I have seen guys stop in training. The combination of agony and disappointment before they stop is always so much better than after. Not one of them has bounced back from it. It damages you in a way that only your deepest mind will register. The trouble is that to repair the damage you have to get back there, into that hole, and prove to yourself that it is a temporary problem, one that, given the same situation again, you would react to differently. It is easy to make the promise to yourself that no matter what, you will never stop, particularly in the warmth of the breakfast room in the springtime. It is harder when you are on the ragged edge of what your body can manage.

Steve never stopped, not in training, not in racing. On occasions, I saw him in more trouble physically than ever before on the rowing machine. He was pulling scores that would have disappointed a schoolboy but he never stopped. Only he knew what kept him going then with no hope of a good score, but he never pulled up. He would carry on rowing, despite the sudden hush that would descend. Normally a rowing machine test fills the gym with a willing crowd, keen to see the technique and the drama, and for the second half of the test they would begin to chip in with shouts of support.

'Go on, Matt! That's looking good.'

'Yeah, Steve! Keep it long.'

Or, with the benefit of your display, they could give you targets to aim for. 'Okay, next 20 strokes get the legs on!'

'Halfway now, let's start getting the score down to 127.'

But if the guy in front of you is obviously in trouble, nothing you can say will get him out of it. You can't offer advice – he has already been through every possible remedy and come up wanting. So the cheers go quiet and, like watching an injured bird in the road, you have to look away and wince in silence.

But there was no looking away for us, stuck out on a hot Italian lake, rowing ourselves into oblivion, pushing on when everything screamed stop. There was one reason why this was happening – we were losing.

Some people can lose and very quickly get out the emotional bandage that is the 'We did our best' routine. That may well be the case. In fact, I can think of races in my career where we were simply outclassed by the opposition. But that is subtly different from saying that you did your best. There are still plenty of winners whose 'best' on paper had no chance of winning and yet went out to overturn the odds, rattle the cages of the favourites and find themselves winners. In my experience, doing my very best and losing don't often go hand in hand. Much more likely is that I settled for second well before it was over, talked myself into a corner and never got out of it. Sport is full of opportunities to learn, but the really useful ones can be painful.

The physical pain of crossing the line in Italy that day in 2003 was short-lived. I spent the last few metres of the race shamefully limping in. The result from the previous year's World Championships was a distant memory. The Australians had bounced back and exacted their revenge on us with the same style and class as we had attacked them in Seville. They took the race to us and, far from responding in an aggressive and enthusiastic way, we had folded. I had been worried about losing all week of the championships, and my lack of leadership and decisiveness had undermined us. The final was the end to a disappointing week, made worse because we knew we could have won. The Australians had done nothing that we could not do. Indeed, we had been going well at the training camp immediately prior to the championships, but the history books don't often record that.

It hurt like hell. I suddenly realised just how Jimmy and Drew had felt in Seville where we had demolished them. Many impartial spectators were full of admiration for the event and the racing. There were now two great pairs knocking chunks out of each other on an annual basis. But I think both pairs knew the stakes were higher than that. Their chief coach had made it plain that if they did not win in Italy, then he would consider any and all options for them for the Olympics. For our part, with the British men's four winning a Silver and the men's eight a Bronze, our fourth place was the worst result of our men's boats. For the first time since joining the team in 1989, I had not won a medal and not been in the top-performing boat.

But the attention of us all was on the future. What would happen next? Jürgen was methodical in his approach.

His first rule was that he was chief coach and the buck stopped with him. He didn't allow us to wallow in the defeat. He sent us away on holiday with as much of a relaxed sense of humour as he could muster, even though in reality the defeat hurt him as much as anyone.

He knew that James would brood and mull over the race much more than I, so we decided to keep in touch with him. With Beverly expecting their baby soon, it would be a busy and stressful time for him anyway, and Jürgen was especially keen that he wasn't left without one of us to talk to for more than a few days.

Third, we had to get the pair back on the rails and moving well enough in the winter to win the Olympic Trials and reassert ourselves at the top of the pile. No one was going to be helped by a sulking and shamefaced duo, so we had to take it on the chin and look ahead, not back.

Lastly, and this took time for me to figure out, he wasn't going to take any advice from us over what to do. This was different from years past, when his door was always open for input about our season. Where we raced, how we trained and what boat class we wanted to do were all up for negotiation. The fact that I had been World or Olympic Champion in the previous 12 seasons had made the boat selection relatively straightforward – you are unlikely to change a winning combination – but a fourth place left a lot to be desired. After the result in Italy, no one else in the team expected to be left unchanged, and we had no right to assume otherwise. The press raised it straight away. With a four winning a Silver medal by a narrow margin and a pair missing by a mile – who is to say that the two should not be combined to create a winning four? The guys in the four were, of course, less than enthusiastic about the prospects, and said so in the press.

But everyone knew there was going to be only one person who made that call, and that was Jürgen.

With tensions expressed publicly between squad members, and a coxless pair on the back foot, the chief coach sent us on a camp to Cyprus.

epilogue

Friday, 13 August, Attica Beach Hotel
Athens Olympic Opening Ceremony day
Eight days till the Final

Difficult day. Wanted to be more a part of the Olympics than we felt today. Stuck out here in the hotel you would be forgiven for thinking we were at a World Championships. Still the logistical advantages make this the right choice; we can be at the lake in 20 minutes, whereas the buses take an hour from the village, plus waiting time in the heat of the day, which can be draining for the village goers. Had a couple of paddles this morning on the lake which went fine, usual last minute niggles and adjustments but we did a burst of rowing just for twenty strokes into the wind that was gorgeous. Got all the hairs standing up on our arms too. After four straight days of tail it had swung to headwind, but it's no big issue, I can't see the oppo liking it either.

Had a pre-race chat at eight p.m. just so we could get it out of the way and went through all the options and targets we have had during the last six weeks, namely good length, power and rhythm. Basically, to try and row our race whatever the oppo throw at us. Went into the TV room afterwards to watch at least the first part of the opening ceremony. Was really impressed by it, well choreographed, not too much of the antique bullshit that the little Greek bit of the Sydney closing had. The five rings of fire in the water was memorable, as was Steve saying the Aussies are a scruffy lot. Classic. Went to bed soon after to make sure I didn't get drawn into waiting for the Brits to come out and staying up too late. Went to bed thinking good things about tomorrow's heat.

Saturday, 14 August. Seven days till the Final

Had the usual night's sleep, fitful with sudden jerking awakenings to stare at the digital clock in the darkness. Got up and had a small bowl of cereal around six a.m. which was an immediate contrast with what happened in Sydney.

First paddle on the lake went smoothly enough and we found a quiet room in the boathouse to lie down and relax. We had been warned the PM was on a visit today and around nine we went back to the boat to meet and greet him and Cherie. They were walking on eggshells, unsure as to what to say to us on a race day, but I think it went okay. Cherie is a dynamo, sparky and confident while Tony, for all his presence, is quieter. Back to the room for another couple of hour's rest and then out to the boat for the last hour build-up.

Felt very quiet and confident throughout, never thought these guys would trouble us even in the strong headwind. Had a fantastic chat right before the race with James – laying down the law about our agenda and our hopes for the race. He genuinely has stepped up this last month and I have never known him as focussed and disciplined. Bloody hot out on the water by the time we boated, it must have been over 35 degrees. You could almost feel the fluid being drawn out of you as the sun hit your head. Doing laps of the warm-up line we had the massive contrast of the tailwind speed and the headwind treacle but both versions felt good and solid. Still didn't feel over-anxious (which should in itself have got me feeling butterflies) but really my nerve scale was hardly flickering.

Start was solid but slow to react apparently, which would have explained why we went behind after ten strokes, then we accelerated in awesome style and took the race right away from the others. Hit a reasonable rhythm at a minute, which took us further ahead and then I just started thinking about finishing the race in first – not how I was rowing or what the boat felt like. As soon as I did that the boat and my legs began to feel heavy and we spent the middle of the race fighting with the Italians rather than destroying them. If I had done that in training I would have had a rocket from the others, and myself, but in the opening round of the Games it is unforgivable. Had a live camera shoved down our noses right after the race which is never pleasant, so put on brave face for the public and gave it the old 'we're happy we are in the semis' routine. All the press seemed happy enough but in the boathouse we were far less complimentary. If we row like that again we won't beat anyone.

Saw Dee and my folks for the first time which was a wonderful foil for the disappointment of our performance but nothing could prevent a quiet afternoon of reflection at the hotel. I need to get more up for this or it's all going to go down. What happened to the guy who used to throw-up in the lake before his Olympic races? I still have confidence he is there… I just have to give him a kick out of bed in the morning.

Sunday, 15 August. Six days till the Final

Felt pretty slow starting this morning, stiff and sleepy as we went down for our morning paddle. Wind had swung round to steady tail-breeze as we did our 12 kilometre outing. No work just mileage, trying to get the heat worked out of our legs. When we got back to the hotel watched the group B heats go off.

Best race of the regatta so far was the eights between Canada and USA, the Yanks never gave up challenging for the lead and came through the Canadians with two hundred left, Brits were miles back after Tom James came down ill overnight. Felt bad for all of them. The USA were inspirational though, a narrow win over the World Champions and a new world record to boot. When I got back to the room the doc was there talking to Steve, apparently he had had a dodgy stomach since the race yesterday. All of a sudden the dreaded illnesses return. I tried to be upbeat, saying to Steve if we had to choose a time to be ill then Monday would be the day to do it. I was immediately moved out of the room in case it was anything contagious and Steve was left to sleep it off. He said he felt okay but several trips to the toilet every few hours can't be good. We still went down to the lake in the evening to train but the famous wind had sprung up and the course looked like the Channel. We got stuck into an ergo for 45 minutes instead.

Steve was still there to train, just at a lower score than he might have been set before. Mood in the hotel a little muted, eight were hammered this morning and need a good repechage to get to the final, the men's quad too. Women's quad was impressive winning their heat well.

Find myself increasingly pissed off with myself over the heat row. Will definitely bring my A game for the semi, we may yet get drawn with Canada.

Monday, 16 August. Five days till the Final

Steve is up and about as usual and despite the wind howling at the balcony we decide to get down to the course and do an ergo. We have plenty here at the hotel but routine is everything, I guess. Racing was cancelled for the day late last night so they knew it was going to get bad. When we get down, there are big rollers at the finish line and all the flags are cracking at the poles behind the grandstand. The warm-up area looks more promising, big waves still but just short of white horses. The venue organiser stops his car to tell us the course is closed but if we want to try it he will send out a safety launch with us and 'if you sink, you sink'.

Anything rather than another bloody ergo so we attach all available defenses to the boat in the boathouse. We have a long continuous strip of plastic attached to the top of the shell to keep the waves out, a big 'V' board behind Steve's back to keep them from rolling in over the bows and a pump in the bottom. However, it turns out we don't need much of it. As soon as we paddle away up the warm-up line it is obvious we'll be okay, the boat rides over much of it and the oars get caught long before the riggers do. It is difficult rhythm-wise but it's not a worry from the sinking point of view. We are allowed out onto the course too and try a few bursts and standing starts. There is a screaming tailwind blowing maybe 20 miles an hour but we make a decent fist of it and get some good pieces in. When we get back the boat is dry, not damp or a pint or two swilling in the bottom, but dry. Good news there then.

Dee came over to the hotel in the afternoon and we went to a local place just to have a drink for an hour. I'm useless company in weeks like this, there is so much that is taboo. But still, great to see her and she seems to be enjoying her cousin and brother being in town.

Good news on Steve too. All seems to go quiet in the p.m. and I am given permission to move back to my bed. Had another afternoon session on the ergo as the course was still rough tonight. We figured we had learned enough in the morning, and besides Jürgen wanted to do a bit more work and set us two eight minute rows and one four which got the blood moving.

Everyone feeling it today I think. Keep catching people with far-away looks in their eyes; James mentioned at dinner that he was especially nervous today too. I find myself on a familiar Olympic rollercoaster, hours spent not feeling worried at all followed by a few feeling really under pressure.

If anything it is reassuring, my body's way of telling me it's nearly time. Find the swimming finals tough to watch too, any medal ceremony gets tears to my eyes double-quick. Team GB not flying quite so high in the pool. At least Ben Ainslie looks like he is going to win one of many Golds at the sailing. At least some of us are enjoying this bloody wind.

Tuesday 17 August. Four days to the Final

Spent a lot of time thinking about the semi today. Down to the lake in our normal routine and out for a paddle. Over the last couple of days we have put a lot of emphasis on our first stroke, trying to improve the aggression and our reaction time. If we get it wrong we snatch at the water and rip the blade through but when we get it right it flies. With the repechages delayed until today we will have no info on whom we will be racing until the afternoon, which is a little strange – we could still get Canada. Back to the hotel to watch the races on the BBC (we have a satellite link here – very nice). The single was amazing; Ian was miles down on some bloke from Uzbekistan then went right through him in the second thousand. Good stuff.

During the post-race interviews Tim Foster mentioned that we had not got the Canadians in our semi; disappointed I have to say, but we had a meeting in the evening to concentrate the minds. Jürgen was adamant we had to raise our game (Games?) from the heat and really focus on our own boat. I don't think the Kiwis are going to win a medal and we should be able to get out in front with ease. The other semi looks more interesting, four crews for three places with Canada, Italy, Australia and Germany all vying for the final.

Went a little quiet after the meeting to try and generate the atmosphere of a big race. Had a dinner with the boys, leg rub in the medical room downstairs and then to bed. Lights-out sure to be early tonight.

Wednesday, 18 August. Three days till the Final

Woke up feeling entirely different to the day of the heat. Nervous, excited and scared in equal measure. We have the easier semi – there can be no doubt of that – but we had to show to ourselves and everybody else that we are more than rank outsiders today. Had a bowl of Alpen for breakfast, because I was unsure about the level of carbohydrate from the night before, and right on cue threw it back up into the lake 40 minutes later. Is there ever a time when you can feel happy about vomiting? I was, and I was pretty sure Ed wasn't too put off by it behind me. I took it as a sign that I was back to normal service, that my body was responding to the situation in exactly the way it had in Atlanta and Sydney.

We had an hour or so in between the warm-up paddle and gathering for the race in the boat house and we spent it stretched out in one of the upstairs bedrooms.

We all came down out of the boat house together, and met with Jürgen. He didn't mince his words, urging us to be hard on ourselves and leave nothing out of the plan to dominate and harness the potential that we have. Pushing away from the stage was a relief after all that, at last there was an outlet for it all. The stands have been poorly filled here but the family one has been full and, whatsmore, draped with flags. It really gets the back of your throat when you see the Union flags waving as you paddle out to the warm-up.

The race was pretty much just what the doctor ordered, although I still managed to fluff the first stoke, which given the practice we had put in pissed me off, but we jumped out to a lead over the Kiwis comfortably enough and before halfway we were in the privileged position of looking back on the field battling to join us in the Olympic

Final. Press were suitably impressed afterwards, and after the Steve Rider chat on camera Steve Redders just gave me a short, definitive nod; translation 'that's more like it'.

The supporting posse has grown from wife, parents and sister to wife, parents, sister, brother-in-law, cousin on Dee's side, uncle, aunt and cousin on mine and now Dee's driver, who has become honorary Brit for the duration of the Games. We all came rattling back to the hotel, me for a quiet lunch and afternoon, them for a boozy fish lunch nearby. We had a coffee afterwards and then said our goodbyes. We won't see each other till after the Final on Saturday. Dee left saying she wanted me to row a last race that befitted my career. Good sentiments indeed.

Thursday, 19 August. Two days till the Final

Bit of a nothing day as far as racing goes. There were a few semi-finals for group B but of course we had nothing to do with it. Morning paddle as ever – getting very used to that routine now, and then we decide on evening routine so head back for long day at the hotel. I can't sleep too long during the days now, too alert and beginning to get the first hint of butterflies. The others seem to have fewer problems, happily sleeping through the afternoon or munching toasties whenever they like. Jürgen calls a meeting in the evening to begin to turn our attention to the Final. He states adamantly that we have to row our race, that he is sure we can win it and that every stroke will count. It takes about 20 minutes for him to talk it through, then he opens it up for us.

My contribution is that I don't want the guys to be surprised when I go quiet in the remaining days. Tomorrow will be hell for all of us, it's part of the deal – building our bodies up for what we have to do – and they should have confidence in me whatever I say or do before the race. Everyone seems happy enough and we all finish the day with a leg rub in the treatment room. The physios have been awesome as ever, jokey and loud when you need it and silent when you prefer that too. Tonight was jokey.

Friday, 20 August. The day before the Final

Worst day of the calendar by far. Rowing was fine for our two sessions down at the lake, indeed, our post-outing chat for the starts *and bursts was glowing. The reaction time and aggression are both getting better on the former, and the length is better on the latter. Back to the hotel and I manage a massive 20 minute sleep after lunch, until the butterflies kick in and leave me lying there, staring at the ceiling. I know I won't sleep much tonight so it would be nice to get some before the race but I don't let it get to me. The BBC coverage in the British lounge is becoming almost impossible to watch now, it's either dotted with small little hopeful titbits or running a massive trailer bigging it up for the weekend, 'Saturday, eight thirty a.m. Matthew Pinsent goes for his fourth Olympic Gold medal' kind of thing, at which point everyone in the room looks at me and I have to play it all cool. I manage to eat steadily through the day not to the same extent as four years ago but enough. Drinking water is easier and I go to the toilet about twice an hour.*

Jürgen convenes the meeting at six and we all go to the meeting-room in the basement ready to talk through it all. Jürgen goes back over the points from yesterday and stresses that he wants to keep emotions out of it if he can. No mention of how we all got to this point, or of me going for four Golds or James two. Just targets. Me; length as ever, rhythm, and keeping the hands moving at the finish of the stroke. Ed; back me up, and be the stroke-man for the tandem. James; sitting up and using his body in the right way and Steve; 'be the speedy man' ie don't take on too much and get tired. Jürgen tries to get me to add something but I can't, it feels like I've got an orange in my windpipe. James steps in to talk about how hard we are going to have to be, how well the Americans rowed to get through the Canadian eight in the last 500 and how we have to get our bodies on the stroke more. Ed talks through the way the crew has come together and how he is sure we are peaking at the right moment and how happy he is with the improvements we have made even this week. We finish up with a final run down of logistics for the morning; six o'clock bus, four k paddle, then sit it out in one of the rooms until an hour before.

We all go for an arranged stroll down to the mini-harbour and sit talking and throwing stones. I put on a brave act but inside it's turmoil. Are we really good enough? Would I honestly say we are favourites? If I was in the Canadian boat would I have more confi-

dence? All bloody hard questions to answer, especially today.

Just before dinner we watch Hoy in the 1km on the track, awesome. How did he manage to watch three guys go before him and break his PB, and then go out and still win? We are all out of the room well before the medal ceremony.

James and Steve are measuring out their bicarbonate of soda, it goes into their system on race day to act as a lactate buffer ie making it less painful in a race. I have never tried it but they say it works, tastes like crap though.

Ask D to call and we spend a miserable couple of minutes trying to get some sense together. I know whatever happens she loves me but I can hardly get my words straight. By the end she is doing the talking and I am forcing out squeaks, totally choked up. She sends a text a minute later: 'There is no one more able than you in the race, trust in your well-earned confidence and that of the entire rowing world and lead your crewmates. I couldn't be prouder of anything than I am of being your wife.'

Fitful sleep.

Saturday, 21 August. Day of the Olympic Final

Am in the lobby well before six with bag packed. No breakfast just a bottle of Lucozade to keep the stomach energy coming in, but even that is a struggle. Down to the course in the bus thinking, 'if Jürgen had an accident now that wasn't his fault and I was slightly injured and couldn't row then all this would be over. I could be loaded into an ambulance smiling'. We arrive safely.

We all split up at the boathouse to stretch, change or sit and I take a little faux jog down the side of the lake. As I turn back and look down the finish area I can see the bloody British flags on the railing already, déjà vu or what? I make sure I have my shades on my head for the warm-up row. Four k goes quickly, a little paddling in pairs, out onto the course near the start and then one complete length of the track. We pause to do a couple of starts and then hit the supporters right on the finish line. It's louder than four years ago – there are hundreds of them.

Back in and we put the boat on slings for Jürgen to check over, he spent all yesterday afternoon sanding down the hull with wet and dry paper so we have a matt finish. We were going to get some stuff from the sailors that they thought could add a second or two, but it breaks our rules so we couldn't. Jürgen urges me to eat something and I go into the restaurant to get a banana. It's very green though and I don't like the sharp taste in my mouth. Ditch it after two bites, finish the Lucozade instead. Have a quick stretch on the mats downstairs then it's into our room upstairs with the bunk beds. I check the time and reckon we have a 100 minutes before it's time to start the land warm-up. I lie on one of the top bunks in the foetal position clutching a bottle of water. Close my eyes.

Eight thirty and the first final starts – the women's sculls. Thankfully can't hear the commentary. Eight fifty and the men are coming down the track. I stand up on the bunks to catch a glimpse of Tufte the Norwegian flashing past the stands.

James is in and out of the room a lot and I can see how red his eyes are, we are all going through it. Steve is, as ever, the quietest, lying out still and calm, he could be asleep again.

Ten past nine; last 20 minutes before we get together and I decide I will watch the women's pair in the athletes' lounge. There are people everywhere including our men's eight and quad waiting to finish their regatta in the B final later in the day. No one says much to me and I can pace up and down the back of the room. The girls start well then the Romanians take charge and we fight our way into the Silver in the second half. I'm happy for them but now it's our turn. Out into the heat and round to the boat. Drop off my bag and give the ticket to Jürgen.

Nine twenty-five and we head out for our warm-up shuffle, out behind the stands and up the course. The stands on the opposite side are nearly full for the first time, it's impressive. The men's pair final is coming down the course towards us but we don't wait for it. As we get back towards the boathouse there is a camera crew with Claire Balding pointing right at us as we jog past. No questions thankfully.

Nine thirty-five; the men's pair is reaching the last 500, Drew and Jimmy are going to win, happy for them.

Nine thirty-eight; last chat on the bench by the boat in the shade. 'I think we had quite a good meeting last night...' Jürgen's classic opener. Only one sentence sticks after that, 'it will be bloody hard, and never, never give up. The last stroke can be the one that counts.'

Nine forty; Ed checks his watch and says 'okay hands on in seven minutes' I remain on the bench because I don't need to pee. Jurgen is with me. 'Remember all those tough times, Massew. A long road to get here but we do this I'm sure.' I nod.

Nine forty-six; we are all ready by the boat and so head out onto the pontoon. As we are getting in Ed and Steve crouch down almost as if in unison and I find myself staring at James. We embrace and he whispers 'enjoy it!' But even at a whisper his voice breaks.

We paddle away into the warm-up lake and begin our circling pattern. Gentle paddle for one length, a couple of bursts back. Practice starts. I am struggling now mentally. The negative thoughts are huge, I just want this to be over. At times, if the rowing God bent down and offered a Silver medal right there and then, I would have taken it. I reign myself in, 'come on Matt, you have come too far to blow this now'. Just as I would tell any schoolboy, I take one technical idea and focus on that. 'Okay, I'm not going to bend my arms too early.'

Ten to eight; Steve takes us up to the bridge that divides the warm-up from the main body of the lake. The double sculls race flashes across the gap and are gone, another group of hopefuls pursuing their destiny. We turn up to the start and go through the final movements of our warm-up.

Ten twenty-two; we attach to the start and hand back the extra kit to the stake boat. T-shirts, caps, bottles, they all go. Now I'm back on an even keel, wanting desperately to get on with it but wanting more desperately to win.

Ten twenty-eight; the starter goes through the call over and turns on the lights. Staring at the red nothing dominates my thoughts more than the first stroke. Make it quick, make it deep.

I know we had a good start and our position relative to the Canadians proves it, level if not a little up after ten strokes. 'Length' Steve calls, quiet almost. We get into our cruise, less energy than the start but the foot hasn't come off the gas much, if at all. Still level, maybe up a bit, then definitely up. 'Don't wait!' We had talked about this and made a point of the mistake we had made in Lucerne two months before. We had slowed after two minutes to row beside the Canadians rather than keep forging ahead. But even though we are trying to get away they are right there, a man down. 750 gone and we are not going to drop them, but we are in position A. We had always felt they put too much into the first half and we needed to be there to punish them in the second.

Halfway, '250 now'; it's a long drawn-out effort, meant to last from the halfway mark to the next, a full 250 metres. We move and then stick, then they start coming back. This should be it, it should be easier from here on in.

'Two-fifty now'; another go at moving, they are just ahead, now we have actually lost ground on them. We are getting close to sprinting but not yet all in. Bad news is we can't seem to shake them from their rhythm, can't get away. Good news, they can't either, it's right in the balance.

Five hundred to go, both boats fly through the last mark locked together. 'Crank it!' It's a different voice, it's James. His favourite call, one we dreamed up in the altitude camp, it's the beginning of the charge. Crank encapsulates everything we want here, relentless, increasing power without losing length.

Four hundred, still together, still we can't get ahead enough to feel we are going to win for sure. The grandstands start on the left side, the roar begins. Okay, I think to myself, this is all over if we get a decisive move here, get a half-length and it's over. Give it 30 strokes, make them the best, as if everything rested on them and win it right here. I go for more power, more length again and start driving the oar through the water with all I've got. We talked about this before too, let's get everything out, let's empty the tank.

'Come on Matt' – James again, not a literal shout for me to do something different, just a reinforcement of his energy, give us more we can take it. Ed is growling too. I reach the end of my 30 and glance over, we have not got the half-length, we are not even leading, we are still behind. One thought is in my head – Silver. But as quick as it arrives I follow it with the old fall back – if I'm going to lose I'm going to make you work, if it has to be second it will be by a tiny margin.

'Yeah!!' James again. I haven't heard anything from Steve for four hundred meters. I am in the end-game, the last ebbs of energy. Row two, look one, the bubble line that marks the finish flashes past. I know it's close, very close.

Two good signs, the Canadians have no idea either and we were at the end of a stroke as I thought we crossed the line. With the blades out of the water, the boat surges and we were right there like a horse at full stretch, head reaching for the line.

'Who got it? Did you win?' Canadian voices across the water.

Twenty seconds pass, heart pumping, legs aching, air scorching through the throat.

Suddenly the stands off to the left erupt, flags waving. I look up and see they are all Union Jacks.

The voices behind me in the boat roar but I can't hear them. It's over, finally over. Tired beyond measure, relieved, proud and overwhelmed I begin to weep into the boat. First quietly, then sobbing, leaning back into Ed's arms.

A few hours later on the BBC I likened the feeling to being in a submarine. All week I had been going deeper and deeper. The pressure building on the outside seemingly every minute. At first there is no discernible difference, then the hull begins to creak and groan fighting against the forces acting on it. I felt like I had rushed around on the inside, propping up bulges and patching leaks. Lack of sleep, loss of appetite, tears welling in the warm-up paddle were all leaks. As the race approached the water pressure got higher and higher until I was sure it was going to crush me. Crossing the line it felt as if someone opened a hatch.

*

From a letter to the crew before it departed for Greece, July 2004: 'The most important thing that I have learned from all this is really enjoy the experience. Even on the really shitty days. Enjoy the people you are with now because for those that aren't carrying on, you will not get the time with your friends ever again. Ask yourself "What does it mean to be here?" and "How much does this crew mean to me?" Then you will remember that the Olympics are special and that special things happen at the Olympics.' Alex Partridge, Great Britain, Men's Coxless Five 2004.